Globalisation and the Asia-Pacific

Globalisation and the Asia-Pacific

Contested Perspectives and Diverse Experiences

Edited by

Iyanatul Islam

Professor of International Business, Griffith Business School and Griffith Asia Institute, Griffith University, Australia and Founding Co-Editor, Journal of the Asia Pacific Economy

Moazzem Hossain

Senior Lecturer in Economics, Griffith Business School and Griffith Asia Institute, Griffith University, Australia and Regional Editor for Australia, World Review of Science, Technology and Sustainable Development

Edward Elgar
Cheltenham, UK • Northampton, MA, USA

Published by
Edward Elgar Publishing Limited
Glensanda House
Montpellier Parade
Cheltenham
Glos GL50 1UA
UK

Edward Elgar Publishing, Inc.
136 West Street
Suite 202
Northampton
Massachusetts 01060
USA

A catalogue record for this book
is available from the British Library

ISBN-13: 978 1 84542 579 1
ISBN-10: 1 84542 579 0

Printed and bound in Great Britain by MPG Books Ltd, Bodmin, Cornwall

Contents

Figures

Tables

Contributors

Jayatilleke S. Bandara, Senior Lecturer, Griffith Business School, Griffith University, Nathan, Australia.

Brendan Berne, Director, Economic Analytical Unit, Department of Foreign Affairs and Trade, Australia.

Bernie Bishop, Senior Lecturer, Griffith Business School, Griffith University, Nathan, Australia.

Tom Conley, Lecturer, Griffith Business School, Griffith University, Nathan, Australia.

Clarisse Didelon, Academic and Research Fellow, UMR 8504, Géographie-Cité, Paris, France.

Moazzem Hossain, Senior Lecturer, Griffith Business School, Griffith University, Nathan, Australia.

Iyanatul Islam, Professor, Griffith Business School, Griffith University, Nathan, Australia.

Leong H. Liew, Head, Department of International Business and Asian Studies, Griffith Business School, Griffith University, Nathan, Australia.

Muhammed Muqtada, Senior Economist, International Labour Organization, Geneva.

Athula Naranpanawa, Griffith Business School, Griffith University, Nathan, Australia.

John Quiggin, Professor, School of Economics, University of Queensland, St Lucia, Australia.

Preface and summary

Globalisation is both a process and a prescription. As a process, it pertains to the evolution of linkages among nations along both economic and non-economic dimensions. As a prescription, many see it as a vehicle for engendering sustainable economic prosperity within nation states, both rich and poor. It is the prescription, rather than the process, that seems to be at the heart of current debates on globalisation. Furthermore, both the agenda of, and discourse on, globalisation cannot be separated from its association with the idealism – and ideology – of the United States. Ever since the end of the Cold War, the United States appears to have taken on the proselytising role of propagating the virtues of a global order built on the principles of a free market economy. Thus, as the 2002 National Security Strategy of the Bush administration proclaims, there is now apparently a single sustainable model of economic success. The Democratic opposition also concurs, arguing for an agenda of 'progressive internationalism' in which the United States is uniquely endowed as the sole superpower to oversee an essentially benign expansion of global capitalism. The international community is, however, divided rather than united in its response to a US-led agenda of globalisation. Is there really a single sustainable model of economic success or are pragmatic alternatives rooted in country-specific circumstances feasible? Is macroeconomic conservatism an essential element of a globalised policy agenda? What about concerns pertaining to economic disparities that seem to be associated with, though not necessarily caused by, globalisation? What should the future of global governance look like, especially in an uncertain era of international relations unleashed by the tragedy of the terrorist attacks on the United States on 11 September 2001 and the two wars (in Afghanistan and Iraq) that have followed from it?

These issues and concerns provided the context for a workshop on the benefits and costs of globalisation held under the auspices of the Griffith Asia Institute (then the Griffith Asia Pacific Research Institute) of Griffith University in mid-February 2003. Scholars from Griffith and other institutions (World Bank, ILO, Department of Foreign Affairs and Trade of the Australian government, Queensland University, Australian National University) participated and deliberated on a wide range of issues, both from a general perspective and from the perspective of specific countries. Most of the scholars who participated in the workshop were kind enough to write updated chapters for this volume that drew on their contributions at the workshop.

This edited volume is divided into two parts. Part I offers an account of selected debates on globalisation. The inaugural chapter by Iyanatul Islam ('Globalisation, economic development and economists') offers a critical account of the nature of disagreements among economists on the outcomes of globalisation. Contrary to popular perception, economists disagree – and often profoundly – on the benefits of globalisation. Brendan Berne ('Keeping the gains of globalisation') adopts a much more optimistic tone by drawing on both Australian and international experience. He suggests an agenda that can consolidate the gains of globalisation while minimising its costs. John Quiggin ('Globalisation: macroeconomic management and public finance') and Muhammad Muqtada ('Macroeconomic stability, growth and employment') contribute two chapters on macroeconomic conservatism. The latter represents a set of ideas in which the primary function of the government is to control inflation and sustain fiscal prudence as a means of creating an investor-friendly policy environment. This is in turn seen as essential for economic growth. Both Quiggin and Muqtada argue the case for shedding the ideological straightjacket that current debates on macroeconomic policy seem to be trapped in. Bernie Bishop ('Foreign investment policy and economic development') concentrates on the influential agenda of wooing foreign direct investment to developing countries and reflects on its promises, pitfalls and perils. He warns against uncritically embracing an agenda of attracting foreign direct investment as a means of engendering development.

Part II of the volume encompasses a collection of chapters on specific country experiences – China, India, Sri Lanka and Australia. The diversity of experiences is quite wide, enabling the reader to appreciate the complex nature of the consequences of globalisation. The chapters range in coverage from issues that are quite broad in scope to those that exhibit an industry-specific orientation.

Leong Liew ('China's changing political economy') charts the evolution of China's embrace of the market economy and the 'uniting and dividing impacts of globalisation'. Whether the 'uniting' effects of globalisation will supersede the 'dividing' consequences of globalisation, and what will be the political responses to such developments, lie at the core of appreciating the complexity of China's political economy. Moazzem Hossain and Clarisse Didelon's contribution ('The "new economy" and India's integration into the global market') represents a cautiously optimistic assessment of India's experience as one of the success stories of the era of globalisation. The chapter admittedly adopts an industry-specific approach but does not eschew the case for the need to reflect on broader indicators of societal well-being.

Concerns about disparities – in both an absolute and a relative sense – permeate the two remaining chapters in this volume. Jayatilekke Bandara and Athula Naranpanawa ('Globalisation, poverty and disparities') suggest, by drawing on the Sri Lankan case, that issues of absolute and relative deprivation cannot be overlooked when celebrating the gains of globalisation, especially in ethnically divided societies. Tom Conley ('It's the government, stupid!') dwells on the Australian experience hailed by many as an exemplar of a mature democracy and a developed economy that weathered the challenges of globalisation in a robust fashion. Certainly, Australia has experienced the longest economic boom in recent decades, but such euphoric proclamations can easily lead one to overlook the contentious issue of inequality and how its satisfactory resolution requires the guiding hand of the government.

The editors of this volume will be remiss in terms of their responsibilities if they fail to acknowledge the role – both financial and inspirational – that the Griffith Asia Institute played in supporting the production of this book. Without sustained encouragement from Professor Bob Elson (now at Queensland University) and Associate Professor Mary Farquhar – both former Directors of the Institute – the book would have not have materialised. Honor Lawler and Wendy Francis were instrumental in ensuring that the workshop on globalisation that provided the genesis for this book was held successfully. Robyn White worked tirelessly on the various chapters to ensure that they conform to a uniform format and meet the style guidelines of the publisher. Of course, the ultimate success of an edited volume depends on the cooperation and scholarly engagement of the contributors. All of them deserve unreserved praise for their role and in particular for their exemplary patience as the editors went through the challenging – and at times agonisingly slow – process of compiling this volume.

Iyanatul Islam and Moazzem Hossain
Griffith Asia Institute
Brisbane, March 2005

PART I

Debates on globalisation: selected issues

1. Globalisation, economic development and economists: voices of dissent

Iyanatul Islam

THE GLOBALISATION WARS . . .

The surest way to do more to help the poor is to continue to open markets. (Mike Moore, former Director General, WTO)

We have to reaffirm unambiguously that open markets are the best engine we know of to lift living standards and build shared prosperity. (Bill Clinton, former US President)

One of the most common claims today is that globalization typically leads to growing income inequality within countries, so that the benefits primarily go to the rich. This claim is simply not true. In fact, it is one of the big myths of the anti-globalization movement. (Dr Nick Stern, former Chief Economist, World Bank)

After more than two decades of application of neoliberal economic policies in the developing world, we are in a position to pass unequivocal judgement on their record. The picture is not pretty. (Professor Dani Rodrik, Harvard University)

Maintaining that globalization as we know it is the way to go, and that if Washington Consensus policies have not borne fruit so far, they will surely do so in the future, is to replace empiricism with ideology. (Dr Branco Milanovic, World Bank)

Complete isolation from the global economy is clearly not good over the long haul for the poor in poor countries . . . Very few people are actually arguing for such isolation . . . What is being debated are the preconditions and the rules of engagement . . . with the global economy, and what is being expressed is a deep concern that integration is being forced on to poor countries too indiscriminately and at too fast a pace . . . (Professor Ravi Kanbur, Cornell University, and ex-Director, World Development Report on Poverty, 2001)

There is a need for change. The world of Bretton Woods is definitely not the world of today, and there is a strong case for far-reaching re-examination of the

institutional structure of the international world. (Professor Amartya Sen, Nobel
Laureate in Economics, 2001)

September 11 has resulted in a global alliance against terrorism. What we now
need is not just an alliance *against* evil, but an alliance *for* something positive – a
global alliance for reducing poverty and for creating a better environment, an
alliance for creating a global society with more social justice. (Professor Joseph
Stiglitz, Nobel Laureate in Economics, 2002)

INTRODUCTION

The professional narrative of economists is preoccupied with the need to
understand how economic linkages *between* nations – inculcated through
movements in commodities, capital and people – improve living standards
within nations.[1] There is a general presumption that 'most economists are,
most of the time, cheerleaders for ... global integration' and are happily
joined in this enterprise by a select club of 'most heads of state, finance
ministers, officials of the World Trade Organization, the IMF and the World
Bank' as well as 'members of the corporate and financial communities'.[2]
There is, however, a growing recognition that, even among mainstream
economists, divisions have emerged in recent years. Some have become
downright cynics who are 'concerned that corporate and financial interests
are shaping the rules of the global system in their own narrow interests'.
Others are critics who 'haven't given up on globalisation altogether, but
worry that more globalisation ... would not produce ... equitable and
sustainable development'.

The emergence of dissent within the economics profession as it pertains to
the contemporary discourse on globalisation has important implications for
the so-called 'anti-globalisation movement' that acquired trans-national
visibility through street protests in Seattle, Genoa and elsewhere.[3] This
movement has often been denigrated by the cheerleaders of globalisation
as a group of Luddites and even demonised by some as no more than an
anti-semitic band of reactionaries.[4] Admittedly, there are malcontents within
this movement who are masquerading as members of a progressive
movement. Nevertheless, when dissident economists voice concerns that
respond to the concerns of the anti-globalisation movement, they vindicate
the profound observation by Goethe that 'the world moves forward because
of those who oppose it'.[5] The Nobel laureate Amartya Sen (2001) offers a
rather similar view, although he invokes the wisdom of Francis Bacon in
making his point. Doubts, Bacon argued more than 400 years ago, enable one
to guard against error while serving as the basis for progress in scientific and
intellectual inquiry. By raising doubts about the current nature of

globalisation, the more strident elements within the anti-globalisation movement may eventually pave the way for 'global solutions' to the challenge of attaining shared prosperity for the world at large.

Dissident economists have an important role to play in seeking global solutions for a better future. By questioning orthodoxy using the tools of scientific and professional investigation, they are more likely to persuade their peers to re-think received ideas. More importantly, they can demonstrate that dissent does not necessarily have to throw the proverbial baby out with the bathwater. After all, John Maynard Keynes, one of the founding fathers of modern macroeconomics, was very much a member of the British establishment. His treatise on macroeconomics persuaded a generation of economists and policy-makers to use the capability of governments to respond to recessions rather than simply rely on the self-healing capacity of the market economy (Krugman 1999). Keynes sought to 'save' rather than rebel against capitalism.

One could argue that today's generation of economists who have refrained from becoming cheerleaders of globalisation are also following in the footsteps of Keynes. They aspire to salvage the agenda of globalisation from their hubristic alter ego.[6] Like Keynes, many are insiders even as they play the role of critics and cynics. It is with such a perspective that this chapter seeks to revisit some key debates on economic globalisation, especially in terms of their relevance to engendering equitable and sustainable growth in developing countries.

SETTING THE CONTEXT: FROM BAUER'S DISSENT TO THE WASHINGTON CONSENSUS

The discourse among economists on the role of globalisation in creating national economic prosperity – and more specifically in enabling poor nations to catch up with their richer counterparts –has its genesis in an earlier debate in the 1960s and 1970s on the efficacy and desirability of inward-oriented vs outward-oriented industrialisation in developing countries.[7] The former was a particular manifestation of the so-called dirigiste doctrine, or the notion that the state had a central role to play in fostering economic development. The latter could be seen as an attempt to restore faith in the virtues of a domestic market economy that established economic links with the rest of the world.

At the time, the intellectual environment was hospitable to dirigiste ideas, given the fact that Keynesianism and a mixed economy model that sought to regulate capitalism held sway in the West.[8] It was at such a juncture that the late Peter Bauer offered a refreshingly radical approach to thinking about development policy.[9] He registered his 'dissent on development' and passionately stated the case for a market-driven strategy to engender development. Other conservative economists lent their dissenting voices to these ideas, with Lal (1983) decrying the 'poverty of development economics'. Responding to such concerns, Sen asked (1983): 'Development – which way now'?

Within a decade of Bauer's polemical piece, dirigisme was discredited as a core plank of economic strategy in developing countries. This paved the way for the ascendency of global neoliberalism, defined here as a specific exposition of the broad principles of mainstream economics.[10] A core policy message was that a 'one-size-fits-all' strategy could be prescribed for both rich and poor nations in producing and sustaining national economic prosperity. Countries were exhorted to pursue 'sound' macroeconomic policies (epitomised by fiscal prudence, monetary restraint and a commitment to low inflation), limit governments to fulfil a set of core functions,[11] privatise public sector activities, deregulate domestic markets, engage in financial sector and trade liberalisation, and provide a hospitable environment for foreign investment.

The international financial institutions (IFIs) – most notably the Bretton Woods institutions (the IMF and the World Bank) – threw their collective weight behind the post-dirigiste economic agenda under the banner of the 'Washington Consensus'.[12] The latter became an ex-post acknowledgement of an informal intellectual alliance among Washington-based organisations – the IMF, the World Bank and the US Treasury (with the last serving as a proxy for the finance ministries of the G7 nations).

In 1980 the World Bank commenced its 'structural adjustment lending' (SAL), designed to reward developing countries that would follow the prescriptions of the Washington Consensus. With the SALs, one could argue that the grand experiment of neoliberalism in development economics began in earnest.[13] Between 1980 and 1998, the Bretton Woods institutions made 958 adjustment loans to developing countries.

Global neoliberalism flourished in the 1990s. It was juxtaposed between the demise of Soviet-led Communism with the end of the Cold War and the onset of one of the longest economic booms in the US economy under the Clinton administration. These developments, as Chomksy (1993) argues, led the Clinton administration in the early 1990s to pursue the hegemonic expansion of the American model of capitalism as the crux of US foreign policy. The demise of Communism meant that the USA could move away from a policy of 'containment' of the Communist threat bred by the seemingly interminable engagement in the Cold War to a policy of 'enlargement' of its ideals. Thus Thomas Friedman of the *New York Times* (2 June 1992) celebrated 'America's victory in the Cold War' and observed that the 'free market is the wave of the future – a future for which America is both gatekeeper and the model'. It was Friedman too who subsequently invented the notion of the 'Golden Straightjacket', a more colourful version of the Washington Consensus. Governments, he opined, would be penalised by an electronic herd of highly mobile investors if they did not don the Golden Straightjacket of 'good policies'.[14]

GLOBAL NEOLIBERALISM UNDER SIEGE: FROM CONSENSUS TO DISSENT

Thirty years after Bauer's pronouncements, the world is once again witnessing a 'dissent on development', but this time it is against the particular prescriptions of neoliberal economics that replaced the dirigiste doctrine of the 1960s. A confluence of several factors has shaken both the complacency and primacy of neoliberalism as a development agenda.

A notable event was the 1997 financial crisis in East Asia, a region that for many years was held as the poster-child of the 'Washington Consensus'.[15] After being hailed for years as the producers of 'miracles', East Asian governments have been blamed for 'causing' the crisis by failing to rectify underlying institutional and structural weaknesses. Other factors that could be linked to the emerging dissent against neoliberalism include the tragic experiences of the ex-Communist economies in Eastern Europe as they sought a rapid transition to a market economy in the 1990s. This has prompted some prominent observers to ponder on the wisdom of using unregulated markets to bring about large-scale societal and political transformation.[16]

There is, in addition, the stark experience of many Latin American economies. Despite more than a decade of experimenting with Washington Consensus-style policies, the outcomes have been disappointing. Growth has been modest, while poverty and inequality have remained entrenched at high levels.[17] At the same time, stagnation, instability and poverty in much of Africa is turning out to be the tragedy of the twenty-first century.

The agenda of global neoliberalism has also been significantly compromised by recent developments in the USA. The euphoria generated by the long boom of the 1990s has been replaced by the anaemic nature of recent economic recovery that is yet to see a return to full employment. To make matters worse, widely reported cases of corporate malfeasance in the USA, following the spectacular collapse of such iconic American companies as Enron and WorldCom, has tarnished the image of Western capitalism.

Geopolitical developments have conspired to impair the legitimacy of a US-led project of global neoliberalism. The tragedy of the terrorist attacks on the USA on 11 September 2001 has spawned an uncertain era of international relations, with a war in Afghanistan and a highly contested and violent occupation of Iraq by the USA and a narrow band of allies. Critics contend that a neoliberal economic model is being crafted in Iraq without popular consent.[18]

Surveys of global attitudes have shown that the international reputation of the USA is at its nadir (Pew Research Center 2004). There is a great deal of anxiety about the aggressive unilateralism of the world's sole superpower.[19] This has been matched by the remarkable critique expressed by Krugman (2003) that the current US administration is in the grip of a radically right-wing movement that has permeated all levels of the American political edifice. It is alleged that the leaders of such a movement do not accept the legitimacy of the current American political system. They are prepared to use their tenure in office to remove the vestiges of the social welfare state in the USA, reward the rich and the powerful through the tax system, engage in military adventures abroad and pass on the costs of such an enterprise to future generations of ordinary Americans by creating record fiscal deficits.[20]

Beyond the paradigm-shifting events noted above, the analytical and empirical foundation of the critique of neoliberalism has been fortified by the work of a number of scholars. Prominent examples include the Nobel Laureate Joseph Stiglitz, Dani Rodrik at Harvard, Branco Milanovic at the World Bank, Ravi Kanbur at Cornell, Jeffrey Sachs at Columbia, Princeton's Paul Krugman, now a *New York Times* columnist, and Mark Weisbrot and his colleagues at the Washington-based Center for Economic and Policy Research (CEPR). Those who have been – and still are – sympathisers of the Washington Consensus, such as William Easterly, an ex-World Bank economist, are also significantly influencing the contrarian literature.[21]

There are a number of strands in the eclectic literature that has affected the intellectual integrity of an ideology that professes faith in globalisation in delivering economic growth. To start with, there is the provocative claim of the 'lost decades'. This maintains that economic growth for the average developing economy in the 1980s and 1990s, the decades of the Washington Consensus, is significantly lower than in the 1960s and 1970s, the decades of the discredited dirigiste doctrine. At the same time, the evidence on global inequality and poverty is being scrutinised with considerable scepticism even as defenders of the faith proclaim that the debate is comprehensively settled in favour of the beneficence of globalisation.[22] Furthermore, several scholars have argued that the basic tenets of the Washington Consensus pertaining to trade liberalisation and macroeconomic conservatism rest on a fragile empirical foundation. Statistically, it has been difficult to establish clear-cut causality between Washington Consensus-style policies, growth and reduced poverty.

In sum, there appears to be a good case for arguing that what was, until very recently, a dominant economic ideology is in some disarray. The attack on global neoliberalism has also turned out to be a virulent critique of the legitimacy of the Bretton Woods institutions. To some extent, these institutions are the victims of guilt by association bred by their proximity to the seat of American power. As the architects of the Washington Consensus, both the IMF and the World Bank are being widely blamed for the failure to engender development, for mismanaging the transition in Eastern Europe, for the lack of results despite reforms in Latin America, and in the case of East Asia for mishandling the 1997 crisis.[23] Not surprisingly, the Washington Consensus now seems to be in a state of 'confusion' (Naim 2002).

EVALUATING GLOBALISATION AND ITS ROLE IN ECONOMIC DEVELOPMENT: THE CONTESTED NATURE OF THE EVIDENCE

The ultimate defence of globalisation by its cheerleaders is that the facts speak for themselves. Critics, on the other hand, maintain that the facts are highly contested.[24] These issues deserve an extended examination.

Globalisation and Growth

The late Michael Bruno, a former Chief Economist of the World Bank, once observed, 'The 1960s look like the golden age of economic development'.[25] Such remarks have turned out to be prescient. In an important study, William Easterly identified a 'puzzle', namely, a significant growth slow-down for the average developing economy during 1980–98 compared with 1960–79, thus prompting him to declare the emergence of the 'lost decades'. As he puts it:

> I document a . . . puzzle that has not received previous attention in the literature. In 1980–98, median per capita income growth in developing countries was 0.0 per cent as compared to 2.5 per cent in 1960–79 . . . [This] stagnation seems to represent a disappointing outcome to the movement towards the 'Washington Consensus' by developing countries.[26]

Others have independently corroborated the troubling fact of a growth slow-down for the average developing economy during the decades hailed as the new era of globalisation. Mark Weisbrot and his colleagues at the

Washington-based CEPR conclude that there was in fact a world-wide slow-down in growth after the 1980s, but some parts of the developing world were particularly hard hit.[27]

Milanovic (2002) has also revisited the notion of the 'lost decades' as part of a broader critique of globalisation. He shows that whether one uses the unweighted regional GDP growth rates, or the population-weighted GDP growth rates, the figures unambiguously show that per capita growth in the first period (1960–78) is better than in the second (1978–98) across *all regions* (Africa, Asia, Latin America, Eastern Europe, Western Europe, North America, Oceania).

The 2003 *Human Development Report* by the UNDP suggests that, in the 1990s, 54 countries (representing 12 per cent of the world's population) experienced negative growth. At the same time, the Human Development Index, encompassing per capita income, life expectancy and literacy, fell in 21 countries in the 1990s (UNDP 2003, p. 40).

Why have the 'lost decades' emerged? Easterly maintains that the policy variables that are often regarded by the advocates of the Washington Consensus as enabling growth to take place either improved or at least did not show any persistent deterioration during the 1980s and 1990s. Thus, the government budget balance (excluding grants), measures of relative price distortions (as proxied by the black market premium) and international competitiveness (as proxied by the real exchange rate) show steady improvements in the 1980s and 1990s. Furthermore, the median inflation rate and degree of openness (as measured by trade/GDP) do not show any persistent deterioration. In other words, it is not possible for the protagonists of the Washington Consensus to rationalise the 'lost decades' by suggesting that the policy environment of the average developing country either did not improve or even worsened because recalcitrant governments failed to follow the standardised recipe of the reform agenda offered to them.

Easterly offers two candidates in explaining the 'puzzle' of the growth slow-down, one pertaining to technical factors, the other to extraneous circumstances. There is suggestive evidence that the standard cross-country 'growth regressions' may be inappropriately specified, with the consequence that the usual explanatory variables in such regressions overstate their impact on growth. It is also possible that the econometric studies cannot capture deeper, underlying causes of growth, such as social cohesion. These are fatalistic conclusions. Despite an enormous literature that has been devoted to an understanding of the process of economic growth, there is a lot that is apparently not known.

Consider now the impact of extraneous circumstances on developing country growth. Easterly contends that the stagnation of the 1980s and 1990s may be attributed to terms of trade shocks, interest rate shocks on external debt payments (caused by an increase in the interest rate in creditor nations) and, most notably, the slow-down in growth in the OECD countries that are the major trading partners of the developing countries.

In seeking to solve one puzzle, Easterly seems to have raised additional questions. Why did growth decelerate in the OECD countries in the 1980s and 1990s? Nevertheless, whatever the reasons behind the 'lost decades', the central evidence of a growth slow-down in the 1980s and 1990s in the world economy in general, and developing economies in particular, may be construed as a robust critique of the empirical foundation of the neoliberal economic agenda. After all, there is near-universal agreement that sustained economic growth is a necessary, though not sufficient, condition in bringing about sustained reductions in global poverty. What, then, has been happening to global poverty?

Globalisation and Poverty

The World Bank, through its 2004 World Development Indicators, has recently released new global poverty estimates for the 1981 to 2001 period.[28] The world's poor are classified by determining whether their income/consumption levels fall below two so-called international poverty lines: $1 a day and $2 a day. Both these thresholds are expressed in terms of 1993 purchasing power parity (PPP). It is customary to treat the $1 a day poverty line as a measure of extreme poverty, while $2 a day is interpreted as the practical minimum for middle-income economies.

The $1 a day poverty line is now enshrined as part of the Millennium Development Goals (MDGs) that the international community – represented by 189 countries – endorsed in September 2000 at the UN millennium summit. The MDGs commit the global community to attain target reductions in both income and non-income dimensions in poverty by 2015 (using 1990 as the base year).

The global figures indicate that extreme poverty in relative terms has apparently fallen significantly (from 39.5 per cent in 1981 to 21.3 per cent in 2001). Projections made by the Bank show that the developing world as a whole appears to be on track to reach the target set by the MDGs.

The overall trends are influenced by a 'China effect'. Rapid growth in China has been accompanied by a rapid reduction in poverty. Given its large weight in the world's population, the trends in the absolute number in extreme poverty have been heavily influenced by developments in China. If one excludes China from the estimates, the absolute number in extreme poverty is slightly higher in 2001 than it is in 1981 (881 million in 2001 versus 845 million in 1981). Regional trends are consistent with this conclusion, where stagnation and negative growth seem to have taken their toll, as in Africa and, for much of the 1990s, in the ex-Communist bloc in Eastern Europe.

In recent years, the global poverty statistics have been mired in controversy. Some argue that the use of the PPP method imparts both a downward bias and considerable volatility to the poverty estimates.[29] Thus, for example, when the Bank decided to update the 1985 PPP series to the 1993 PPP series, it caused large and arbitrary changes in poverty counts for a number of countries.[30]

At the other extreme are those scholars who demonstrate that the trend decrease in extreme poverty has been much faster than the evidence compiled by the Bank and that the MDG goal of halving extreme poverty has already been reached. Bhalla (2002) has made the astonishing claim that the Bank deliberately overstates the incidence of poverty so that it can continue to justify its large operations in developing countries.

As Deaton (2003, 2004) has argued, the nature of the controversy can be traced to the fact that some scholars have relied on readily available national accounts data to generate the poverty estimates, while the Bank relies on household surveys. The average consumption/income that can be derived from the national accounts is usually significantly lower than the corresponding mean from the survey data. In some important cases, such as India, the discrepancy has grown over time. This suggests that household surveys understate the income/consumption growth of the poor and thus overstate poverty levels.

One should not, however, jump to the conclusion that the national accounts data are more reliable than survey data. The former aims to measure macroeconomic aggregates, while the latter are geared towards estimating living standards at a household level. It is a perilous procedure to conflate the two. This has motivated Deaton to argue that the professional community concerned with global poverty estimates must come to an agreement on appropriate protocols for monitoring global poverty. At the same time, he suggests that the Bank should seriously consider abdicating its current position as the sole official producer of global poverty statistics and either transfer the enterprise to an independent, accountable body or pursue its current obligations jointly with the UN.

In a refreshingly radical paper, Pritchett (2003a) has rejected the idea that one should continue to measure global poverty in terms of the $1 a day benchmark. He makes the important point that the current approach does not measure global poverty because its application inevitably means that there is hardly any poverty even in a middle-income country such as Malaysia. Any measure of global poverty should have a uniform standard against which all the poor in the world – from Chad to Canada – can be assessed. Using this novel approach, Pritchett (ibid.) argues that a measure of global poverty would need to rely on $15 a day (in terms of PPP dollars) which corresponds to the practical minimum for OECD economies. In this scheme, $1 a day is a measure of destitution, while $2 a day is a measure of extreme poverty. The message clearly is that the world in the last two decades of globalisation has witnessed some progress against destitution – thanks mainly to changes in China – but any meaningful progress against global poverty is a long way off and is certainly not going to be achieved by 2015.

Preoccupation with the $1 a day measure of extreme poverty has also deflected attention from assessing changes in non-income dimensions of poverty within the framework of the MDGs, especially target reductions in hunger and malnutrition and child and maternal mortality, as well as provision of universal primary schooling for boys and girls. Here is the latest report card compiled by the World Bank. Less than 50 per cent of the countries are on track to reach the 2015 target for reductions in hunger and malnutrition; children in more than half the developing world will not receive primary education by 2015; most regions in the developing world will not achieve the target reductions in child and maternal mortality by 2015.

Globalisation and Inequality

Over the past two years, a great deal of debate has surrounded the issue of global inequality. Is it declining, as some argue, or is it rising, as others contend? The issue of global inequality is an important element of the broader discourse on the benefits and costs of globalisation. To the cheerleaders who would like to see a deeply integrated world economy, a decline in global disparities in income is evidence that poor countries – and the poor within such countries – are catching up with their richer counterparts. Critics and cynics contest such optimism, arguing that the world is much more unequal now than it has ever been. To the uninitiated, such discourse is not easy to make sense of. As Ravallion (2004) has argued, the protagonists in this debate often do not clarify the implicit value judgements that are embedded in the evidence.

It turns out that there are two ways of measuring disparities across nations. In one approach, all countries are treated equally, a case of 'one country, one vote'. Thus, tiny Chad in this framework gets the same weight as gigantic China. The resulting inequality index of real per capita income across nations is a so-called 'unweighted' measure. It typically yields a disturbing trend of what Pritchett (1997) has called 'divergence, big time'. Poor countries, with some notable exceptions, have progressively fallen behind rich countries.

The alternative is to allow for variations in population size across nations when measuring global inequality, a case of 'one person, one vote'. This engenders a so-called 'population-weighted' inequality index of real per capita income across nations. It yields a rather optimistic picture of declining global inequality. Why?

The reason is not difficult to fathom. Two of the world's most populous economies – China and India – have grown rapidly in recent years, with the former managing this feat over a much longer period and in a much more visible fashion than the latter. Not surprisingly, as Milanovic (2004) points out, China's per capita real GDP (measured in 1995 purchasing power parity or PPP dollars) has increased from 17 per cent of the world average to 60 per cent between 1980 and 2000. India's progress has been much less dramatic, but is still noticeable, with its per capita real GDP (also measured in 1995 PPP dollars) rising from 16 per cent of the world mean to 25 per cent over the same period. Scholars who highlight these undeniably positive developments – such as Sala-i-Martin (2002) and Bhalla (2002) – thus question the credibility of those who document the 'disturbing' rise in global disparities.[31]

Critics have seized on the 'China effect' in contesting the evidence of declining global inequality. When China is taken out of the available estimates, the outcome of a sharp decline in world inequality dissipates. Growth has blessed some countries in the age of globalisation far more than others. Thus, even as one celebrates the rise of China, should one forget less fortunate nations?

The rather different value judgements that are reflected in different measures of global inequality have not been satisfactorily resolved. Those who defend the 'one country, one vote' could, for example, argue that this is a time-honoured convention enshrined in the UN system. Yet the 'one person, one vote' principle is intrinsically democratic and its reflection in measures of inequality is able to incorporate the rising economic fortunes of populous economies in Asia.

Some scholars, such as Birdsall (2001) and Firebraugh (2003), argue that the preoccupation with inequality *between* nations overlooks the important issue of inequality *within* nations. One is struck by the irony that disparities within China and India have actually gone up in the 1990s even though these countries are held as distinguished exemplars that have contributed to the decline in global inequality (Milanovic 2004).

There is a growing consensus among economists that the interaction between growth, inequality and poverty represents the eternal triangle (Bourguignon 2003). Growth reduces poverty, but such gains can be offset by rising inequality. Furthermore, rising inequality may retard growth through multiple channels. Examples include the way in which inequities in society can constrain the capacity of the poor to invest in health and education and undermine social and political stability.

Some scholars, such as Sen (2001) and Pogge (1989), emphasise that the concern for global inequality lies at the core of developing a system of global ethics. Sen argues that one should always reject the 'comforting conservatism' that leads the international community to quietly accept the grotesque inequities that characterise the world today. To Pogge, concern about inequality is an integral component of global citizenship. In Singer's scheme of global ethics, the world at large needs to embrace the view that the welfare of someone living 10 000 kilometres away matters as much as the welfare of a fellow citizen who lives 10 kilometres away. This is a prerequisite for laying the foundations of a truly egalitarian global community.[32]

Macroeconomic Policy, Growth and Poverty

So far the discussion has focused on the highly contested nature of the evidence on global growth, poverty and inequality. This sets the broad context for a brief discussion of the empirical foundation of two basic tenets of the Washington Consensus: the respective roles of macroeconomic and trade policy in determining trends in growth and poverty in developing countries. The evidence pertaining to the nexus between macroeconomic policy and economic performance is discussed first, followed by trade policy.

Macroeconomic prudence in engendering national economic prosperity receives pride of place in the original version of the Washington Consensus. Yet the empirical evidence corroborating a link between macroeconomic conservatism (as reflected in fiscal prudence and the single-minded pursuit of low inflation), growth and poverty is fragile. On the basis of the available literature and some estimates done by the author (Islam 2003), one can highlight the following stylised facts.

* Macroeconomic conservatism implicitly focuses on 'special cases' because it is a parable of the misfortunes that await countries if they engage in macroeconomic extremes – such as untenable fiscal deficits and hyperinflation. New findings by Easterly (2001) confirm that statistical studies that rely on cross-country data are particularly sensitive to extreme cases. Their removal from cross-country regressions impairs the validity of the standard view that macroeconomic and related policies have a significant impact on growth.
* Moderate rates of inflation are not harmful to growth. Inflation rates need to be quite high (in the 15 to 40 per cent range) before they become prejudicial to growth (Bruno and Easterly 1995).
* Studies using OECD data also show that countries that aimed for very low rates of inflation (0–3 per cent) do not necessarily exhibit either lower inflation or lower unemployment than countries that did not adopt inflation targeting (Debelle et al. 1998).

- While some studies have demonstrated a statistical link between fiscal deficits and poor growth performance, others focusing on both poverty and growth have not been able to endorse the findings. More specifically, there is no statistical link between fiscal deficits and higher incidence of poverty, as scholars sympathetic to the neoliberal cause have themselves discovered (Dollar and Kray 2000).
- Some studies have demonstrated that inflation has a negative impact on the living standards of the poor, but the estimated elasticities are quite low and can be easily offset by countervailing factors. For example, a 1 per cent increase in inflation leads to a 0.01 per cent decline in the average income of the poor, but a 1 per cent increase in per capita GDP leads to a 0.94 per cent increase in the average income of the poor (Ghura et al. 2002).
- While growth is a key determinant of the incidence of poverty, it can be offset by rising inequality (Ghura et al. 2002). Hence, what matters to poverty reduction is equitable growth rather than the single-minded pursuit of fiscal prudence or low inflation.
- One should not rely on cross-country studies to draw policy lessons. There is no alternative to in-depth studies of the experiences of individual countries or a specific set of countries (Cashin et al. 2001).

Perhaps the last word on the role and relevance of macroeconomic policy in understanding variations in national economic performance should be given to a seminal World Bank study that was published more than a decade ago. It concludes that 'a country's macroeconomic policies can only explain a part, often a small part, of its economic performance'.[33]

Trade Policy, Growth and Poverty

Among dissident economists, Rodrik (2001) has probably been the most influential in casting doubts on the veracity of the voluminous empirical literature on trade and growth that seeks to show that the former is primarily determined by the latter. Rodrik's point is that such studies usually conflate outcomes with policy variables. Trade volumes are outcomes of both trade and non-trade policies. A better approximation of trade policies is tariff and non-tariff barriers, compliance with WTO regulations and so forth. When tariffs, for example, are used in simple, cross-country regressions to 'explain' growth, no statistically significant result emerges. Indeed, the association seems to be positive, with higher economic growth being correlated with greater propensity to trade. This may simply be capturing the well-known historical pattern that many countries initially grow under relatively protected domestic markets. As they get richer, they begin to liberalise their trade regime.

In more recent studies, Rodrik et al. (2002) have sought to show that trade policy plays a much less significant role in explaining growth vis-à-vis variables that approximate the quality of institutions across countries. Warner (2003) has responded to this finding by presenting new results that show that trade policy still plays a significant role in determining cross-country differences in economic growth even in the presence of institutional variables. He concedes, however, that his empirical methodology is really constructed to test a dichotomous 'closed vs open economies' framework. It is as yet not suited to test the much more interesting intermediate cases of the consequences of incremental variations in trade policy. Furthermore, he notes that his results represent a description of the past, not necessarily a prescription for the future.

Recent studies that are sympathetic to the Washington Consensus have also failed to identify any meaningful impact of trade (as conventionally measured in terms of trade volume as a proportion of GDP) on both growth and poverty (as measured in terms of the average income of the poorest 20 per cent of the population). For example, in a cross-country econometric study that received considerable publicity in the international media, Dollar and Kraay (2000) failed to demonstrate a statistically significant impact of trade performance of countries on the average income of the poor. A similar finding is reported in an IMF study (Ghura et al. 2002).

DISSENT ON GLOBALISATION: WHICH WAY NOW?[34]

The Bretton Woods institutions have not been passive in the face of emerging dissent on globalisation. The Washington Consensus has, in recent years, mutated into the 'augmented Washington Consensus' (AWC), in which the original agenda has been supplemented by a concern with poverty reduction and a range of 'governance' issues – see Table 1.1.[35] The prerequisites of 'good' governance revolve around democratic reform, the promotion of civil society, institution and capacity building, transparency, a renewed commitment to poverty reduction, and the creation of social safety nets. This has naturally bred the suspicion among both dissident economists and those who favour a simpler development agenda that the AWC is straining the limits of what is possible in poor economies afflicted by scarce administrative, intellectual and managerial capital.[36] Why go for such an ambitious agenda of reform that ends up describing the desirable features of development but does not suggest a feasible way of getting there?

Table 1.1   Re-inventing global neoliberalism: the 'augmented' Washington
*   Consensus*

Washington Consensus (the original ten)	Augmented Washington Consensus (original ten plus . . .)
1. Fiscal discipline	11. Central bank independence and inflation targeting
2. Redirection of public expenditure towards basic education, primary health care, infrastructure	12. Reform of both public sector and private sector governance
3. Tax reform	13. Flexible labour markets
4. Interest rate liberalisation	14. WTO agreements and harmonisation of national standards with international standards in business and finance, but with exceptions (most notably environment and labour)
5. Competitive exchange rate	15. Strengthening national financial systems to facilitate eventual capital account liberalisation
6. Trade liberalisation	16. Sustainable development
7. Liberalisation of FDI flows	17. Protecting the vulnerable through safety nets
8. Privatisation	18. Poverty reduction strategy (PRSP and PRSF)
9. Deregulation	19. Country ownership of policy agenda
10. Secure property rights	20. Democratic participation

Notes:
This is an amended version of a suggested interpretation offered by Rodrik (2002a).
PRSP = poverty reduction strategy papers; PRSF = poverty reduction strategy framework.
The left side column of the table is based on Williamson (1999).

From Structural Adjustment to PRSPs: More of the Same

In the light of the AWC, the 1980s version of structural adjustment programmes appears to have been jettisoned in favour of so-called 'poverty reduction strategy papers' (PRSPs) that low-income economies are now expected to prepare in order to gain access to external assistance. The PRSPs – of which there have been quite a few – are supposed to be prepared in a participatory and consultative manner using the principle of 'country ownership'.[37] Distinguished observers of the development scene, such as Ranis (2004), are concerned that this has not happened and the PRSPs are likely to suffer, as did the previous genre of structural adjustment lending, from an over-reliance on IMF/World Bank tutelage.

The Need for Institutional Eclecticism in Devising Development Strategies

What, then, is the way forward? It is necessary to move away from the formulaic principles that drove the 'Washington Consensus' and rediscover the virtues of a mixed economy model with its many institutional variants.[38] This means that both states and markets have critical roles to play in economic development. The appropriate combination of the two varies over time and across countries. Hence it is necessary to devise context-specific approaches to deal with problems of poverty, inequality and sustainable development.

Moving Beyond the Preoccupation with Trade Liberalisation

Dissident economists contend that policy-makers in developing countries should also recognise that the benefits of further trade liberalisation of goods and services have probably been oversold. The WTO as a forum has so far evaded meaningful discussion of liberalisation of labour flows across the world. Given that low-skilled labour is one of the plentiful resources available to developing countries, and given large global disparities in wages, even a modest scale of regulated labour migration can engender benefits that substantially outweigh the benefits from all remaining trade liberalisation (Pritchett 2003b).

Dissident economists counsel caution on an uncritical agenda of economic integration because there is likely to be a trade-off between the imperatives of globalisation and domestic democratic politics. When policy-makers gear their entire national development strategy to the preferences and sentiments of global markets – often subsumed under the rubric of attracting and sustaining investor confidence – they may be forced to shun the voices and concerns of domestic constituencies and the strategic directions that a nation ought to take. This inadvertently undermines democratic governance and may well cause the tensions between domestic stakeholders and foreign constituencies to become unmanageable. Under such circumstances, crafting a credible national development strategy becomes rather difficult.[39]

The Reform of Global Economic Governance

There is also the contentious issue of the reform of global economic governance. Despite the commendable attempts that the IFIs have made in recent years to improve transparency and accountability in their operations and decisions, a growing number of influential voices are now arguing that, to remain at the forefront of development policy and practice, institutions of global economic governance, most notably the IFIs, must confront their impaired legitimacy.[40]

The thesis of impaired legitimacy starts from the premise that the prevailing ownership structure of the IFIs, in which rich countries are disproportionately favoured by the current voting formula, creates powerful incentives for the G7 nations, and the USA in particular, to pursue their commercial and national interests, often at the expense of the interests of developing countries. This pursuit of self-interest is usually cloaked in the language of the Washington Consensus, suggesting that there is a universally agreed set of ideas on what constitutes a national development agenda.

One solution, some argue, lies in changing the voting formula so that the developing countries have more influence over the IFIs. Yet another is to disband the durable, but entirely undemocratic, practice whereby the head of the World Bank is chosen by the USA and the head of IMF is chosen by the North Western European nations.

Others have argued that that there should be clear separation between policy analyses, research and the operational activities of the IFIs by ensuring that the former are carried out by independent agencies. Currently the research departments are located within these institutions, creating the risk that some of the politically sensitive policy-oriented research could be used to justify the operational imperatives of the World Bank and IMF.[41] Critics maintain that it is through the lending operations and 'country assistance strategies' that the largest shareholders of the two institutions seek to exercise their strategic influence. While it is easy to dismiss the above proposals as too contentious and hence unlikely to be ever seriously considered by the international community, what is clear is the need to move away from an artificial consensus on global policy issues. It is necessary to nourish the spirit of eclecticism and intellectual diversity anchored in the idea of country-specific approaches to development.

THE NEED FOR AN ENABLING INTERNATIONAL ENVIRONMENT

Crafting pragmatic alternatives to neoliberalism at the national level will also require an environment in which developing countries can harness an increased inflow of external resources to meet national development goals through both aid and access to export markets of the rich nations. Access to such markets depends not just on dismantling trade barriers by both rich and poor countries, but also on the ability of the developed world to create the necessary demand for developing country exports. This means fostering and sustaining buoyant domestic markets in the industrialised countries – a task that surely belongs to the domain of macroeconomic policy. Trade flows would have to be complemented by appropriate aid flows. Current calculations suggest that present annual flows of development assistance of US$40 to 56 billion will have to double if the world community wishes to make a credible commitment to financing the Millennium Development Goals (UNDP 2002, p. 31). At the same time, renewed efforts will have to be made in ensuring that the available quantum of aid is allocated to priority areas that directly affect growth and poverty. The rich nations of the world need to make a credible commitment to 'development-friendly' policies. The empirical record for the past 20 years suggests that global neoliberalism has failed to live up to its promise.

NOTES

1. Scholars working within the analytical tradition of political science and international relations take a much broader view and emphasise the multiple forces of globalisation entailing cultural, social, economic, political, military and strategic dimensions. See Keohane and Nye (2002).
2. Birdsall (2003, p. 1).
3. See Klein (2002) for dispatches from the front lines of this movement.
4. See Strauss (2003).
5. As cited in Ali (2003, Ch. 1).
6. Drawing on the Australian experience, Edwards (2002, p. 24) makes the point that the true believers of the market economy (known as 'economic rationalists') are also afflicted by righteousness.
7. Ranis (2004) offers a comprehensive review of debates on development policy.
8. See Beeson and Islam (2004).
9. Bauer (1971). Peter Bauer passed away on 2 May 2002. In a review of Peter Bauer's work, Amartya Sen (1982, p. 1) described him as 'one of the most distinguished development economists in the world, and undoubtedly the foremost conservative one'. Despite this, Sen disagreed profoundly with Bauer's ideas, finding them 'fundamentally flawed'. The Cato Institute posthumously awarded Bauer the first Milton Friedman Prize (US$500 000) for Advancing Liberty on 7 May 2002. Helen Hughes (2002, p. 64), Emeritus Professor of the Australian National University, described the award-giving ceremony as a 'gathering of thinkers whose promotion and defence of liberal ideas against dirigiste policies has delivered comfortable living standards and political freedom for the majority of people in the industrial countries'. She proceeds to note, 'If the Cato award, to be given every second year, continues to go to thinkers as outstanding as Peter Bauer, it will rank well above the Bank of Sweden's tarnished Nobel prize in economics'.
10. Others have used the term 'market fundamentalism' to denote neoliberalism. See Stiglitz (2002) and Soros (1998). The unifying vision of mainstream economics is that an appropriate combination of state intervention and a reliance on the market mechanism is necessary for engendering and sustaining economic development. While this vision suggests a presumption in favour of a mixed economy model and its many institutional variants, neoliberal economics displays a presumption in favour of the market mechanism This, in turn, reflects a conviction that the limits of the government (or 'government failure') are much more pervasive than the limits of the market (or 'market failure'). See

Islam (1992) on the way the constant tension between 'government failure' and 'market failure' has shaped the evolution of political economy in East Asia.

11. This list typically includes specification and protection of private property rights, and provision of strictly defined public goods, such as national defence and security. Of course, maintaining macroeconomic stability is also seen as one of the 'core' functions of governments.

12. Williamson (1990, Ch. 2) is widely attributed for inventing this term. Williamson (1999) has lamented the fact that both reputable economists and populist commentators have abused his conception of the term 'Washington Consensus'. He argues that he never intended it to become a synonym for 'neoliberalism' or 'market fundamentalism'. He developed the term within the specific context of Latin America. His original intent was to convey the proposition that there were ten 'core' policy elements that unified mainstream economists, US policy-makers (and, by implication, policy-makers in the G7 nations), and IFIs. These policy elements covered fiscal discipline, reorientation of public expenditure towards basic health, infrastructure and education, tax reform, financial liberalisation, unified and competitive exchange rates, openness to foreign investment, privatisation, deregulation and secure property rights (or the rule of law). The paper defends the use of Washington Consensus as a reasonable reflection of the neoliberal consensus in the developing world. It draws on the rationale offered by Kanbur (1999) that, despite the subtleties embedded in the original intent of Williamson, critics of the Washington Consensus judged what they saw in practice. Kanbur maintains that practitioners from the Bretton Woods institutions used the notion of the Consensus to adopt an aggressive negotiating stance with (recalcitrant) developing countries.

13. Yet the consensus was by no means universal, as some practitioners expressed disquiet that the ascendency of neoliberalism was a case of a 'reaction too far'. See, for example, Killick (1989).

14. Friedman (2000).

15. See Islam and Chowdhury (2000) for an account of the rise and decline of East Asia as rare exemplars of 'Washington Consensus' policies.

16. See, for example, Stiglitz (1999) and Kolodko (1999).

17. See ILO (2002a), Birdsall and Szekely (2003), Equidad (2000), Lustig and Arias (2000).

18. See Brian Whitaker in *The Guardian*, 13 October 2003 ('Spoils of war'). See also Naomi Klein in *The Nation*, 28 April 2003 ('Privatisation in disguise').

19. See Prestowitz (2003).

20. See Krugman (2003, Ch. 1). In an interview with *Der Spiegel* (29 July 2003) Nobel Laureate George Akerlof has made the provocative proclamation that the current US government is 'the worst . . . ever . . . in more than 200 years of history. It has engaged in extraordinarily irresponsible policies not only in foreign policy and economics but also in social and environmental policy.'

21. Both Stiglitz and Kanbur held distinguished positions at the World Bank, but both resigned. Stiglitz was Chief Economist of the World Bank until November 1999, while Kanbur resigned from the Directorship of the World Bank's 2000 World Development Report on May 2000. For details, see Wade (2003).

22. Thus one hears the proclamation that the 'the best available evidence shows . . . the current wave of globalisation, which started around 1980, has actually promoted equality and reduced poverty' (Dollar and Kraay 2002, p. 1).

23. See Islam (2003).

24. See Kanbur (2004) for an insightful account of the 'hard questions' that need to be answered in evaluating the evidence.

25. Bruno (1995, p. 9).

26. Easterly (2001, p. 1).

27. Weisbrot et al. (2000). See also Weisbrot et al. (2001) where they argue that progress in terms of a broad range of social indicators was also slower in the 1980s and 1990s than in previous decades.

28. World Bank (2004, Ch. 1).
29. See Pogge and Reddy (2002) who question the credibility of global poverty statistics.
30. See Quibria (2003).
31. The venerable conservative journal *The Economist* ('More or less equal', 14 March 2004) hails the cases of China and India as great exemplars of the benefits of 'international economic integration'.
32. These ideas are antithetical to the classic libertarian theory of justice developed by Rawls (1971).
33. Little et al. (1993).
34. This section draws on Beeson and Islam (2004).
35. Rodrik (2001) coined the term the 'augmented Washington Consensus', while Stiglitz (1998) talked about a 'post-Washington Consensus'. He seems to have moved away from that idea in subsequent work.
36. See Rodrik (2002b) and McCawley (2000).
37. Reviews of 'first generation' PRSPs are available in Ames et al. (2002), ILO (2002b), Levinsohn (2003) and Stewart and Wang (2003).
38. See Kuttner (1997) for an elegant statement for the case of the eclectic mixed economy model. Freeman (2003) concludes, on the basis of cross-country regressions, that capitalism can take many institutional forms without any particular form 'outperforming' others.
39. Rodrik (2002b) makes this argument forcefully.
40. See, for example, UNDP (2002). See also Stiglitz (2002). Williamson (2000) offers a comprehensive guide to reform proposals pertaining to the IMF, while Pincus and Winters (2002) examine the 're-invention of the World Bank'. Kapur (2002) offers a critique of G7 proposals to reform the 'multilateral development banks' (MDBs).
41. Deaton (2002), Kanbur (2002) and Wade (2002) make these suggestions.

REFERENCES

Ali, T. (2003), *The Clash of Fundamentalisms*, London: Verso.
Ames, B., G. Bhatt and M. Plant (2002), 'Taking stock of poverty reduction efforts', *Finance and Development*, **39** (2), 1–5.
Bauer, P. (1971), *Dissent on Development*, London: Weidenfield and Nicholson.
Beeson, M. and I. Islam (2004), 'Neoliberalism and East Asia: resisting the Washington Consensus', *Journal of Development Studies*, **41** (2), 197–219.
Bhalla, S. (2002), *Imagine There's No Country: Poverty, Inequality, and Growth in the Era of Globalization*, Washington, DC: Institute for International Economics.
Birdsall, N. (2001), 'That silly inequality debate', mimeo, Brookings Institution, May.
Birdsall, N. (2003), 'Manuscript on globalisation', prepared for *The Global Agenda Magazine*, Washington, DC: Center for Global Development.
Birdsall, N. and M. Szekely (2003), 'Bootstraps, not band-aids', mimeo, Washington, DC: Institute for International Economics.
Bourguignon, F. (2003), 'The poverty–growth–inequality triangle', paper presented at the Conference on Poverty, Growth and Inequality, Paris: Agence Française de Developpement and EU Development Network.
Bruno, M. (1995), 'Development issues in a changing world: new lessons, old debates, open questions,' *Proceedings of the World Bank Annual Conference on Development Economics 1994*, Washington, DC: World Bank.
Bruno, M. and W. Easterly (1995), 'Inflation crises and long-run growth', *Journal of Monetary Economics*, February, **41**, 3–26.

Cashin, P. et al. (2001), 'Macroeconomic policies and poverty reduction: stylised facts and an overview of research', IMF Working Paper, WP/01/135, September.

Chomsky, N. (1993), 'The Clinton vision', *Z Magazine*, December, 1–13.

Deaton, A. (2002), 'Is world poverty falling?', *Finance and Development*, **39** (2), 1–5.

Deaton, A. (2003), 'How to monitor poverty for the millennium development goals', mimeo, March, Princeton University: Research Program in Development Studies.

Deaton, A. (2004), 'Measuring poverty in a growing world', mimeo, February, Princeton University: Research Program in Development Studies.

Debelle, G. et al. (1998), 'Inflation targeting as a framework for monetary policy', *Economic Issues*, (5).

Dollar, D. and A. Kraay (2000), 'Growth is good for the poor', Policy Research Working Paper No. 2587, World Bank.

Dollar, D. and A. Kraay (2002), 'Spreading the wealth', *Foreign Affairs*, January/February.

Easterly, W. (2001), 'The lost decades: developing countries' stagnation in spite of policy reform 1980–1983', mimeo, February, Washington, DC: World Bank.

Edwards, L. (2002), *How to Argue with an Economist,* Cambridge: Cambridge University Press.

Equidad (2000), 'Poverty and inequality: recent trends', InterAmerican Development Bank, March.

Firebraugh, G. (2003), *The New Geography of Global Income Inequality*, Cambridge, Mass: Harvard University Press.

Freeman, R.B. (2003), 'Institutional differences and economic performance among OECD economies', October, London School of Economics and Political Science: Centre for Economic Performance.

Friedman, T. (2000), *The Lexus and the Olive Tree*, New York: Anchor Books.

Ghura, D., C. Leite and C. Tsangaridies (2002), 'Is growth enough? Macroeconomic policy and poverty reduction', IMF Working Paper, WP/02/118, July.

Hughes, H. (2002), 'A tale of two refugees: Heinz Arndt and Peter Bauer', *Policy*, **18** (2), 63–4.

ILO (2002a), *Globalisation and Decent Work in the Americas: Report of the Director General,* 15th American Regional Meeting, Lima, December.

ILO (2002b), 'Poverty reduction strategy papers (PRSPs): an assessment of the ILO experience', mimeo, November, Geneva.

Islam, I. (1992), 'Political economy and East Asian economic development', *Asian-Pacific Economic Literature,* **6** (2), 69–101.

Islam, I. (2003), 'Avoiding the stabilization trap: towards a macroeconomic policy framework for growth, employment and poverty reduction', Employment Paper No. 53, Geneva: ILO.

Islam, I. and A. Chowdhury (2000), *The Political Economy of East Asia: Post-Crisis Debates,* Oxford and Melbourne: Oxford University Press.

Kanbur, R. (1999), 'The strange case of the Washington Consensus', mimeo, Cornell University.

Kanbur, R. (2002), 'IFIs and IPGs: operational implications for the World Bank', mimeo, June, Cornell University, paper prepared for the G24 Technical Group Meeting, Beirut, 1–2 March.

Kanbur, R. (2004), 'Growth, inequality and poverty: some hard questions', commentary prepared for the State of the World Conference, Princeton Institute for Regional and International Studies, Princeton University, 13–14 February.

Kapur, D. (2002), 'Do as I say, not as I do', Working Paper No. 16, October, Washington, DC: Center for Global Development.

Keohane, R.O. and J.S. Nye (2002), 'Globalization: what's new? what's not? (and so what?)', *Foreign Policy*, Spring.

Killick, T. (1989), *A Reaction Too Far: Economic Theory and the Role of the State in Developing Countries*, London: Overseas Development Institute.

Klein, N. (2002), *Fences and Windows: Dispatches from the Front Lines of the Globalization Debate*, London: Flamingo.

Kolodko, G.W. (1999), 'Ten years of post-socialist transition: lessons for policy reform', World Bank Policy Research Working Paper, No. 2095, April, Washington, DC: World Bank.

Krugman, P. (1999), *The Return of Depression Economics*, New York: WW Norton.

Krugman, P. (2003), *The Great Unravelling: From Boom to Bust in Three Scandalous Years*, London: Allen Lane.

Kuttner, R. (1997), *Everything for Sale: The Virtues and Limits of Markets*, New York: Alfred A. Knopf.

Lal, D. (1983), *The Poverty of Development Economics*, Hobart Paperback, No. 16, London: Institute of Economic Affairs.

Levinsohn, J. (2003), 'The World Bank's poverty reduction strategy paper approach: good marketing or good policy?', G–24 Discussion Paper No. 21, April, UNCTAD.

Little, I.M.D. et al. (1993), *Boom, Crisis and Adjustment: The Macroeconomic Experience of Developing Countries*, Washington, DC: World Bank.

Lustig, N. and O. Arias (2000), 'Poverty and inequality trends in Latin America and the Caribbean, *Finance and Development*, March.

McCawley, P. (2000), 'Poverty in Indonesia: the role of the state in the post-Soeharto era', paper presented to the 50th Anniversary Conference, Faculty of Economics, University of Indonesia, Jakarta, 4–5 October.

Milanovic, B. (2002), 'The two faces of globalisation: against globalisation as we know it', April, World Bank.

Milanovic, B. (2004), 'Half a world: regional inequality in five great federations', April, World Bank and Carnegie Endowment for International Peace.

Naim, M. (2000), 'Washington Consensus or confusion?' *Foreign Policy*, Spring.

Naim, M. (2002), 'Washington Consensus or Washington confusion'? *Foreign Policy*, Spring.

Pew Research Center (2004), 'A year after Iraq: mistrust of America in Europe ever higher, Muslim anger persists', *The Pew Global Project Attitudes*, Washington, DC: The Pew Research Center for the People and the Press, 16 March.

Pincus, J.R. and J. Winters (eds) (2002), *Re-inventing the World Bank*, Ithaca, NY: Cornell University Press.

Pogge, T. (1989), *Realizing Rawls*, Ithaca, NY: Cornell University Press.

Pogge, T.W. and S. Reddy (2002), 'Unknown: the extent, distribution and trend of global income poverty', mimeo, 16 August, Columbia University.

Prestowitz, C. (2003), *Rogue Nation: American Unilateralism and the Failure of Good Intentions*, New York: Basic Books.

Pritchett, L. (1997), 'Divergence, big time', *Journal of Economic Perspectives*, **11** (3), 3–17.

Pritchett, L. (2003a), 'Who is not poor? Proposing a higher international standard for poverty', Working Paper No. 33, November, Washington, DC: Center for Global Development.

Pritchett, L. (2003b), 'The future of migration', Yale Global Online, 5 November.
Quibria, M.G. (2003), 'The Millennium Development Goals: are we counting the world's poor right'?, ERD Policy Brief No. 20, Manila: Asian Development Bank.
Ranis, G. (2004), 'The evolution of development thinking: theory and policy', paper presented at the Annual World Bank Development Economics Conference, Washington, DC, 3–4 May.
Ravallion, M. (2004), 'Competing concepts of inequality in the globalization debate', World Bank Policy Research Working Paper No. 3243, March.
Rawls, J. (1971), *A Theory of Justice*, Oxford: Oxford University Press.
Rodrik, D. (2001), 'The global governance of trade as if development really mattered', Background Paper, October, New York: UNDP.
Rodrik, D. (2002a), 'Trade policy reform as institutional reform', in B.M. Hoekman, P. English and A. Mattoo (eds), *Development, Trade, and the WTO: A Handbook*, Washington, DC: World Bank.
Rodrik, D. (2002b), 'Feasible globalisations', mimeo, June, Harvard University.
Rodrik, D., A. Subramaniam and F. Trebbi (2002), 'Institutions rule: the primacy of institutions over geography and integration in economic development', October, Kennedy School of Government, Harvard University.
Sala-I-Martin (2002), 'The "disturbing" rise of global income inequality', mimeo, 12 March, Columbia University Press and National Bureau of Economic Research.
Sen, A.K. (1982), 'Just deserts', *New York Review of Books*, 4 March.
Sen, A.K. (1983), 'Development: which way now?' *Economic Journal*, 93, December.
Sen, A.K. (2001), 'Global doubts and global solutions', The Alfred Deakin Lectures, 15 May, Australia.
Soros, G. (1998), *The Crisis of Global Capitalism*, New York: Public Affairs.
Stewart, F. and M. Wang (2003), 'Do PRSPs empower poor countries and disempower the World Bank, or is it the other way round?'. Queen Elizabeth House Working Paper Series No. 108, Oxford.
Stiglitz, J (1998), 'More instruments and broader goals: moving towards the post-Washington Consensus', 1998 WIDER Annual Lecture, Helsinki.
Stiglitz, J. (1999), 'Whither reform? Ten years of the transition', paper presented at the World Bank Annual Conference on Development Economics, Washington, DC.
Stiglitz, J. (2002), *Globalisation and its Discontents*, New York: WW Norton.
Strauss, M. (2003), 'Globalism's Jewish problem', *Foreign Policy*, November/ December.
UNDP (2002), *Human Development Report 2002*, New York: Oxford University Press.
UNDP (2003), *Human Development Report 2003*, New York: Oxford University Press.
Wade, R. (2002), 'Globalisation, poverty and income distribution: does the liberal argument hold?', in D. Gruen, T. O'Brien and J. Lawson (eds), *Globalisation, Living Standards and Inequality,* proceedings of a conference, 27–28 May, Reserve Bank of Australia and Australian Treasury.
Wade, R. (2003), 'US hegemony and the World Bank: the fight over people and ideas', *Review of International Political Economy*, 9 (2), 215–43.
Warner, A. (2003), 'Once more into the breach: economic growth and integration', Working Paper No. 34, December, Washington, DC: Center for Global Development.

Weisbrot, M., R. Naiman and J. Kim (2000), 'The emperor has no growth: declining economic growth rates in the era of globalisation', 26 September, Washington, DC: Center for Economic and Policy Research.

Weisbrot, M. et al. (2001), 'The scorecard on globalisation: twenty years of diminished progress', 11 July, Washington, DC: Center for Economic and Policy Research.

Williamson, J. (1990), 'What Washington means by policy reform' in J. Williamson (ed.), *Latin American Adjustment: How Much Has Happened?*, Washington, DC: Institute for International Economics.

Williamson, J. (1999), 'What should the bank think about the Washington Consensus?', paper prepared as a background paper to the *World Development Report 2000*, July.

Williamson, J. (2000), 'The role of the IMF: a guide to the reports', International Economics Policy Briefs, Working Paper No. 00–5, May, Institute for International Economics.

World Bank (2004), *World Development Indicators*, Washington, DC: World Bank.

2. Keeping the gains of globalisation

Brendan Berne

While some high-profile groups oppose globalisation, believing it harms labour, increases global poverty and inequality and degrades the environment, evidence suggests globalisation helps drive economic growth, reduces poverty and improves global equity and in the long run contributes to better environmental outcomes. History shows globalisation is not inevitable, as it arises from individual economies actively choosing to engage with the global economy. Only in the 1990s have levels of international economic integration surpassed those of a century ago, the first great age of globalisation. In the early twentieth century, depression and a deterioration in global security turned away governments from interaction with the global economy, imposing trade barriers, restricting investment and migration and, as a consequence, lowering national incomes and growth.

For globalisation to continue, it is vital governments understand how best to use it to maximise community welfare and so maintain local support. The deterioration in world security due to terrorism makes this task more urgent. To do this, governments must adopt sound domestic policies, build strong institutions and ensure their domestic markets function. Far from weakening governments' influence, as some critics claim, globalisation increases the need for sound domestic policies and institutions to allow citizens and corporations to prosper in open markets.

GLOBALISATION GOOD FOR GLOBAL GROWTH AND EQUITY

On balance, evidence suggests opening economies to international trade and investment promotes their growth, reduces poverty levels and improves equity. All else being equal, openness to trade and foreign investment helps an economy grow. However, domestic policies strongly influence whether short-term capital flows benefit an economy; promoting such capital inflows to an economy with a weak institutional environment can create a financial crisis.

Globalisation and Growth

Openness to trade boosts growth

Trade helps an economy grow in several ways. First, trade enables economies to specialise and produce in areas where they have a cost advantage over other economies. Over time, this encourages economies to place more of their resources in the most productive areas, increasing productivity. For example, abundant unskilled labour advantages developing economies in producing labour-intensive products like clothing and footwear and in low-value-added assembly processes. Second, trade increases the size of the market producers can access, increasing scope for economies of scale. Even in populous developing economies, low incomes make producers' potential local market small, so trading with the world is vital. Third, trade diffuses new technologies and ideas, increasing productivity. For example, US evidence suggests imports introduce new technologies to the local economy, with a doubling of research and development spending in other economies increasing US productivity by 2 per cent (Lewis and Richardson 2001). Finally, trade allows consumers to buy products more cheaply, increasing their purchasing power and living standards.

Good evidence exists that trade boosts growth, especially for poor economies. A recent study of 73 developing economies found that since 1980 those increasing their ratio of trade to GDP grew on average faster than those that did not; these poor economies also grew faster than developed economies (Figure 2.1) (Dollar and Kraay 2001). These economies include China, India, Brazil, Malaysia, Mexico and the Philippines. In the 1990s, these economies' GDP grew an average 5.0 per cent annually, up from 1.4 per cent in the 1960s, closing the gap with rich economy income levels. Notably, these economies reduced tariffs by an average 34 percentage points since 1980, increasing their trade exposure (Dollar and Kraay 2001). By contrast, economies that did not increase their exposure to international trade reduced their average annual growth from 3.3 per cent in the 1970s to 0.8 per cent in the 1980s and 1.4 per cent in the 1990s (Dollar and Kraay 2001).

An earlier study also found an increase in the ratio of trade to GDP by 1 percentage point raised per capita income by 0.5–2.0 per cent (Frankel and Romer 1999); another found developing economies with open economies grew an average of 4.5 per cent between 1970s and 1980s, while those with more closed economies grew an average of 0.7 per cent (Sachs and Warner 1995). Other studies find mixed evidence of the links between trade and growth. However, no economy closed to trade enters the ranks of the fastest growing economies (Temple 2001).

Firm-level studies also confirm freer trade benefits workers. In Australia, exporting companies provide higher wages, greater job stability, safer workplaces and more training; they also invest in new technology (Lewis and Richardson 2001). In Taiwan and China, exporting companies' productivity increases faster than similar companies which do not export (Lewis and Richardson 2001; Perkins 1997).

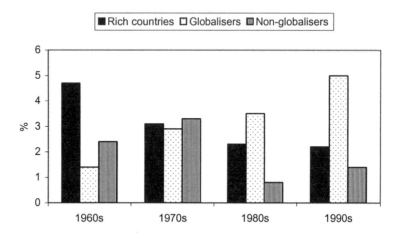

Notes:
'Rich countries' refers to the 24 OECD countries plus Chile, Hong Kong, Republic of Korea and Singapore.
'Globalisers' refers to the top one-third of 72 developing countries in terms of their growth in trade as a share of GDP between 1975–79 and 1995–97 in constant local currency units.
'Non-globalisers' refers to the remaining developing countries in this group.

Source: Dollar and Kraay (2001)

Figure 2.1 Decadal average annual GDP growth for rich, globalising developing and non-globalising developing countries

Openness to FDI beneficial
FDI has many benefits for economies, particularly developing economies. Accessing foreign savings can help economies grow faster and, in the case of developing economies, catch up with rich economies (Barro et al. 1995). FDI can increase competition in the host economy, making domestic companies more efficient and improving living standards. FDI also transfers new technology and skills; FDI in services proves particularly effective in accelerating take-up of 'new economy' technologies (APEC 2001; Graham 2001). FDI also increases employment including in local companies supplying the foreign companies, increasing wages and living standards (Graham 2001).

A recent study of 20 developed and 20 developing economies found that FDI had a strong positive effect on economic growth, after holding other factors constant (McLean and Shrestha 2002). FDI remained a powerful contributor to economic growth even when the study excluded developed economies, with a 1 per cent increase in FDI in developing economies on average increasing growth in GDP per capita by close to 0.5 per cent (McLean and Shrestha 2002).

But capital flows risky
Inflows of foreign savings benefit economies by allowing more investment and growth. However, opening economies to foreign capital inflows is good for living standards only when domestic and international capital markets are reasonably efficient, the domestic institutional regulatory framework is adequate, and borrowers and lenders believe that they will bear the consequences of their commercial decisions (McLean and Shrestha 2002). As the Asian financial crisis showed, many developing economies do not meet all these assumptions; in this environment large, unregulated capital inflows can undermine living standards.

Globalisation critics claim it increases world poverty and inequality, but the latest evidence suggests this is not the case. Economies that chose to globalise have grown more quickly than others, catching up to rich economies; by contrast, non-globalisers have languished. Poverty reductions in large globalisers like China and other East Asian economies have more than offset rising poverty in non-globalising Africa, reducing the total number of people living in poverty. Domestic factors still drive inequality within an economy, with international trade and investment playing only a minor though positive role. Government policy remains a powerful determinant of poverty and equality outcomes even in economies that trade and invest freely.

Globalisation and Equity

Developing economies abundant in unskilled labour can use trade to expand their employment and raise their living standards. Over the past two decades, poor economies choosing to globalise grew more quickly than those that did not, reducing inequality between developing and developed economies; several other studies confirm open developing economies are catching up with developed ones, reducing the major source of world inequality (Figure 2.1) (Dollar and Kraay 2001; Sachs and Warner 1995; Clark et al. 2001).[1] Inequality between developed economies, which all feature comparatively low trade barriers, more than halved between 1960 and 1995 (World Bank 2002a).

Globalisation and Poverty

Over the past two decades, rapid growth and stable income distributions
combined to reduce poverty in open developing economies (World Bank
2002a). Between 1993 and 1998, the number of people in absolute poverty in
globalising developing economies declined by 14 per cent, or 107 million
people, to 762 million. Most people still in poverty were concentrated in the
rural sector, which usually is less open to world trade and investment than
other sectors. Other indicators of these globalising economies also improved,
including average years of schooling and life expectancy, reaching levels of
the developed economies in 1960 (World Bank 2002a). By contrast, poverty
in the less globalised economies rose by 4 per cent, or 17 million people,
between 1993 and 1998, to 437 million; these economies also suffered from
lower school enrolments and life expectancy than globalisers (World Bank
2002a). Between 1980 and 1998, the net effect of these diverging trends in
globalisers and non-globalisers was a reduction in global poverty of around
200 million people (Figure 2.2) (Bourgignon and Morrisson 2001; Chen and
Ravallion 2001).[2] Impressively, these declines in world poverty took place
despite the world population increasing by 2 billion over the same period.

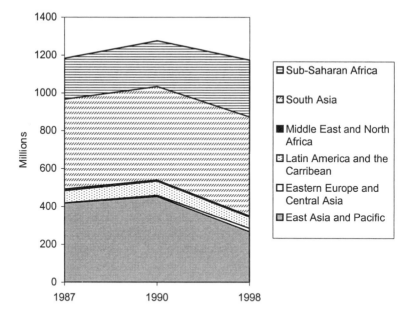

Source: World Bank (2002a)

Figure 2.2   Global poverty by region

Other studies also point to poverty falling globally but with a striking divergence in regional experiences. One study shows that while the overall number of people living below US$1 per day has fallen by over 200 million between 1970 and 1998, the number in Africa has risen by over 175 million. In 1960 Africa was home to only around one in ten of the world's extremely poor, but by 1998 this share had risen to two out of three (Sala-i-Martin 2002).

DOMESTIC FACTORS INTERACT WITH OPEN MARKETS TO DRIVE OUTCOMES

Weak domestic policies and institutions undermine the benefits from globalisation. Some economies with poor domestic policy environments can for a while attract significant foreign investment inflows but generally fail to improve their populations' socio-economic conditions (Table 2.1). Also, some developing economies fail to maintain strong growth despite reasonably high ratios of trade to GDP because they lack the domestic policies that support for development (Birdsall and Hamoudi 2002). Typically, such economies continue to export a few commodities with long-term falling prices because their weak education, infrastructure and economic policies prevent them diversifying into more profitable export lines.

Table 2.1   Foreign direct investment flows, per capita growth rate and percentage point decline in human development index shortfall, selected economies

	Foreign direct investment flows US$ billions		Per capita growth rate %	Reduction in human index development shortfall %
	1985	1997	1985–97	1985–97
FDI boosts growth				
Chile	0.2	5.2	3.7	47
China	2.3	43.5	8.3	45
Republic of Korea	0.3	2.2	6.5	35
FDI failing to boost growth				
India	0.1	3.1	3.7	13
Romania	0.0	1.1	−0.6	−2.0

Source: United Nations Development Fund (1998)

Domestic governments must provide the right environment to maximise and better distribute the benefits globalisation offers. As well as opening their economies to world markets, governments must undertake a wide range of domestic economic reforms if they are to reduce poverty and reach developed economy income levels.

Local Markets That Work

To capture the gains from free trade, consumers and investors need well functioning goods, services, labour and capital markets to respond to new global opportunities and incentives; governments must ensure these markets work. To function properly, markets require property rights and legal systems, a state that enforces anti-trust regulation and does not interfere with market prices.

A domestic economy in which producers and consumers are used to responding to market prices is better placed to exploit the gains of globalisation. Firms relying on state ownership, monopoly power, regulated exchange rates, prices or subsidies can find it difficult to adjust suddenly to lower world prices. Hence, prior to opening their economies, governments should remove as many distortions to market prices as possible. This is especially important for key infrastructure sectors like electricity and transport, as these provide key inputs to other sectors. By promoting competition throughout the economy governments can help keep input prices low so that local producers can compete internationally.

For example, over the past 20 years, Chinese authorities have dismantled the great majority of price controls, which once covered virtually all goods and many services, allowing producers to compete in China's increasingly open markets. In 2001, anticipating WTO entry, authorities eased price controls on another 128 categories of goods and services; markets now determine 90 per cent of all retail and agricultural prices (Economic Analytical Unit 2002a; *South China Morning Post*, www.scmp.com, 12 July 2001). Only strategic commodities like petroleum, coal, wheat and rice retain price controls and many of these prices are close to international levels. The Mexican government dismantled many price controls as it liberalised trade under the North American Free Trade Agreement, helping Mexican manufacturers compete; however, some remaining controls hamper sectors like agriculture.

In many developing economies, legislating high minimum wages makes labour too expensive, preventing local firms from succeeding in global labour-intensive industries and reducing the gains world market access offers. For example, the Philippines legislates high minimum wages for low-skilled workers, undermining the capacity of labour-intensive industries like clothing and footwear to export, even from export processing zones which provide duty free inputs (Philippines Export Processing Zone 2002). Strong unions can have a similar effect (Fosu 2000). Centralised wage bargaining which compresses real wage differences across sectors also reduces the influence of comparative advantage on trade performance and the gains from trade (Sapir 2000). Restrictive workplace dismissal laws also deter firms from hiring new workers. India and many Latin American economies like Argentina and Brazil suffer from such restrictions, keeping formal sector employment growth low (Economic Analytical Unit 2001a, 2001b).[3]

Institutional Strength

Economies with good economic governance and strong institutions benefit much more from globalisation than those with weak, non-transparent governments and legal systems. For example, without reasonably sound property rights or enforceable contracts, economies are unlikely to attract domestic or foreign investment, restricting export industries' expansion. Similarly, good governments are needed to provide sufficient public infrastructure, encouraging private and foreign direct investment.

Irrespective of the extent of trade openness, economies with strong institutions grow more quickly, reducing the gap between developed and developing economies (Figure 2.3). For example, secure property and contractual rights can increase the speed at which developing economies grow and nearly double the rate at which they catch up with rich economies (Knack and Keefer 1995). By contrast, poor domestic governance that allows elites to capture most of globalisation's benefits and encourages firms to lobby for rents rather than pursue productivity gains significantly reduces developing economies' growth rates (Rama 1993). High corruption levels also reduce growth amongst developing economies, increasing risks and deterring investment, a major source of growth (Knack and Keefer 1995). Bureaucrats, judges and politicians who allocate public goods or licences or fail to enforce the law or regulations in return for bribes undermine their country's legal and regulatory framework, encouraging inefficient investment, reducing growth and exacerbating inequality (Knack and Keefer 1995).

Also, weak economic and legal institutions reduce globalisation's benefits. Inefficient and corrupt bureaucracies deter local and foreign direct investment in many developing economies (Garibaldi et al. 2001; Hoekman and Saggi 1999). For example, legally starting a business in Bolivia takes 20 procedures, 88 business days and 266 per cent of average annual income; in Australia it takes two procedures, two days and 2 per cent of average annual income (World Bank 2002c).

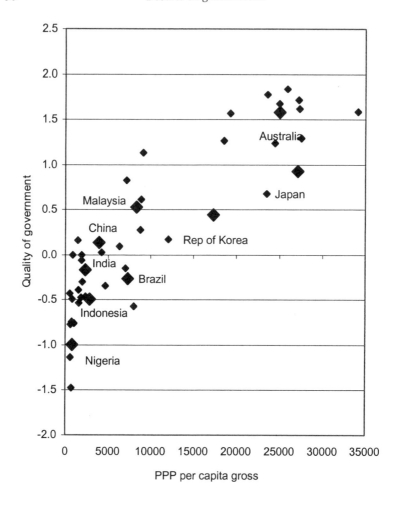

Notes: Based on 46 countries' surveys of quality of public service provision, quality of
bureaucracy, civil service competence and credibility of government policy. See Kaufmann and
Kraay (2002) for more details. The purchasing power parity measure of GDP recognises that the
same product can cost less in poorer countries, increasing the amount of goods and services a
given amount of income can buy.

Source: Kaufmann and Kraay (2002)

*Figure 2.3 Scatter plot of economies' national income, per capita
            purchasing power parity basis and quality of government
            measures*

A Tale of Two Economies

Russia and Poland faced serious challenges transitioning to market economies. While both opened to trade, foreign direct investment and capital flows, Poland also comprehensively reformed its institutions, improved policy-making procedures and boosted community participation, producing superior economic and social outcomes to Russia. Authorities strengthened property rights, implemented strong prudential controls for the financial system and built a competitive market sector through targeted privatisations and industrial modernisation. Policies aimed to improve both growth and equity outcomes. Parliament and the media led inclusive debates on economic reforms, increasing community ownership and support for new policies. Human development indicators improved markedly over the 1990s.

In contrast, Russia did not reform governance and property rights systems prior to opening its economy, increasing corruption and crime. Poorly targeted, non-transparent privatisations and economic restructuring aggravated inequality and concentrated economic power in a few hands. Between 1989 and 1996, inequality doubled and labour's share of national income fell from 74 per cent to 55 per cent. By 1996 Russian life expectancy had declined by more than four years.

These policies meant Poland was better placed to benefit from globalisation. Between 1991 and 1997, it attracted US\$18 billion in foreign direct investment or US\$4 657 per capita, compared with Russia's US\$13 billion, or only US\$88 per capita.

Source: United Nations Development Program (1999)

Property Rights

Successful market economies need to exchange goods, services, savings and ideas safely and efficiently. Many developing economies fail to define or protect basic property rights, limiting consumers', investors' and producers' activities. For example, few people in the urban Philippines or India can demonstrate they own their dwelling or business, preventing them from obtaining credit for investing (Borgonos 2002; Economic Analytical Unit 2002b). Also, in Ghana limited titling of rural land reduces farmers' incentives to invest (Besley 1995). In the last decade, the Australian aid programme has successfully titled traditional landowners in Thailand and Indonesia, significantly increasing farmers' economic security and investment capacity. In transition economies where property rights remain weak, firms on average reinvest less of their profits than firms in economies with better defined property rights (Johnson et al. 2001). In other cases, weak intellectual property rights make it extremely difficult for inventors to keep the gains from their inventions, discouraging their efforts. Hence weak physical and intellectual property rights deter new investment, reducing growth.

Weak property rights also reduce gains from opening to world markets, as they can undermine local producers' ability to compete. For example, farmers without secure title to their land may be unable to invest in more efficient farming techniques to compete with cheaper agricultural imports. Weak property rights in Nigeria, Burma, Pakistan and the Russian Federation prevent farmers from participating in the world economy (World Bank 2002a).

Several economies successfully reformed property rights as part of an overall market reform programme. For example, in 1992 Mexico reformed its property rights, transferring communal *ejido* lands to private hands, eliminating irregularities in land tenure and improving contract enforcement. Poland also undertook significant property right reforms, increasing the success of its transition to a market economy (United Nations Development Program 1999). Since the early 1980s, authorities have given Chinese farmers long-term leases on their land, but recently the government announced it would give them secure title to their land to encourage necessary plot consolidation and improve farm efficiency.

Weak Institutions Undermine Africa's Exports

Strengthening African institutions would have a powerful impact on Africa's struggling export sector. A study of 49 African countries showed the quality of institutions has a powerful impact on real export growth. Among indicators of institutional quality, the rule of law and the security of property rights have the clearest influence on export performance, even when controlling for other factors including policy distortions and political stability. The export sector often plays little part in setting economic policies, increasing the incidence of policy surprises and undermining rates of investment in the sector. Corruption imposes a series of informal taxes on exporters' efforts to distribute their products abroad, reducing their success.

Source: Weder (1998)

Investing in Public Goods

Governments must invest in people to develop the economy and help them to prosper from globalisation.

Education
Public investment in education strongly influences the rate at which economies grow; adults' average years of secondary school attendance strongly influences growth rates, with a one-year increase in average schooling lifting the growth rate 0.7 per cent per annum. Quality of education also matters; students' average science test results strongly correlate with growth (Barro 1998).

Investing in education also improves the gains from globalisation (Barro 1998). Adequate investment in education ensures locals possess the skills to access the technologies that trade and foreign direct investment introduce and secure better-paid managerial, professional and technical positions, as well as lower-skilled positions. Foreign direct investment in technologically more advanced industries increases the need for good local absorptive capacity to diffuse technologies (Borensztein et al. 1998).

Health
Investment in health strongly influences economic growth and the gains from globalisation. High adult survival rates increase incentives to save and invest and good nutrition and low disease incidence improve learning outcomes, productivity and technology transmission; all these support growth and increase the gains from globalisation. Studies show that improved health outcomes most benefit growth in very poor economies, especially in tropical countries where disease control is more difficult (Bhargava et al. 1998).

Physical infrastructure
Adequate public investment in efficient infrastructure increases incentives for private and human capital investment, boosting growth and the gains from globalisation. Investing in transport, electricity and water supply and telecommunications infrastructure typically produces higher rates of return than private capital investment (Easterly et al. 1993; Canning et al. 1994). In the early 1990s, World Bank estimated China's transport and other infrastructure shortages were taking one percentage point off its GDP growth each year (East Asia Analytical Unit 1998).

Poor domestic transport provision damages Africa's export performance, limiting the gains from globalisation. In land-locked Uganda, prior to reforms, outlays on transport and insurance to local monopolies that government cargo reservation policies support absorbed 70 per cent of merchandise export value (Yeats 1997). Overall, transport costs absorb as much as 40 per cent of African export revenues (Figure 2.4) (Yeats 1997).

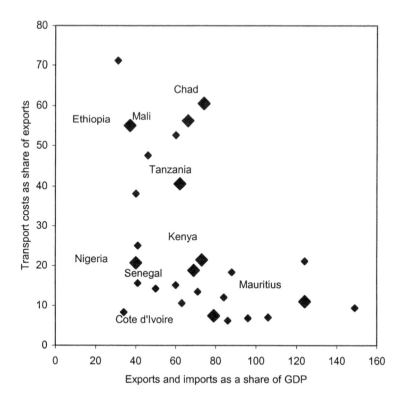

Note: Statistical analysis suggests that transport costs explain around one half of the variation in economies' share of trade in GDP.

Source: Yeats (1997)

*Figure 2.4   Scatter plot of transport costs as a share of exports, and exports
             and imports as a share of GDP, in African countries*

Infrastructure spending also attracts foreign direct investment and
increases its benefits. Developing transport hubs helps local firm numbers
reach a critical mass, increases links between foreign and domestic firms and
accelerates the spread of new technologies, as Singapore and Hong Kong
demonstrate. Governments also should encourage private sector infrastructure
investment, to increase funding available and improve service delivery.
However, governments must ensure infrastructure providers do not secure
local monopolies. For example, Mexico privatised its publicly owned
telephone monopoly, TELMEX, and only later implemented a regulatory

framework to guard against it exploiting its private monopoly. Breaking up monopolies to ensure they operate in competitive markets usually is essential to ensure infrastructure service costs are kept as low as possible for local producers and consumers (East Asia Analytical Unit 1998).

MAINTAINING EQUITY

Most studies find freer international trade contributes little to inequality, with other domestic policy settings and initial conditions, including technological change, land distribution and access to education and training, more important (Dollar and Kraay 2001). For example, technological change has a far greater impact on wage inequality within economies than trade or foreign investment, suggesting government education and training policies are vital to reducing inequality by ensuring the maximum number of people benefit from new technologies and more open markets.

Nevertheless, in developed economies open trade regimes can contribute to inequality by allowing labour-intensive goods to enter more freely, reducing demand for unskilled workers. This creates a role for governments to do more to spread the gains from globalisation, particularly by enhancing the skills of low-skill workers.

To promote equity, governments should target a number of policies.

Education Crucial

Investing in education and training protects against inequality arising from technological change. Investing in workers' education and training to adapt to new technologies can reduce the incidence of inequality. For example, the Republic of Korea invests heavily in education, minimising the deterioration in equality due to rising skilled wages, whereas Brazil invests considerably less, resulting in widening inequality (Cornia 1999). Similarly, Canada's investment in education prevented the increase in inequality seen in the United States (Cornia 1999).

Despite this evidence, investment in education in many developing economies has declined. Since 1980 per capita public spending on education has fallen by 60 per cent in sub-Saharan Africa and South Asia and by 33 per cent in Latin America (Oxfam International 1999).

Within developing economies, unequal access to education between genders and ethnic and regional groups also contributes to overall inequality. For example, in Peru rural illiteracy rates are three times those of urban areas, while in Pakistan twice as many urban 10 to 14-year-old children have completed school as rural children (Oxfam International 1999). These trends aggravate urban–rural divides that contribute significantly to national inequality trends. Rural Zambians have fewer teachers and over 50 per cent of rural children live more than 10 kilometres from a school, contributing to rural poverty (Oxfam International 1999). In Brazil the poorest 50 per cent of the population live in the northeast states, where half the children receive on average less than 4 years' schooling. Even in the Philippines, which enjoys relatively good overall educational outcomes, regional differences are considerable, with only one in three children in northern Mindanao completing primary school, compared with four out of five in Central Luzon. As a result poverty rates in Mindanao are twice those of Central Luzon (Oxfam International 1999).

Building a Social Safety Net

Progressive taxation and social safety nets offer another way governments can improve equity outcomes and minimise the social costs of adjusting to international competition. Especially in developed economies, temporary support for retraining or education is effective in assisting people move out of unskilled positions vulnerable to import competition.

However, excessive minimum wage provisions and social safety nets can have unintended negative impacts on low-income earners. For example, in Europe high minimum wages for unskilled workers have reduced inequality between employed workers but resulted in higher long-term unemployment, increasing inequality between employed and unemployed people (Sapir 2000). Expensive social protection programmes can discourage workforce participation and squeeze out other spending priorities. For example, the Netherlands spends 12 per cent of its GDP on cash programmes for the non-elderly alone.

In developing economies, with more limited financial resources, safety nets need to target disadvantaged groups carefully, be easy to administer and take account of regional and ethnic disparities. Containing the costs of administering programmes improves their sustainability. Programmes also should minimise incentive distortions to avoid poverty traps (World Bank 2002a). Governments have adopted a range of successful schemes including food price subsidies, food stamps, school feeding and micro-enterprise credit (World Bank 2002a).

Maintaining Macroeconomic Stability

Effective macroeconomic policy is vital to reducing inequality and minimising any negative impacts of globalisation on the poor. High inflation increases inequality, as the poor are least able to protect themselves against its effects (Cornia 1999). In Turkey, Argentina and Mexico repeated bouts of inflation and currency devaluation favoured rich households that could afford to buy property which was a hedge against inflation or move their assets offshore, increasing inequality (Birdsall and Hamoundi 2002). Also, recessions usually threaten unskilled workers' employment more than skilled workers (Cornia 1999; Birdsall and Hamoundi 2002). Overvalued exchange rates also increase inequality. Generally lower-income workers are concentrated in traded agricultural and manufacturing sectors which are more exposed to cheaper imports or reduced export opportunities. Many higher-income people work in the more naturally protected services sector, but benefit from cheaper imports and lower costs of international travel and assets. Such unequal impacts can encourage elites to maintain overvalued exchange rates.

Prematurely opening economies to international capital flows can be disruptive and aggravate inequality. Financial crisis on average affects poor households in developing economies more harshly than wealthy ones, reducing equity (Birdsall and Hamoundi 2002). In Latin America and Asia inequality increased in 73 and 62 per cent of cases of financial crisis; by contrast, in Finland, Norway and Spain stronger safety nets prevented adverse equity outcomes from financial crisis (World Bank 2002a). Finally, large-scale taxpayer-funded bail-outs of banks and depositors on average favour wealthier groups (Birdsall and Hamoundi 2002).

Promoting Rural Development

Urban–rural income gaps in developing economies greatly exceed those of OECD economies. Urban communities often enjoy strong advantages over their rural counterparts, including better access to education, lower birth rates and higher per capita government spending (Eastwood and Lipton 2000). Urban communities also tend to gain relatively more from economic reforms. For example, lower agricultural tariffs benefit urban consumers but lower rural producers' lower incomes (Eastwood and Lipton 2000). Reflecting this, developing urban areas generally enjoy better overall living and health standards than rural areas, with the gap rising since the 1970s (Eastwood and Lipton 2000).

Several governments have successfully addressed this divide, indicating policy priorities. First, rural producers need access to land and markets where they can sell surplus produce and obtain inputs. Second, rural credit schemes are important in assisting rural households or business invest in new technologies and increase their productivity. Third, maintaining low inflation is important for rural areas. In Brazil, urban–rural inequality declined over the 1990s, largely owing to reduced inflation which had relatively disadvantaged rural households (Ferreira and Litchfield 1999). Finally, decentralising the provision of public goods and infrastructure to the provincial level can improve rural services but investing in administrative capacity is critical (International Fund for Agricultural Development 2002).

Growth in smallholder agriculture sharply reduced rural poverty in Indonesia and Malaysia in 1970–80, as it did in Japan, South Korea and Taiwan in the 1950s and 1960s. In China rising grain yields, a relatively equal redistribution of land among households, rising producer prices, better access to free markets and the phasing-in of prices for food grains which markets set reduced rural poverty in 1978–84 (International Fund for Agricultural Development 2002).

AUSTRALIA'S ENABLING ENVIRONMENT A MODEL OF SUCCESS

From the early 1980s, Australia has opened its markets to world trade and investment; combined with other domestic reforms this has driven faster growth in output and living standards.

Australia Globalises

Since the mid-1970s, Australia aggressively liberalised its trade regime, dramatically increasing trade as a share of overall economic activity. By 2000–01, average effective rates of manufacturing assistance had fallen to 5 per cent from 22 per cent in 1984–85 (Industry Commission 1995; Productivity Commission 2001).[4] As tariffs fell Australia's trade increased dramatically, with imports and exports as a share of GDP rising steadily through the 1980s and 1990s to above 22 per cent by 2001. Notably, although lower tariffs boosted imports, increasingly competitive Australian producers were able to increase exports at the same pace.

Also, from the early 1980s, Australia has had one of the region's most liberal foreign direct investment regimes; this attracted large FDI inflows, boosting investment and competition. Limited restrictions remain in aviation, media and established residential real estate. While the Foreign Acquisitions and Takeovers Act 1975 empowers the federal government to examine FDI proposals over $20 million, it may only reject proposals it finds are contrary to the 'national interest'. Since 1975 only two major foreign investment proposals have failed to meet this criterion.[5] At the same time, Australian investment abroad increased as other countries liberalised their investment regimes and Australian firms sought to exploit their global competitive advantage.

After opening its capital account in 1983, Australia also continued to attract an increasing inflow of international investment in Australian shares and debt, boosting inflows.[6]

Reforms Complement Open Markets

At the same time as Australia opened its markets to goods and capital, it embarked on a broad programme of economic reform that enabled consumers, firms and workers to respond better to global markets' demands. This allowed Australians to seize the opportunities globalisation presented and dramatically improve their living standards.

Market reforms

Successive governments undertook a range of reforms to make goods markets more competitive and to help local firms compete in global markets. First, Australia overhauled its competition legislation, establishing an independent regulator, the Australian Competition and Consumer Commission, to implement this legislation.[7] In the 1990s, the commission has become more active in taking court actions against firms abusing market power (Australian Competition and Consumer Commission 2000). In industries where insurmountable entry barriers create a natural monopoly, Australia now has a national access regime promoting competition in service provision that uses this monopoly network infrastructure. Electricity transmission now operates within a national code and telecommunications services have guaranteed access to the national fixed line grid.

Since the early 1980s, successive governments have liberalised domestic financial markets. In the 1960s and 1970s a small group of domestic banks dominated Australia's financial services industry. The government set interest rates below market clearing levels forcing banks to ration credit, restricting the level of funding available to firms (Edey and Gray 1996). In the early 1980s, authorities allowed the market to determine interest rates and foreign banks to enter, increasing operational flexibility, competition and funding levels.[8] Consequently, the financial sector nearly doubled its size by the mid-1990s (Edey et al. 1996).

From the early 1980s, growing access to foreign capital, rapidly evolving financial products, including derivatives, reduced regulation of financial institutions' activities and the rise of institutional investors have rapidly developed financial markets. This increased banking sector competition and efficiency, cutting margins and allowing firms to access funds more cheaply (Davis 1996). Increasing competition generated a rush of new investment and technological innovation, including automatic teller machines and later electronic banking.

A banking crisis in the late 1980s and early 1990s greatly increased Australian banks' focus on risk measurement and management. For example, Australian banks maintain credit bureaus, separating credit management from credit origination, and manage credit risk at the group level. More recently, banks have established independent risk management groups to assess all risks bank groups face.

These financial sector reforms created an ideal environment for Australians to access and use foreign capital efficiently, avoiding the type of crisis Asia experienced in the late 1990s. Also, reforms improved firms' access to new capital, helping them grow and adapt to globalisation's competitive pressure.

As Australia globalised, governments and analysts believed regulated labour markets impeded firms' ability to respond to changes in global markets. Regulations kept wages in some declining sectors artificially high and maintained archaic relativities between different skill categories. As tariffs declined, companies needed more wage flexibility to compete (Hilmer 1989). Hence, in the late 1980s, Australia began to move away from the centralised wage bargaining that had characterised wage setting for decades, introducing the two-tier wage system whereby unions and employers could choose to negotiate wage increases outside the centrally determined wage system (Sloan and Wooden 1998). At the 1988 National Wage Case, increases to previously centralised award wages were tied to industry productivity gains. By the 1990s pressure for a more competitive labour market grew, and in 1991 the Australian Council of Trade Unions accepted the need for enterprise bargaining endorsed in the Industrial Relations Reform Act 1993 (Sloan and Wooden 1998). Finally, the Workplace Relations Act 1996 allowed workers and employers to negotiate Australian Workplace Agreements, firm or industry employee-based wage and salary agreements.

Building and strengthening institutions

Australia possesses strong institutions and governance standards, increasing firms' and citizens' ability to benefit from globalisation. Australia ranks highly in broad measures of institutional quality, ranking equal twelfth out of 159 countries in government effectiveness, eleventh out of 168 countries in regulatory quality, twelfth out of 169 countries in rule of law, and thirteenth out of 160 countries in control of corruption.

Over the past two decades, Australia has undertaken significant institutional and regulatory reform, strengthening the economy's ability to adapt to globalisation. For example, in the financial sector, the Wallace inquiry in the late 1990s further reformed bank and financial institution supervision, securities market regulation and corporate governance, producing the Australian Prudential Supervision Agency and the Australian Securities and Investments Commission (Economic Analytical Unit 2002a). In corporate regulation, the Corporate Law Economic Reform Program resolved legal inconsistencies arising from Australia's federal system of government. It also modernised regulation of financial reporting and financial markets, corporate governance, takeovers, directors' duties, fundraising and investment products to enhance transparency and accountability (Australian Treasury 1999).

Recent macroeconomic policy innovations include adopting an inflation target to guide monetary policy and the Charter of Budget Honesty to increase the public transparency of fiscal policy. In 1996 the *Statement on the Conduct of Monetary Policy* guaranteed the Reserve Bank operational independence from the Federal Government and formalised an inflation target of between 2 and 3 per cent over the economic cycle. In 2001 new taxation reforms introduced a broad-based consumption tax, reducing income taxes and taxing goods and services more equitably.

Impact on the Economy

Over the past two decades, opening to world markets and other reforms markedly altered how Australian businesses operate, forcing some to transform quickly to survive. The most important changes were improved management practices, greater specialisation and more rapid technological uptake.

New management techniques
Facing greater domestic and foreign competition, Australian firms have upgraded management practices and workplace arrangements, adopting a more strategic approach. A growing number of firms now benchmark their performance against leading global firms to maintain competitiveness and use production processes that conform to international quality standards (Productivity Commission 1999). For example, the automotive industry has adopted 'lean production' in assembly processes and more carefully manages inventory and quality, forcing change on component suppliers. Increasingly firms, governments and public utilities contract out non-core activities to improve efficiency (Productivity Commission 1999). In over half of Australian workplaces with more than 20 employees, workplace agreements link pay to employee performance (Productivity Commission 1999).

Increased specialisation
Greater market discipline forces firms to rethink their areas of expertise, dropping activities in which they cannot compete globally. From the mid-1980s, trade between firms within a given industry rose sharply, indicating firms were specialising more and relying on others to supply inputs they once produced themselves (Productivity Commission 1999).[9] In white goods, for example, the number of firms fell from 18 in 1978 to 3 by the mid-1990s. The remaining firms specialised in larger refrigerators and top-loading washing machines to gain economies of scale (Productivity Commission 1999).

Greater technology uptake
Since Australia reduced its trade barriers and reformed other key aspects of its economy, firms have been investing more in technology. The proportion of manufacturing businesses with 10 or more employees using advanced technologies increased from 33 per cent in 1988 to 44 per cent in 1997 and expenditure on foreign capital goods and research and development has increased strongly (Productivity Commission 1999). In white goods, where protection now is low, research and development spending rose sharply; this has not yet occurred in the more highly protected textiles, clothing and footwear industries (Productivity Commission 1999).

In the early 1990s, a survey of 900 firms showed international competitive pressure was the major incentive firms cited for increasing research and development spending (Bureau of Industry Economics 1993). Other studies confirm the prospect of lower tariffs proved the most effective trigger of firm innovation across Australia.

Although Australia is a net importer of information technology, it has adopted these technologies aggressively, bringing tremendous gains to consumers. Australia's use of computer technology is amongst the highest in the world, especially in telecommunications, finance, retailing and insurance industries (Economic Analytical Unit 2002b; Simon and Wardrop 2002). Rapid information and communication technology take up has allowed producers to reduce the prices of their services, benefiting consumers and in some cases increasing export competitiveness (Simon and Wardrop 2002).

Industry responds
As a result of these strategies, most industries with a genuine comparative advantage adjusted well to open markets and reforms. For example, the Australian Pork Council reported open markets changed the industry's defensive inward-looking stance to a more competitive and export focused position, boosting export growth from 3 per cent in the early 1990s to 6 per cent in 1999. Similarly, the Australian citrus industry successfully

became more export orientated as it faced increased international competition (Australian Commonwealth Parliament Joint Standing Committee on Treaties 2001).

Australian Society Reaps the Rewards

As producers upgraded their management and labour practices and adopted new technologies, Australian society benefited; higher productivity growth pushed living standards higher and faster. Openness to world markets also internationalised Australian consumption patterns, providing consumers with new goods more cheaply than they could be produced at home, boosting community purchasing power and living standards.

Productivity growing faster

Higher productivity means the economy can provide more goods and services for each Australian, increasing average living standards; productivity growth means living standards rise at a faster rate. Globalisation combined with other reforms to sharply increase the rate at which Australia's productivity grew through the 1990s, reversing the trend in the pre-reform period. After Australia's productivity ranking amongst developed countries slipped from third in 1950 to sixth in 1973 and tenth in 1992, its productivity growth rose sharply in the 1990s, outpacing nearly all developed countries (Productivity Commission 1999). Australia's economic performance during the 1990s was especially impressive, when its real per capita GDP grew faster than in any other decade except the 1960s (Figure 2.5) (Australian Treasury 2002).[10]

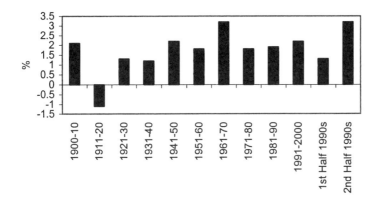

Source: Australian Treasury (2002)

Figure 2.5   Australia's productivity level, decade averages, 1900–2000

New products, cheaper

As tariffs came down, Australians could purchase most consumer goods, including major ones like cars, more cheaply (Figure 2.6). As tariffs declined between 1993–94 and 1998–99, spending on clothing and footwear fell by 5 per cent. Also, household incomes rose sharply, further boosting the affordability of many traded goods.

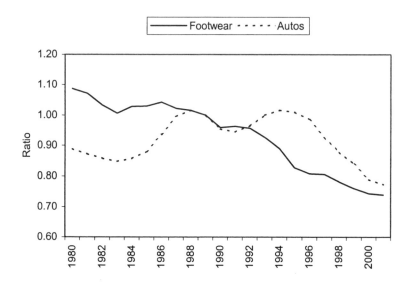

Source: CEIC (2002)

*Figure 2.6   Price of footwear and autos relative to all other prices
(1980=1), 1980–2001*

Globalisation also allowed Australians to access a much more diverse array of goods and services than in the past. For example, Australia is home to over 4000 Chinese restaurants and thousands of other types of restaurant, markedly more than there were a few decades earlier (Henry 2002).

Inequality Trends Steady

Since the 1980s, inequality has remained roughly steady, mainly because the welfare system has offset a slight rise in income inequality (Figure 2.7) (Harding and Greenwell 2002). Taking taxes and transfers into account, the living standards of Australia's low-income earners have increased substantially since 1980 (Johnson et al. 1995).

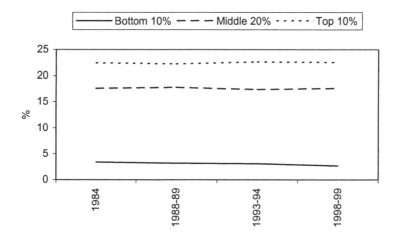

Source: Harding and Greenwell (2002)

Figure 2.7 Shares of household disposable income, selected deciles 1984–99

GLOBAL POLICIES MUST PROMOTE DEVELOPMENT

Australia's experience shows what small open economies can achieve with the appropriate market and institutional environment. However, for many developing countries, international policies could do more to promote development.

International Trade Barriers Hinder Development

Despite 50 years of trade reforms, remaining global trade barriers still impose considerable costs on developing and developed economies alike. International trade barriers hinder developing economies from specialising in and exporting products they produce most competitively and reaping the maximum gains from free trade. By removing all developed economy barriers to developing economy imports, developing economies could gain over US$40 billion extra a year (Figure 2.8) (World Bank 2002a).[11] Adding in gains from removing developed economy subsidies, total potential gains would exceed international aid flows to developing economies.

Developing economies' trade policies also damage one another. While their markets are smaller, developing economies on average impose up to three times higher trade barriers than developed economies. Hence

developing economies could increase their welfare by over US$65 billion if
they liberalised their own trade regimes (Figure 2.8) (Yeats 1997; World
Bank 2002a).

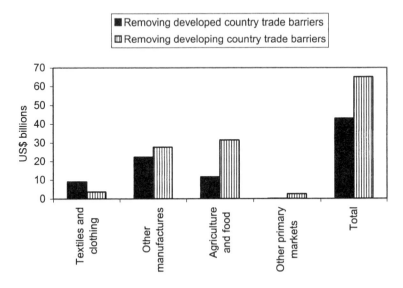

Note: These figures are lower bound estimates of the gains from liberalisation as they assume
developed countries have implemented their Uruguay Round commitments, ignore dynamic and
scale effects and do not consider services trade liberalisation.

Source: World Bank (2002a)

*Figure 2.8   Potential annual developing economy incomes gains from
removing developed and developing economy trade barriers*

Developed economies like the EU, the United States and Japan finance
huge domestic agricultural production and export subsidy schemes that
depress world agricultural prices by an estimated 12 per cent every year
(United States Department of Agriculture 2001).[12] For example, in 2001 12
per cent of African agriculture was worth US$7.1 billion, only slightly lower
than bilateral aid flows to Africa of US$8.3 billion (Economic Analytical
Unit 2003). These subsidies significantly undermine developing economies'
agricultural export income. When subsidised products are dumped on
international markets, they also disrupt developing economies' own
agricultural markets and third economy export markets.

Subsidised agricultural products can swamp developing economy markets
when they open their own markets in the absence of international disciplines.

For example, after the Jamaican dairy market was opened to competition in the early 1990s, shiploads of subsidised milk powder from Europe severely damaged Jamaica's dairy farmers. Domestic producers now meet less than one fifth of domestic consumption, impacting heavily on Jamaica's mainly small-scale operators (Oxfam International 2002a). Support for US cotton farmers has virtually wiped out Mali's efficient cotton industry, sending many farmers into poverty (Oxfam International 2002b). Mainly for this reason, many developing economies retain high barriers to agricultural imports, pushing up food prices and undermining potential farm efficiency gains (Economic Analytical Unit 2003a).

Improving Global Public Good Provision

Keeping and expanding the gains of globalisation also requires ongoing cooperation on many global governance issues. Many activities that economies and companies undertake have beneficial or adverse transnational impacts that governments can control only through international cooperation. Major global economic cooperation priorities include improving international financial architecture, cooperating on international investment and competition issues and controlling communicable diseases. In the past decade, through multilateral organisations and agreements, the global community has begun tackling international financial architecture and investment issues. In other areas, however, including combating abuses of global market power, international cooperation is at an early stage.

Strengthening international financial architecture
As the 1997 Asian financial crisis demonstrated, the international financial system is increasingly interdependent; events in one market can rapidly affect others. The costs of a single institution failing are much greater than the loss of its private capital, as it can lead to a loss of confidence in otherwise sound institutions, even triggering their collapse. Developing economies which are open to foreign capital flows but do not have sound domestic regulatory regimes are particularly vulnerable.[13]

Since they were established soon after World War II, the International Monetary Fund and to a lesser extent the World Bank have played a central role in helping maintain international financial stability. In 1999 the International Monetary Fund and the World Bank commenced the Review of Standards and Codes to identify weaknesses in member economies' regulatory arrangements which could contribute to economic and financial instability. This initiative is designed to foster increased market efficiency and discipline and ultimately to contribute to a more robust and less crisis-prone global economy. International standards in a range of regulatory, corporate governance and macroeconomic data areas provide a benchmark to help member economies identify vulnerability and guide policy reform. Hence the programme aims to increase transparency about global economic governance standards for markets and encourage governments to adhere to core international codes (International Monetary Fund 2003).

In 1999 11 major economies including Australia also convened the Financial Stability Forum to promote international financial stability through information exchange and cooperation in financial supervision and surveillance. The forum regularly brings together national authorities responsible for financial stability in international financial institutions, sector-specific international regulatory and supervisory groups and committees of central bank experts. The Financial Stability Forum seeks to coordinate the efforts of these various bodies to promote international financial stability, improve market functioning and reduce system-wide risk in financial markets (East Asia Analytical Unit 1999). The Financial Stability Forum also coordinates with other agencies including the International Monetary Fund to offer recommendations to develop effective bank deposit guarantee schemes, identify financial sectors at risk of instability, enhance securities regulators' information exchange and more closely involve the private sector in combating financial crises and financial market volatility.

Competition rules

While most developed and some developing economies enforce domestic competition policies which prohibit anti-competitive behaviour by firms, no international agreement enforces competition internationally. In 1996 a WTO Working Group on the Interaction between Trade and Competition Policy was created to explore and analyse the link between competition and trade (Center for International Development 2002). In 2003, in the context of the Doha Round, the working group examined a range of competition policy issues including provisions for export cartels and the need to support developing economy capacity building in regulating competition.

Tackling global health issues

The greater movement of people as the world globalises has increased the rate at which communicable disease spreads across borders. The incidence of many serious diseases like malaria, tuberculosis and HIV/AIDS and now recently SARS is on the rise, increasing governments' need to coordinate their efforts to combat them. In particular, the future growth of many African economies is under serious threat if they cannot contain the HIV/AIDS pandemic (Word Bank 2002b).[14] Since the mid-1990s, UNAIDS has coordinated the global response to the AIDS crisis. Since then, the World Bank has initiated a regional AIDS prevention programme, the

Multi-Economy AIDS Program, the first stage of which covers Ethiopia and Kenya (World Bank 2002b). Similar international coordination efforts are needed in a range of areas affecting international health, including vaccinating against common childhood and communicable diseases, spraying for malaria-carrying mosquitoes and improving water quality.

NOTES

1. 'Globalisers' refers to the top one-third of 72 developing countries in terms of their growth in trade as a share of GDP between 1975–79 and 1995–97 in constant local currency units. 'Non-globalisers' refers to the remaining developing countries in this group (Dollar and Kraay 2001).
2. This figure differs slightly from that which Figure 2.2 implies because of the different period used.
3. Opening to trade without freeing up the labour market can be costly. For example, Chile saw unemployment rise 3.5 per cent after reducing tariffs because the high minimum wages prevented the export sector from absorbing labour from sectors that were previously protected.
4. Effective rates of assistance measures include trade barriers, budgetary assistance and other assistance that raises the return to producers.
5. These were proposals to demolish and redevelop the historic inner-Sydney harbour-side suburb of Woolloomooloo and Shell's bid to take over Woodside Petroleum in 2001.
6. In 1981 the Committee of Inquiry into the Australian Financial System (Campbell Inquiry) recommended liberalising the banking system and exchange rate, to promote financial system efficiency, competitiveness and stability; this resulted in authorities dropping capital controls.
7. The Trade Practices Act 1974 prohibits mergers or acquisitions which result in a substantial lessening of competition, prohibits monopolies from misusing their market power and outlaws firms preventing or deterring market entry. It specifically prohibits horizontal and vertical arrangements between firms which result in a substantial lessening of competition and prohibits individual firms with substantial market power from taking advantage of that power.
8. Reforms allowed banks to decide whether to lend to firms at interest rates they chose. Large government deficits in the 1970s and early 1980s coupled with high inflation increased demand for market determined interest rates so that financial institutions could better price risk.
9. One index of intra-industry trade rose from 66 in 1984–85 to 80 in 1996–97 (Productivity Commission 1999).
10. Normally, countries' growth rates slow as they reach higher-income levels, making this achievement even more impressive.
11. This estimate is the lower bound of actual benefits because it excludes efficiency gains developing economies would achieve from operating at larger production scales and using more advanced technologies they could afford if they increased their market share; it also excludes the benefits from services liberalisation. These estimates provide an income equivalent of the welfare gains, rather than an estimate of the rise in GDP.
12. Most developed economies pay farm subsidies on the basis of production volumes, so they artificially encourage farmers to produce more, increasing world supply and depressing prices.
13. Because financial markets are highly liquid and the cost of undertaking transactions is relatively low, the volume of international flows of funds can change suddenly, shifting

exchange and interest rates rapidly, affecting economies. Furthermore, changes in market sentiment can quickly undermine confidence in a group of economies.
14. Africa includes the top 19 economies for HIV/AIDS prevalence in the world. In 2000 the World Bank estimated 25.3 million Africans were living with AIDS, 3.8 million of whom were infected with HIV during that year. About 12 million African children have been orphaned by AIDS (World Bank 2002b).

REFERENCES

APEC (2001), 'The New Economy and APEC', APEC Economic Committee, Singapore: APEC Secretariat, October.
Australian Commonwealth Parliament Joint Standing Committee on Treaties (2001), 'Who's Afraid of the WTO?', Canberra, September.
Australian Competition and Consumer Commission (2000), 'Annual Report 1999–2000', Canberra: AusInfo.
Australian Treasury (1999), 'Making transparency transparent: an Australian assessment', available at www.treasury.gov.au, accessed April 2001.
Australian Treasury (2002), information supplied to the Economic Analytical Unit, June.
Barro, R. (1998), 'Human capital and growth in cross-economy regressions', Harvard University, available at http://hassler-j.iies.su.se/conferences/papers/barro.pdf, accessed 20 June 2002.
Barro, R.J., N.G. Mankiw and X. Sala-i-Martin (1995), 'Capital mobility in neoclassical models of growth', *American Economic Review*, **85** (1), 103–15.
Besley, T. (1995), 'Property rights and investment incentives: theory and evidence from Ghana', *Journal of Political Economy*, **103** (5), 903–37.
Bhargava, A., D.T. Jamison, L. Lau and C. Murray (1998), 'Modelling the effects of health on economic growth', Global Programme on Evidence for Health Policy Discussion Paper Series, no. 33, World Health Organization, available at www-nt.who.int/whosis/statistics/discussionpapers/pdf/paper33.pdf.
BIE (1993), 'Monitoring micro economic reform', available at www.pc.gov.au, accessed 14 November 2002.
Birdsall, N. and A. Hamoudi (2002), 'Commodity dependence, trade and growth: when openness is not enough', paper presented at Reserve Bank of Australia and Department of Treasury conference, Globalisation, Living Standards and Inequality, Sydney, 26–28 May.
Borensztein, E., J. De Gregorio and J. Lee (1998), 'How does foreign direct investment affect economic growth?', *Journal of International Economics*, (45), 115–35.
Borgonos, T. (2002), Economic Analytical Unit interview with Researcher, Labor Education and Research Network, Manila, 3 May.
Bourguignon, F. and C. Morrisson (2001), 'Inequality among world citizens: 1820–1990', mimeo, Paris: DELTA.
Canning D., M. Fay and R. Perotti R. (1994), 'Infrastructure and growth', in M. Baldassarri, M. Paganaetto and E.S. Phelps (eds), *International Differences in Growth Rates*, New York: St Martin's Press.
CEIC (2002), Economic Database, Hong Kong.
Chen, S. and M. Ravallion (2001), 'How did the world's poorest fare in the 1990s?', *Review of Income, Wealth*, **47** (3), September.

Clark, X., D. Dollar and A. Kraay (2001), 'Decomposing Global Inequality', World Bank, available at www.worldbank.org, accessed 18 October 2002.

Cornia, G.A. (1999), 'Policy reform and income inequality', paper presented at World Bank conference, Stiglitz Summer Research Workshop on Poverty, Washington, DC, 6–8 July.

Davis, P. (1996), 'The role of institutional investors in the evolution of financial structure and behaviour', paper presented at the RBA conference, The Future of the Financial System, 8–9 July, Sydney

Dollar, D. and A. Kraay (2001), 'Trade, Growth and Poverty', Development Research Group, World Bank, available at www.worldbank.org, accessed 8 November 2002.

East Asia Analytical Unit (1998), *Asia's Infrastructure in the Crisis: Harnessing Private Enterprise*, Canberra: Department of Foreign Affairs and Trade.

East Asia Analytical Unit (1999), 'Asia's financial markets', Department of Foreign Affairs and Trade, March, Canberra, available at www.dfat.gov.au/eau.

Eastwood, R. and M. Lipton (2000), 'Rural–urban dimensions of inequality change', University of Sussex Discussion Papers in Economics, no. 200, June, Brighton, United Kingdom.

Economic Analytical Unit (2002a), 'China embraces the world market', Canberra: Department of Foreign Affairs and Trade.

Economic Analytical Unit (2002b), 'Connecting with Asia's tech future – ICT export opportunities', Canberra: Department of Foreign Affairs and Trade, November.

Edey, M. and B. Gray, B. (1996), 'The evolving structure of the Australia financial system', paper presented at the 1996 RBA conference, The Future of Financial Systems, 8–9 July, Sydney.

Ferreira, F.G. and J.A. Litchfield (1999), 'Education or inflation? The roles of structural factors and macroeconomic instability in explaining Brazilian inequality in the 1980s', Discussion Paper, Distributional Analysis Research Programme no. DARP43, March, Toyota Centre.

Fosu, A.K. (2000), 'International trade and labour market adjustment in developing economies', paper presented at International Economic Association Conference, Globalisation and Labour Markets, University of Nottingham, 7–9 July.

Frankel, J. and D. Romer (1999), 'Does trade cause growth?', NBER Working Paper, No. 5476.

Garibaldi, P., N. Mora, R. Sahay and J. Zettelmeyer (2001), 'What moves capital to transition economies?', IMF Staff Paper, vol. 48, Special Issue, Washington, DC.

Graham, E. (2001),'Fighting the wrong enemy', Institute for International Economics, available at www.iie.com, accessed 13 July 2002.

Harding, A. and H. Greenwell (2002), 'Trends in income and consumption inequality in Australia', paper presented at the 27th General Conference of the International Association for Research into Income and Wealth, Stockholm, 18–24 August.

Henry, K. (2002), 'Spreading the benefits of globalisation: "selling" the compounding benefits of reform', speech presented at Australian Treasury and Reserve Bank of Australia conference, Globalisation, Living Standards and Inequality, Sydney, May.

Hilmer, F.G. (1989), *New Game, New Rules*, North Ryde: Angus and Robertson.

Hoekman, B. and K. Saggi (1999), 'Multilateral disciplines for investment-related policies', in P. Guerrieri and H. Sharer (eds), *Global Regionalism and Economic Convergence in Europe and East Asia: The Need for Global Governance Regimes*, Rome: Instituto Affari Internazionali.

IMF (2003), 'IMF reports on the Observation of Standards and Codes', available at www.imf.org, accessed 16 August 2003.

Industry Commission (1995), *Assistance to Agricultural and Manufacturing Industries*, Information Paper, Canberra: AGPS

International Fund for Agricultural Development (2002), 'IFAD strategy for rural poverty reduction in Asia and the Pacific', available at www.ifad.org/ operations/regional/2002/pi/pi.htm, accessed 25 June 2002.

Johnson, D., I. Manning and O. Hellwig (1995), 'Trends in distribution of cash income and non-cash benefits', National Institute of Economic and Industry Research, report to the Department of Prime Minister and Cabinet, Australia.

Johnson, S., J. McMillan and C. Woodruff (2001), 'Property rights and finance', mimeo, Cambridge, MA: Sloan School of Management, MIT.

Kaufmann, D. and A. Kraay (2002), 'Growth without governance', available at www.worldbank.org, accessed 16 December 2002.

Knack, S. and P. Keefer (1995), 'Institutions and economic performance: cross-economy tests using alternative institutional measures', *Economics and Politics*, November, **7** (3), 207–26.

Lewis, H. and D. Richardson (2001), 'Why global commitment really matters!', Institute of International Economics, available at www.iie.com, accessed 13 July 2002.

McLean, B. and S. Shrestha (2002), 'International financial liberalisation and economic growth', Research Discussion Paper, available at www.rba.gov, accessed 14 July 2002.

Oxfam International (1999), 'Education now: break the cycle of poverty', available at www.caa.org.au/oxfam/advocacy/education/report/index.html, accessed 24 June 2002.

Oxfam International (2002a), 'A genuine development agenda for the Doha Round of WTO negotiations', joint NGO statement, 28 January.

Oxfam International (2002b), 'Cultivating poverty', available at www.oxfam.org, accessed 31 March 2003.

Perkins, F.C. (1997), 'Export performance and enterprise reform in China's coastal provinces', *Economic Development and Cultural Change*, April, 501–39.

Philippines Export Processing Zone (2002), information supplied to the Economic Analytical Unit, 7 May.

Productivity Commission (1999), 'Impact of competition policy reform on rural and regional Australia', available at www.pc.gov.au, accessed 2 September.

Productivity Commission (2001), 'Trade and Assistance Review 1999–2000', Annual Report Series 1999–2000, Canberra: AusInfo.

Rama, M. (1993), 'Rent-seeking and economic growth: a theoretical model and some empirical evidence', *Journal of Development Economics*, (42), 35–50.

Sachs, J. and A. Warner (1995), 'Economic reform and the process of global integration', *Brookings Papers on Economic Activity*, **96** (1), 1–118.

Sala-i-Martin, X. (2002), 'The world distribution of income', 21 April unpublished, available at www.columbia.edu, accessed 9 September 2002.

Sapir, A. (2000), 'Who is afraid of globalisation? The challenge of domestic adjustment in Europe and America', paper presented at Harvard University conference, Efficiency, Equity and Legitimacy: The Multilateral Trading System at the Millennium, Harvard University, 1–2 June.

Simon, J. and S. Wardrop (2002), 'Australian use of information technology and its contribution to growth', Reserve Bank of Australia, Research Discussion Paper, 2002–02, Sydney.

Sloan, J. and M. Wooden (1998), 'Industrial relations reform and labour market outcomes: a comparison of Australia, New Zealand and the United Kingdom', paper presented at Reserve Bank of Australia conference, Unemployment and the Australian Labour Market, Sydney, July.

Temple, F. (2001), 'Evidence shows globalisation has benefited the poor', World Bank Economy Director for Bangladesh, available at www.lnweb18. worldbank.org, accessed 4 June 2002.

United Nations Development Fund (1998), available at www.undp.org, accessed September 2001.

United Nations Development Program (1999), 'Human Development Report', available at www.undp.org, accessed May 2002.

USDA (2001), 'Profiles of Tariffs in Global Agricultural Markets', Washington, DC: Market and Trade Economics Division, Agricutural Economic Report, no. 796, January.

Weder, B. (1998), 'Africa's trade gap: what should Africa do to promote exports?', paper presented at United University Headquarters conference, Asia and Africa in the Global Economy, Tokyo, 3–4 August.

World Bank (2002a), 'Doing business in a hostile investment climate', available at http://rru.worldbank.org/HotTopics/Hot_Topics_Djankov.asp, accessed 20 June 2002.

World Bank (2002b), *Globalisation, Growth and Poverty*, Washington, DC: World Bank and Oxford University Press.

World Bank (2002c), 'Intensifying Action Against HIV/AIDS in Africa'.

Yeats, A.J. (1997), 'Did domestic policies marginalize Africa in international trade?' Washington: World Bank, available at www.worldbank.org, accessed 13 August 2002.

3. Globalisation: macroeconomic management and public finance

John Quiggin

The received wisdom about globalisation and its implications for public policy are perhaps best summarised by Friedman's (1999) metaphor of the Golden Straitjacket. The metaphor embodies the claim that, while globalisation constrains the options available to governments, it offers unparalleled prosperity to those countries that comply with its requirements.

To fit into the Golden Straitjacket, a country must adopt the following (rather redundantly expressed) golden rules:

- making the private sector the primary engine of its economic growth;
- maintaining a low rate of inflation and price stability;
- shrinking the size of its state bureaucracy;
- maintaining as close to a balanced budget as possible, if not a surplus;
- eliminating and lowering tariffs;
- getting rid of quotas and domestic monopolies;
- increasing exports;
- privatising state-owned industries and utilities;
- deregulating capital markets and the domestic economy;
- opening banking and telecommunications to private ownership and competition;
- allowing citizens to choose from an array of competing pension options.

Like other proponents of globalisation, Friedman argues that governments must adopt the neoliberal policy agenda or face the wrath of the 'Electronic Herd' of global financial traders. These arguments have been strongly contested. On the one hand, many critics of globalisation, notably Hirst and Thompson (1996) have rejected the claim that globalisation is the inevitable result of technological progress. On the other hand, many writers have rejected claims that globalisation is beneficial (for example, Baker et al. 1998).

In this chapter, I will consider both parts of Friedman's metaphor. First, is Friedman correct in describing globalisation as offering 'golden' opportunities? More precisely, have the fiscal and macroeconomic policies advocated by Friedman produced sustained improvements in economic performance in countries where they have been implemented? I will argue, on the contrary, that few of the policies listed above have yielded the claimed benefits and most have been positively harmful.

Second, regardless of the benefits and costs, does globalisation impose a straitjacket? Is the power of financial markets such that governments have no alternative but to accede to their demands? I will argue that, in reality, governments have considerably more room for manoeuvre than is commonly supposed. Moreover, while financial markets can impose substantial economic costs on countries in the event of a loss of confidence, adherence to the policy agenda of the 'Golden Straitjacket' does little or nothing to reduce the likelihood of such an adverse outcome. The only adequate response is the construction of a new regulatory framework for international financial markets.

Four sets of issues raised in Friedman's list will be addressed in this chapter. First, there is the general claim that financial markets promote sound economic policies, rewarding governments that adopt them and punishing those that do not. Second, there are issues related to macroeconomic policy and the injunction to focus on fighting inflation. Third, there are questions of taxation and public expenditure. Finally, there are issues concerned with privatisation and deregulation. In each case, the neoliberal policy framework is assessed. The final section consists of an assessment of the options open to governments.

FINANCIAL MARKETS AND THE WASHINGTON CONSENSUS

The policy settings advocated by Friedman have also been referred to as the 'Washington Consensus'. John Williamson of the Institute for International Economics coined this term to describe the set of economic assumptions and policy prescriptions favoured by major Washington-based institutions including the IMF, the World Bank and the United States Treasury (Williamson 1990).

The Washington Consensus arose following the breakdown of the system of fixed exchange rates adopted by the victorious allies meeting at Bretton Woods in 1945. By the late 1960s, the Bretton Woods system was breaking down under the strain of inflation in the major developed economies (which rendered fixed exchange rates untenable) and the gradual erosion of capital controls through developments such as the 'Eurodollar' market (trade in financial assets denominated in US dollars, but outside the control of US monetary authorities). The abandonment, during the 1970s, of fixed exchange rates and controls on capital movements paved the way for massive growth in the volume of financial transactions and led to the current era of globalisation.

During the 1970s, governments, particularly in less developed countries, engaged in large-scale borrowing. When the world economy declined at the end of the 1970s, many found themselves unable to service their debt, leading to a series of crises. In responding to these crises, the International Monetary Fund typically required governments to cut public expenditure, sell or close loss-making public enterprise and remove a variety of regulatory policies. Although these policy responses were far from uniformly successful, they appeared to work better than any alternative, and formed the basis of the Washington Consensus.

A central point in the Washington Consensus was the belief that the debt crisis was the result of mistaken policies in the debtor countries, and not of problems in the financial markets that had made the borrowings possible. The Washington Consensus discouraged the use of capital controls as a way of managing debt problems, and encouraged countries to deregulate their financial systems.

Faith in the Washington Consensus reached a peak in the mid-1990s. The breakdown of Communism and strong growth in stock prices, particularly in the United States, supported the view that financial markets were the main engine of liberal capitalism. Less developed countries that had embraced the Washington Consensus experienced large inflows of private capital and strong economic growth. Important examples included Argentina, which tied its currency to the US dollar in 1992, and East Asian economies which deregulated financial markets in the early 1990s.

Since the mid-1990s, international financial crises have occurred regularly. The majority have occurred in developing and formerly-Communist countries including Mexico in 1994, a large number of Asian countries in 1997 and 1998, Russia in 1998, and Turkey and Argentina in 2001 and 2002. However, the failure of Long Term Credit Management, an unregulated 'hedge fund' based in the United States, threatened the solvency of a number of major banks and raised the possibility that even developed countries were not immune from serious financial breakdown.

The crises of the 1990s exposed weaknesses in the Washington Consensus approach to financial stabilisation. In general, the crises arose much more rapidly than in the 1980s. More importantly, the countries affected were generally perceived, at least prior to the crises, as having followed the policy prescriptions of the Consensus. Far from rewarding countries that followed sound policies, financial markets appear to have contributed to the crises, first by financing unsound investments and then by facilitating capital flight when the crises began.

Events in the United States have also cast doubt on the idea that financial markets promote sound policy. The financial bubble of the late 1990s swept the entire financial markets into a speculative frenzy (Shiller 2000). Stock market analysts promoted worthless stocks, auditors signed accounts showing high profits for companies that were actually insolvent, and bond market analysts failed to predict defaults caused by fraud and mismanagement.

The series of financial crises since the 1990s has undermined faith in financial markets, but has yet to give rise to significant initiatives that would reduce their power or improve their operations. The status of financial market institutions today is something akin to that of the Communist Party in the declining years of the Soviet Union. The claims of omnipotence and omniscience made by writers such as Friedman are still the official orthodoxy, but few really believe them any longer.

MACROECONOMIC POLICY

The core of the neoliberal macroeconomic policy agenda may be summed up by the slogan 'fight inflation first'. This approach may be seen, in its strongest form, in the policy framework adopted in New Zealand in the 1990s (Quiggin 1998). The neoliberal approach eschewed any active form of fiscal policy, seeking instead to keep budgets as close as possible to balance. Monetary policy was directed solely at a target of controlling inflation. In the case of New Zealand the target was a range of 0–2 per cent, with no allowance for variations over the course of the economic cycle. Macroeconomic policy was not concerned with reducing unemployment, which was assumed to be determined by the institutional structure of the labour market.

A more moderate and eclectic version of the neoliberal framework was adopted in Australia. Having rejected active fiscal policy (pejoratively referred to as 'pump-priming') in the early stages of the 1989–92 recession, the Hawke–Keating Labor government embraced it in the One Nation package.

The Coalition government elected in 1996 has taken a somewhat ambivalent view of fiscal policy. Initially, the government adopted a neoliberal stance to justify cuts in public expenditure, in violation of its campaigning commitments. More recently, Keynesian rhetoric has accompanied policies such as assistance to first-home buyers. Assessment of the Coalition's position is complicated by the complexity of Australian macroeconomic developments since 1996. Although economic growth has generally been fairly strong, suggesting that budget surpluses would be an appropriate fiscal policy, unemployment has remained high, and there have been a series of occasions on which an economic downturn appeared likely, including the Asian crisis of 1997–98 and the post-GST slowdown in late 2000.

Although fiscal policy has not been abandoned, monetary policy has clearly become the primary tool of macroeconomic management in Australia. At first sight, the policy framework adopted by the Australian Reserve Bank looks very similar to that of New Zealand, being based on an inflation target of 2–3 per cent per year. There are, however, important differences. First, the Australian target allows for slightly higher rates of inflation and, more significantly, allows for higher inflation rates in peak periods, with the target being specified as the average rate of inflation over an economic cycle (typically about five years). Second, inflation targeting is not seen as an end in itself but as a summary statistic for a policy aimed at stabilising output and employment as well as inflation.

The Australian approach succeeded during the 1990s, whereas the New Zealand approach failed and was ultimately abandoned (Quiggin 1998). Although the failure of the New Zealand approach was due, in part, to bad luck, and in part to poor implementation, most studies have concluded that the rigidly neoliberal approach was fundamentally flawed because of the lack of concern about stabilising output and employment.

TAXATION AND PUBLIC SPENDING

The first item in Friedman's list of 'golden' constraints is the claim that the private sector should be the primary engine of growth. An obvious corollary, and a central item in the neoliberal policy programme is the desirability of reducing the share of national resources allocated to the public sector. Beginning with the Thatcher government in the United Kingdom, neoliberal governments have made strenuous attempts to reduce the size of the public sector.

Several strategies have been adopted in attempts to achieve this goal. The first has been to reduce the quantity and quality of those services that are normally provided by the public sector, including health, education and social welfare services. For example, Australian governments in the 1990s have reduced education expenditure, leading to larger classes in schools and, more dramatically, in universities. (The ratio of students to academic staff rose by approximately 70 per cent between 1990 and 2000.) Eligibility for a wide range of social welfare benefits has been tightened and, in some cases, the level of benefits has been reduced.

A second strategy, commonly referred to as 'user pays', involves the imposition of charges for services that were previously funded from general revenue. If imposed on a limited scale, as in the case of admission fees for museums and galleries, such charges simply change the financial basis of provision. More systematic commercialisation, as in the application of National Competition Policy to local government services, generally involves a change in the nature of the services provided and is a first step on a path leading to corporatisation and, ultimately, privatisation.

A third strategy has been the replacement of publicly-provided services by private alternatives, usually with some public funding. Examples include voucher systems for education, tax incentives for reliance on private superannuation in place of age pensions and subsidies to private health insurance.

As with other aspects of globalisation, it has been claimed that reductions in the size of the public sector are both inevitable, if an internationally competitive economy is to be maintained, and beneficial. The first part of this claim does not stand up to empirical scrutiny. Analysis such as that of Mitchell (1991) has shown that the share of government expenditure in GDP tends to be positively correlated with economic openness, as measured by the ratio of trade to GDP, not negatively correlated as the inevitability argument would imply. It is possible that, by increasing exposure to international shocks, economic openness enhances the demand for government intervention to manage risk.

Economic analysis gives little guidance with respect to the desirability of reducing the ratio of government expenditure to GDP, which is primarily a political question. Thus far, despite the political dominance of neoliberal governments in many countries, policies aimed at reducing the size of the state have had only limited political success. Resistance to neoliberal policies, and the failures of many policy initiatives, have meant that only limited steps have been taken to implement the neoliberal programme with respect to taxation and public spending. In particular, growth in the share of national income taken by governments as taxation revenue and returned in the form of public services and transfer payments has been slowed, but not reversed or even, in most places, halted.

PRIVATISATION AND DEREGULATION

The public and private sector boundaries established in most developed countries after 1945 remained largely unchanged until the 1980s. The private sector dominated agriculture, mining, manufacturing and retail and wholesale trade. The public sector dominated health, education and other community services and the provision of infrastructure services (roads, railways, electricity, communications and so on). Occasional nationalisations and denationalisations (for example, steel in the United Kingdom) did little to change this.

The first government to adopt a systematic policy of privatisation was the Thatcher–Major Conservative government in the United Kingdom. Over 15 years, the Conservatives privatised a wide range of industries including telecommunications, gas, water, electricity and railways. The Conservatives also pioneered the systematic contracting-out of the provision of publicly-financed services such as health and education.

In retrospect, it is generally conceded, even by advocates of privatisation, that the Thatcher government's fiscal rationale for privatisation as a device for reducing budget deficits and public sector borrowing requirements was faulty, that many of the assets were sold at bargain-basement prices and that subsequent regulation of privatised industries left much to be desired. Nevertheless, the popularity of privatisation spread rapidly to other English-speaking countries (except the United States, where public ownership had never been important) and then to the rest of the world. The popularity of privatisation was enhanced by the collapse of Communism in 1989.

In the last few years, the process of privatisation in the English-speaking countries has slowed drastically, and in some cases been reversed. Renationalisation has been necessitated in some cases by the collapse of privatised firms such as Railtrack in the United Kingdom and Air New Zealand. Apart from these emergency measures, New Zealand, which led the way in adopting the neoliberal agenda, has now taken the first steps in reversing it, with the renationalisation of accident compensation insurance and the re-establishment of a publicly-owned bank.

The slowdown in privatisation has arisen, in part, from the gradual realisation that the profits generated by well-run public enterprises are, in many cases, greater than the interest savings that can be generated by selling assets and using the proceeds to repay debt. The first-stage privatisation of Telstra, in Australia, provides a fairly typical instance. In the first three years after privatisation, the interest savings resulting from privatisation totalled about $2.9 billion. By contrast, the public was deprived of dividends of $2.3 billion and retained earnings of $2 billion, for a loss of $1.4 billion. Since earnings are likely to grow over time, if only as a result of inflation, while interest savings are fixed, the loss can be expected to grow steadily. Far from increasing the net worth of the public sector, the Telstra privatisation reduced it by around $15 billion.

Utility Deregulation

The first privatisations undertaken by the Thatcher government did little more than replace public monopolies with private monopolies, and, in the process, transfer wealth from the public to the private sector. Advocates of the neoliberal agenda saw the introduction of competition, rather than a mere change in ownership, as the crucial objective. As a result, privatisation gave rise to radical changes in the regulation of infrastructure services such as electricity and telecommunications. Similar changes took place in the United States where, although nominally private, the regulated monopoly providers of these services had acted, in many respects, like public enterprises.

The move towards competition had two main components. The first was to provide retail consumers with a choice between competing service providers. The second was to end central planning of infrastructure investment and replace it with market-generated signals. Experience with retail competition has been mixed, but, on balance, modestly positive. However, the shift away from planning infrastructure investment has been almost uniformly disastrous.

On the one hand, there have been financial bubbles leading to wasted and duplicated investments on an unprecedented scale. In the United States, investment in telecommunications infrastructure such as fibre-optic cable totalled $500 billion in 1999 and 2000 alone. More than 95 per cent of this cable remains 'dark', that is, it has never been used to carry signals. Paradoxically, the resulting string of bankruptcies has meant that this overcapacity has been accompanied by repeated service failures. Millions of users of broadband services have been disconnected, in some cases by four or five successive providers. Similarly, in Australia, competition between Telstra and Optus produced the bizarre result that half the country was wired up with two sets of broadband cables, while the other half got none (Quiggin 1996).

Meanwhile, in the electricity industry, vitally-needed investment has not been undertaken. At a time when improvements in electricity supply technology and the needs of computer users for uninterrupted power supplies should have led to substantial improvements in reliability, the new systems of regulation have produced repeated blackouts wherever they have been introduced, most notably in Auckland, California, Victoria and South Australia.

WHAT CAN GOVERNMENTS DO?

The Impossible Trinity

In macroeconomic terms, the choices available to governments can be described in terms of the 'impossible trinity'. A government cannot simultaneously pursue an independent macroeconomic policy, maintain a fixed exchange rate and allow free international capital movements.

Over the last century, governments have responded to this dilemma in very different ways. The economy of the nineteenth century, like that of the late twentieth century, was one of unrestricted capital flows and tight constraints on government policies. The nineteenth-century global economy was disrupted by the outbreak of the Great War in 1914. Attempts to reconstruct it after 1918 failed, leading to the Depression of the 1930s and the renewal of war in 1939.

As noted above, a radically different system was adopted in 1945. The Bretton Woods system relied on fixed exchange rates and restrictions on international capital flows. With these restrictions in place, the main policy instrument used to stabilise the economy, avoiding recessions and excessive booms, was fiscal policy. In periods of depressed activity, governments stimulated demand by cutting taxes and increasing public expenditure. The opposite measures were used to restrain potentially inflationary booms.

The abandonment of controls on capital flows and the shift to floating exchange rates has had mixed effects on the scope for fiscal and monetary policy. As the impossible trinity idea shows, with no controls on capital flows governments can adopt an independent monetary policy only if they are prepared to abandon any control over the exchange rate.

Few governments or central banks have been willing to disregard the exchange rate, often seen as an indicator of national economic worth, but Australian experience suggests that this is probably the optimal response. The willingness of the Reserve Bank to accept a sustained depreciation in the value of the Australian dollar, rather than raising interest rates to support the currency, was the main reason why Australia, unlike New Zealand, suffered little or no adverse effect from the Asian crisis in 1998.

Even assuming that the exchange rate is not targeted, it is necessary to determine the appropriate stance of monetary policy. It is generally agreed that monetary policy should focus primarily on keeping inflation rates low and stable, but the details of inflation targeting are important. A comparison between Australia and New Zealand is useful here. The New Zealand monetary system involved an exclusive focus on inflation, with a tight (0 to 2 per cent) annual target. The results included violent fluctuations in interest rates and unemployment that ultimately forced the abandonment of the system. By contrast, the Australian Reserve Bank takes unemployment and other variables into account in a more flexible system in which the average inflation rate, over the course of the economic cycle, is targeted.

The impact of globalisation on the scope for fiscal policy is complex and, in some respects, paradoxical. In some important respects, the removal of controls on capital flows makes it easier for governments to adopt a flexible fiscal policy. In a closed economy, attempts to stimulate economic activity through tax cuts or higher public spending, financed by the issue of government bonds, tend to raise interest rates and may therefore 'crowd out' private investment (including the purchase of homes and consumer durables).

By contrast, in the absence of exchange controls, interest rates are set on world markets. Provided that budget deficits are not so large or sustained as to raise concerns that governments may repudiate their debt or resort to inflationary financing, budget deficits have no direct effect on interest rates.

There is, however, an indirect effect. The central bank, which is normally independent in an economy of this kind, will in general have a view as to the desired degree of stimulus arising from the combined impact of fiscal and monetary policy. Other things being equal, central banks will respond to an unexpected shift to a more stimulatory fiscal policy by raising interest rates and offsetting the stimulus.

In recent years, however, many central bankers and others have concluded that exclusive reliance on monetary policy as a tool for economic management is misguided and potentially dangerous. There has been an increasing resurgence of interest in the active use of fiscal policy to stabilise the economy.

The International Financial System

Since the Asian crisis, the deficiencies of the existing system of international financial relations have been recognised quite widely. This recognition has grown with subsequent crises, particularly that of Argentina. Proposals for reforms, often referred to, rather grandly, as a 'new global financial architecture', have been canvassed, and widely discussed among central banks and international financial institutions. However, as yet, little progress has been made. The most innovative suggestion to gain widespread support has been for the creation of a procedure analogous to bankruptcy that could be pursued by national governments unable to service their debts. Although potentially valuable, this idea would have been more useful as a response to the crises of the 1980s, which typically arose because governments were unable to repay their debts, than to the more complex financial problems of the 1990s, which typically involve breakdowns in the financial system.

An alternative that has been frequently proposed, but remains at the margins of the international policy debate is the idea of a tax on international financial transactions, commonly referred to as a 'Tobin tax' after James Tobin, the economist and Nobel prize winner who first proposed it (Tobin 1991; ul Haq et al. 1996).

The most obvious objection to a transactions tax is that the tax could be avoided/evaded either by substitution of exempt for taxable transactions or by shifting transactions to a financial centre that does not levy the tax. In particular, it is argued that unless a tax is imposed universally it would be nullified by such a shift in transactions. This latter claim appears premature. After all, it is, in principle, possible to completely avoid income tax by making all income-generating contracts in jurisdictions that levy no income tax (tax havens) and considerable tax is in practice avoided in this fashion. Nevertheless, countries do succeed in levying income taxes (at widely divergent rates) on their inhabitants.

On the other hand, arguments concerning the possibility of substitution of exempt domestic transactions for taxable transactions appear well founded. In many cases, it is possible to replace an international financial transaction with a set of domestic transactions that have the same ultimate effect. It would appear that the only feasible approach is to tax all financial transactions, domestic and international, at a common rate (Quiggin 2001). Many countries, including Australia, already tax a range of 'retail' financial transactions (for example, bank debits and credits, mortgages), often at rates higher than those envisaged for a tax on international transactions.

Taxation and Public Spending

In the absence of effective controls over global capital markets, the free movement of capital must be taken into account as a constraint on the policy options available to governments. However, this is a constraint, not, as Friedman would have it, a 'straitjacket'.

In the absence of restrictions on capital movement, capital will naturally flow where it can secure the highest post-tax returns. Hence governments are likely to face increasing difficulty in levying tax on income from capital. The difficulties in taxing income derived from capital are not as great as have been suggested by some commentators. Particularly in Europe, moves are being made to harmonise rates of tax on income from capital, so as to prevent competitive bidding down of tax rates. Moreover, governments retain the option of taxing the capital income of residents, whether that income is derived from foreign or domestic assets. Nevertheless, the capacity of governments to tax income from capital has clearly declined.

By contrast, globalisation in itself does not impose significant constraints on the revenue that can be raised from taxes on consumption and personal income. During a decade in which globalisation has dominated public discussion, the ratio of tax revenue to national income has remained stable or increased in most countries. Moreover, contrary to what is implied in many discussions, the ratio of tax revenue to national income is generally higher in countries that are more exposed to international markets, because trade forms a larger share of total income.

Although there are economic limits above (and below) which it is very difficult to raise (or lower) tax revenues, the key issues are political. The Australian community must decide what proportion of income to allocate to improved public services and what proportion to allocate to private consumption. Unfortunately this issue has never been seriously debated, and outcomes have been produced by a mixture of policy drift, bracket creep, unfunded tax cuts and expenditure cuts justified by incoming governments on the basis of spurious 'black holes'.

CONCLUDING COMMENTS

The neoliberal policy agenda associated with globalisation is, in some respects, a return to the classical liberal economic orthodoxy of the nineteenth century, the first great era of globalisation. However, as the prefix 'neo' implies, neoliberalism can only be understood in relation to its historical background, namely the reaction against the social-democratic and Keynesian mixed economy which prevailed from the end of World War II until the early 1970s.

The mixed economy undoubtedly needed restructuring. Nevertheless, despite having dominated the policy agenda for the past two decades, neoliberal globalisation has failed to produce the promised benefits. What is needed is not more market-oriented reform, but a modernised and internationalised version of Keynesian social democracy.

ACKNOWLEDGEMENTS

I thank Nancy Wallace for helpful comments and criticism. This research was supported by an Australian Research Council Senior Fellowship and Australian Research Council Large Grant A00000873.

REFERENCES

Baker, D., G. Epstein and R.E. Pollin (1998), *Globalization and Progressive Economic Policy*, Cambridge: Cambridge University Press.
Friedman, T. (1999), *The Lexus and the Olive Tree: Understanding Globalization*, New York: Farrar Strauss Giroux.
Hirst, P. and G. Thompson (1996), *Globalization in Question: the International Economy and the Possibilities of Governance*, Cambridge, UK: Polity Press.
Mitchell, D. (1991), *Income Transfers in Ten Welfare States*, Aldershot: Avebury.

Quiggin, J. (1996), *Great Expectations: Microeconomic Reform and Australia*, St Leonards, NSW: Allen and Unwin.
Quiggin, J. (1998), 'Social democracy and market reform in Australia and New Zealand', *Oxford Review of Economic Policy*, **14** (1), 76–95.
Quiggin, J. (2001), 'The fall and rise of the global economy: finance', in C. Sheil (ed.), *Globalisation: Australian Impacts*, Sydney: University of New South Wales Press, pp. 19–34.
Shiller, R.J. (2000), *Irrational Exuberance*, Princeton, New Jersey: Princeton University Press.
Tobin, J. (1991), 'International currency regimes, capital mobility, and macroeconomic policy', *Greek Economic Review*, (August), Special Issue on monetary integration.
ul Haq, M., I. Kaul and I. Grunberg (1996), *The Tobin Tax: Coping With Financial Volatility*, Oxford, UK: Oxford University Press.
Williamson, J. (1990), 'What Washington means by policy reform', in J. Williamson (ed.), *Latin American Adjustment: How Much has Happened?* Washington: Institute for International Economics, pp. 7–33.

4. Macroeconomic stability, growth and employment: issues and considerations beyond the Washington Consensus

Muhammed Muqtada[1]

INTRODUCTION

This chapter is essentially a cursory exercise in raising a few issues and debates, drawing upon the lessons and non-lessons from the practice of macroeconomic policy formulation undertaken by most countries of the world since the second oil price shock of 1979. The oil price hike triggered off serious recessionary tendencies globally. That recession evidently was not on a scale anywhere comparable to the Great Depression of the 1930s, but certainly initiated a new wave of macroeconomic practice, underpinned by the macroeconomic principles of the so-called *counter-revolution* thinking, across countries. The outcomes of the pursuit of this line of prescriptions, over the past two decades, have been less than encouraging, especially in terms of growth, employment and levels of living (see ILO's *World Employment Report, 2000–01*, for recent trends in global and regional output and employment). Global output growth declined to nearly one-third of the rates achieved during the 1950s and 1960s (and till 1973, when the first oil price shock came in).

This phenomenon (see Figure 4.1) must strike as worrisome, especially to the bulk of the policy-planners and academic community who trust that employment generation and poverty reduction are closely (though not automatically) related to accelerated growth. At the country level, Table 4.1 contrasts the real per capita GDP of the 1980s with that of the 1990s for a random sample of 20 countries.[2] Barring a few exceptions, real per capita income grew very slowly, and in fact declined in some cases. This then could hardly contribute much to the alleviation of poverty[3] and the unemployment situation. Furthermore, inequality increased. If one introduces this, as a simplistic welfare content of growth, social justice becomes far removed. Table 4.1 also provides some estimates to show that *'welfare-weighted'*

increase in real per capita GDP (see note to Table 4.1 on such an index
proposed by Sen) was even lower.

Table 4.1 Per capita growth and welfare

Countries	1980s		1990s	
	Per capita real GDP	Welfare GDP	Per capita real GDP	Welfare GDP
Bangladesh	253.16	167.97	314.85	217.40
Barbados	6795.97	3475.46	7232.71	n.a.
Bolivia	867.93	503.05	897.61	368.92
Brazil	4093.27	1612.75	4299.32	1665.56
Bulgaria	1588.11	1194.02	1485.10	1047.00
Chile	2737.87	1317.46	4383.90	1863.16
Egypt	859.03	558.37	1044.54	726.48
Hungary	4657.75	3305.37	4528.13	3274.52
Indonesia	616.93	405.01	961.49	650.01
Kenya	335.51	148.14	339.53	171.65
Nepal	164.25	114.87	203.60	128.88
Pakistan	384.64	256.15	487.61	335.60
Peru	2378.30	1280.36	2140.66	1185.93
Philippines	1085.38	619.75	1093.11	584.81
Sri Lanka	514.29	320.15	692.99	469.50
Tanzania	183.84	104.51	182.41	93.75
Thailand	1429.74	814.95	2570.14	1486.83
Uganda	236.35	158.36	293.20	183.54
Ukraine	2038.85	1526.49	1220.01	866.21
Zimbabwe	648.94	280.34	680.69	n.a.

Notes:
n.a.: not available
Sen (1983) tried to provide a *welfare* measurement of growth through weighting the latter by the
Gini ratio: $Y^* = Y (1-g)$, where Y = per capita real GDP; g = Gini ratio. For the 1980s the per
capita real GDP is for the period 1980–90, and for the 1990s the figure is for the period 1990–
99. The Gini ratio figure is related to the average of the available data for the 1980s and 1990s
respectively.

Sources: UNCTAD (2001), *Handbook of Statistics*, CD-ROM; WB, UNDP and ILO for Gini
ratio

The following pages attempt to trace the above outcomes to the
macro-policy framework adopted across almost all countries, developed and
developing, and to draw attention to the need for a return to the goal of full
employment[4] (compare ILO, *Global Employment Agenda*) as the central
objective of macroeconomic policy. The exercise, in short, is focused on the
campaign towards 'full, productive and freely chosen employment' and
draws inspiration from the need 'To promote opportunities for women and

men to obtain decent and productive work, in conditions of freedom, equity, security and human dignity' (ILO 1999).

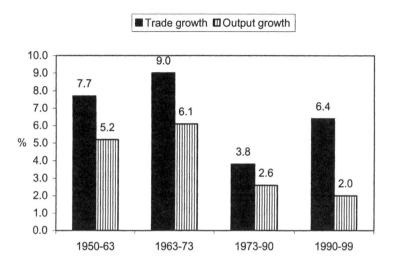

Source: WTO (2001) *World Trade Statistics*

Figure 4.1   World merchandise trade and output, 1950–99 (average annual percentage change in volume terms)

MACROECONOMIC POLICY AND THE SEARCH FOR AN OBJECTIVE

A macroeconomic policy framework must serve a well-defined objective. A test of its success would thus lie in how far it has contributed to achieving that objective.

The period of the 1980s and 1990s, the hey-days of the World Bank (WB) and IMF's stabilisation and structural adjustment programmes, saw a return to 'growthmanship' values, and the 'trickle-down' advocacy of distributive justice. The so-called counter-revolution period (1980s and 1990s) had its own value judgement, deeply embedded in the neoliberal paradigm. It largely focused on the individual consumer, the individual firm – both operating under conditions of free competition and perfect information. Disorders and malaise in the economy were seen as policy distortions, and there was a need to return to *getting the prices right* (WB/IMF model). As contended by Keynes during the Great Depression of the 1930s, and by Keynesians now, such a system fails to predict, or to suggest ways to get out of, prolonged recessions, since aggregate demand equalling aggregate supply could produce an equilibrium that is less than a full-employment equilibrium (that is, *the GNP gap*). The persistently high levels of un/underemployment and poverty, coupled with lack of sustained economic growth, provide a necessary rationale to rethink the objective of macroeconomic policy.

In a free democratic society, stabilising and empowering markets are indeed critical goals. Markets are also a social entity that mediates exchange and relations (through the product, services and labour markets). Prior to the counter-revolution of the 1980s and 1990s, there was a critical focus on a development agenda, on society, social classes and institutions. Economic considerations and policy-making were embedded in the overall goals of the society, and intermediated by various social classes (see, for example, Kalecki on 'intermediate regimes'). In point of fact, the concern over societal order and societal values defined economic, social and political institutions and policies: 'As a rule, the economic system was absorbed in the social system, and whatever principle of behaviour predominated in the economy, the presence of the market pattern was found to be compatible with it' (Polanyi 2002, p. 71).

It appears that the IMF/WB's campaign, during the two decades of stabilisation and adjustment, contained an overriding focus on one social institution, the market, with a macro-policy drawn up for 'getting the prices right'. In the process of moving the economy through the 'self-regulating market', governments (especially in the developing countries) were weakened (by a reduction in civil services, public expenditure and, importantly, several of their functional roles), while workers felt less certain and less organised, as capital became freer to flow in and out of a country. A growing asymmetry of power allocation between labour and capital, and of power allocation among social institutions, implied, *inter alia*, that workers were moving further away from *decent work*, and capital (especially big businesses) tended to move away from establishing what Charles Handy termed *decent capitalism*.[5]

Provided that the ultimate objectives of growth and development are shared prosperity and social justice, policies and policy reforms need to be seen linked to these objectives. Hence, for policy reformers who have undertaken economic reforms, it would be futile, or at best half-hearted, to confine themselves to addressing the 'negative effects of liberalisation' or 'social effects of stabilisation'. Social 'add-ons' (such as transfers, subsidies) may indeed be necessary to support the weaker and vulnerable groups in societies, but these do not add up to a 'corrective' factor to the process that, in the first place, denies social justice. *An integrated economic and social policy framework is warranted.*

The overarching objective of the ILO being the promotion of social justice, encapsulated in *Decent Work* (ILO 2001), it is important that we recognise the explanatory and the contextual factors that would best promote the value-basis of the organisation. The promotion of socially just societies requires campaigns, persuasion, economic policies and political willingness. Thus, while the legal considerations are contained in the ratification and the full implementation of the conventions, it is equally important that side-by-side sound and mutually supportive economic and social policies are formulated and implemented to serve the same objective in a consistent manner. The design of a macroeconomic policy framework is a critical core in this, and is required to 'serve' the objective at stake.

WASHINGTON CONSENSUS ON THE MACRO-POLICY FRAMEWORK

'There are many kinds of macro models of various shapes and sizes' (Bruton 2001), and the one which was adopted by the so-called Washington Consensus (WC) focused predominantly on 'getting prices right'. The policy prescription on the macro-framework was on the attainment of *price* and *balance of payments* stability. If the prices were stable and the exchange rate realistic, a country, other things being equal, would not face balance of payment difficulties. The intellectual stimulus for this position came from Anne Krueger (1992), Bela Balassa (1982), Bhagwati and Srinivasan (1983) and others, who claimed that the success of the East Asian miracle was largely due to the 'macro correctness' and openness of these economies. Alternative views exist on this explanation (Wade 1990; Amsden 1989).

Since the 1980s, the IMF/WB have predicated their core macro-policy focus on, and conditionalised their lending programme to, controlling inflation and reducing fiscal and current account deficits. Voluminous literature, analytical and empirical, has evolved, to establish credibility on why stability matters, and how stability is attained, following the above line of prescriptions.[6] These include the following well-known policy instruments (Bird 2001):

- fiscal and monetary discipline;
- tax reforms;
- strict control of public expenditure;
- financial liberalisation designed to encourage domestic saving;
- the elimination of over-valued exchange rates;
- trade liberalisation designed with the objective of raising domestic economic efficiency and exploiting comparative advantage.

A critical precondition for economic growth is an enabling economic and political environment that encourages both domestic and foreign investors and facilitates longer-term capital accumulation and enterprise development. Macroeconomic stability is a crucially necessary element in establishing such an environment. From the mid-1980s, the developing countries, one after another, adopted, and experimented with, various measures of stabilisation in order to reduce seemingly unsustainable fiscal and current account deficits.

There are those who argue that stabilisation policies performed reasonably well, especially when accompanied by structural adjustment programmes, and that growth is negatively affected if prices are unstable (inflation, fiscal deficits and black market premium in the foreign exchange market have been used as indicators; compare Fischer 1993).

The need to keep prices stable can hardly be a disputable subject. The worry comes, as expounded by Fischer (1993), from the following logic: 'The usual emphasis on the stability of the macroeconomic framework (rather than its conduciveness to growth) suggests that the main reason macroeconomic factors matter for growth is through uncertainty.' He then identifies two main channels through which uncertainty affects growth: first, policy-induced macroeconomic uncertainty affects the price mechanism, and second, 'temporary uncertainty' about the macroeconomy tends to reduce investment. Fischer (1993) uses a regression analogue of growth accounting, and panel data for a large number of countries, to establish how growth is negatively related to inflation and low budget deficits. The first of the two channels is treated at some length, which leaves open the issues of how investment is affected by the price mechanism, and whether investment could be affected by other factors as well.

There are many other studies labouring on the same point (especially inflation being the main indicator of macroeconomic uncertainty). The results are, however, not quite straightforward, and often mixed. A series of recent studies by the IMF staff states the following: 'Notwithstanding the theoretical appeal of the arguments that high inflation is damaging to growth, the empirical support for this relationship has been mixed' (Bredenkamp and Schadler 1999).

Such studies and results, useful pointers as these are, still keep begging the question. First of all, from the point of view of the individual country, such a cross-sectional panel data review is unremarkable. Second, at the country level, what is the cut-off point for inflation, crossing which would initiate unhealthy effects? Surely, here, one is not talking about hyperinflation as we have occasionally seen in some Latin American and Eastern European countries. One also has to consider, in this regard, the contention that mild inflation, especially in developing countries, is often conducive to resource mobilisation and to utilisation of capacity.

The two, presumably inter-related, channels of uncertainty mentioned by Fischer that affect growth adversely are indeed critical. However, the *causes* of such uncertainty are not fully explained by inflation and other price variables alone.[7] Thus, for instance, investment is certainly likely to be favourably affected if the price environment is conducive. But investment depends on a host of other, possibly no less important, factors. Hence, regressing growth on price variables is likely to show a weaker relationship than when directly regressed on the investment–GDP ratio. One could then concentrate on what explains investment in an economy.

A series of UNU–WIDER studies (whose main findings are summarised in Taylor 1988) argued that growth often appeared less related to macro reforms than, say, to governance and institutions, and that the efficacy of specifically-targeted macro-policies (such as inflation control) often depended on structural constraints, institutions and group bargains (Banuri 1990). The ILO has produced its critique of stabilisation and structural adjustment via the negative employment/income and institutional effects, both at the global level (ILO 1996/97), and at the country level (van der Geest and van der Hoeven 1999).

A cursory review of some cross-section and panel data, by the present author, on the performance of 20 randomly selected developing countries during the past two decades (1980–99) tends to stress the following:

1. Nearly 20 years of stabilisation policy measures, largely through strict conditionalities, have generally produced substantial price discipline. Tables 4.2 and 4.3 and Appendix Figures 4A.2 (a) to 4A.2 (e) show quite clearly the declining trends as well as the reasonably low levels of inflation and budget deficits that currently exist.
2. The substantial reductions in the inflation rate and in budget and current account deficits are yet to trigger off sustained and adequate growth rates in the individual economies, barring the very few. Not only has growth been inadequate (relative to labour force growth rates and unemployment, for example), it has also remained highly volatile (see Appendix Figures 4A.1 (a) to 4A.1 (e) for growth fluctuations in selected countries). Such volatility in the economic *performance* can possibly occur despite price stability, whether owing to financial sector inadequacies or to shocks from short-term debts or other non-price variables (Little et al 1993). This, in turn, can further affect investment (Fischer's second channel of uncertainty), and adversely affect aggregate demand, the individual's income and the firm's economic viability.[8]
3. There appears to be a weak causal relationship between growth and the price variables (see Table 4.4 for a cross-country regression). GDP

growth rate has a weak relationship with inflation and budget deficit. In fact the latter shows a weak positive relationship.

Table 4.2 Growth, inflation and budget deficit

Countries	RGDPGR[*]	Inflation (CPI, %)	BD (%, GDP)
Bangladesh	4.8	6.23	n.a.
Barbados	1.8	1.56	n.a.
Bolivia	4.2	2.16	−2.27
Brazil	3	4.86	n.a.
Bulgaria	−2.7	2.57	1.53
Chile	7.2	3.34	−1.47
Egypt	4.4	3.08	n.a.
Hungary	1.1	10	−3.62
Indonesia	4.8	20.49	−1.1
Kenya	2.2	2.64	n.a.
Nepal	4.8	8.04	−3.93
Pakistan	3.8	4.14	−3.88
Peru	5.1	3.47	−2.09
Philippines	3.2	6.71	−3.73
Sri Lanka	5.2	4.69	−6.85
Tanzania	2	7.89	n.a.
Thailand	4.7	0.31	−10.9
Uganda	7.2	6.36	n.a.
Ukraine	−10.7	22.7	n.a.
Zimbabwe	2.6	58.5	n.a.
France	1.5	0.53	n.a.
Japan	1.3	−0.33	n.a.
UK	2.5	1.56	0.03
US	3.3	2.19	1.34

Notes:
n.a: not available
RGDPGR: real GDP growth rate, BD (per cent, GDP): budget deficit-including grants
[*] Growth rate related to 1990–99 period

Sources: UNCTAD (2001), *Handbook of Statistics*, CD-ROM; WDI (2001), CD-ROM

4. The negative relationship between inflation and growth is further corroborated by our panel (pooled) data for the 20 countries, spread over 1980–99, relatively more significant and with a slightly higher R^2 (see column (1) in Table 4.5). Furthermore, growth is negatively (and significantly) related to current account deficit, but positively (but insignificantly) related to budget deficit (see columns (2) and (3) in Table 4.5).

5. It may be noted from our panel results that the level of investment (investment–GDP ratio) as a single variable explains growth far better, and more significantly, than all the three 'price' variables taken together

(columns (4) and (5) in Table 4.5). It may be noted that although the level of investment in our snapshot, cross-section analysis makes for a positive explanation of growth at the individual country level, investment trends, with a few exceptions, are declining (Table 4.6) across almost all countries. Thus, despite broad tendencies towards declining inflation and budget deficits, investment has failed to pick up significantly (see Figure 4.2 for cross-country illustrations of these relationships).

Table 4.3 Inflation and budget deficit: trends across countries, 1980–99

Countries	Inflation rate		Budget deficit		GDP growth rate
	1980–82	1997–99	1980–82	1997–99	
Bangladesh	7.96[c]	6.57	1.36	−0.65[h]	4.56
Barbados	12.38	2.67	−3.67	−3.72[h]	1.48
Bolivia	85.39	4.85	0.34[g]	−2.31	1.82
Brazil	118.38[a]	5.00	−2.60	−7.59[i]	2.40
Bulgaria	2.53[b]	360.84	n.a.	2.13	0.09
Chile	22.54	4.86	2.21	0.30	5.41
Egypt, Arab Rep.	17.74	3.96	−14.39	−1.02[j]	5.20
Hungary	8.15	14.15	−1.90	−4.13	0.77
Indonesia	13.75	28.29	−2.08	−1.49	5.59
Kenya	17.26	6.82	−6.12	−2.74[k]	3.18
Nepal	13.19	7.36	−4.08	−4.14	4.44
Pakistan	8.92	7.25	−5.21	−6.04	5.44
Peru	61.80	6.43	−2.80	−0.52	1.82
Philippines	13.59	7.42	−2.97	−1.84	2.38
Sri Lanka	18.49	7.88	−16.15	−6.46	4.70
Tanzania	29.56	12.26	n.a.	n.a.	3.33
Thailand	18.49	7.88	−5.61	−6.89	6.26
Uganda	66.40[a]	7.27[d]	−3.25	n.a.	5.27
Ukraine	n.a.	157.67[e]	n.a.	n.a.	−6.93
Zimbabwe	8.02	24.00[f]	−8.59	−6.78[j]	4.15

Notes:
Inflation rate, CPI (per cent, annual); years: [a]1981–83, [b]1986–88, [c]1987–89, [d]1996–99, [e]1995–97, [f]1996–98
Budget deficit, including grants (per cent, GDP); years: [g]1986–88, [h]1987–89, [i]1993–97, [j]1995–97, [k]1994–96
GDP growth rate quoted from UNCTAD (per cent per annum) for period 1980–99; (based on constant 1995 USD GDP)

Sources: WDI (2001); UNCTAD (2001), CD-ROM

These illustrations appear to be arguably consistent with the following. Stabilisation policies and measures undertaken by the developing countries over the past two decades have indeed yielded substantial price discipline, inflation in particular. Therefore, if growth were found to be negatively related to inflation *during this period*, the likely acceptable explanation is *not* that growth has been damagingly negative owing to high inflation, but that declining inflation must have been associated with positive growth! Our illustrations show a weak/negative relationship between the two. A recent IMF study admits that evidence on the relationship can be mixed. Barring a few exceptions, growth in the developing countries was relatively low and/or volatile. This implies that even a low positive growth could return a negative relationship with inflation rates that were largely declining over the period. Thus it appears that, while inflation rates were falling, growth has remained slow, volatile and far from reaching the sustained levels required to make tangible progress in reducing unemployment and poverty. More significantly, investment trends were largely on the decline (see Table 4.6). These trends would tend to suggest *tendencies toward a low-level equilibrium trap* (a stabilisation trap?).

Table 4.4   Macro-stability and growth: cross-country regression analysis

Independent variables	Dependent variable: real GDP growth rate coefficient
Constant	4.060^b
	(0.705)
INF avg	-0.002^a
	(0.001)
BD avg	0.032
	(0.145)
No. of countries	18
R^2	0.140

Notes:
[a] significant at 0.15 per cent level
[b] significant at 0.01 per cent level
INF avg: inflation average, and BD avg: budget deficit average for the period 1980–99
Standard errors in parentheses

Sources: WDI (2001), CD-ROM; World Bank

Our empirical evidence would further contend that growth is far better explained by investment levels than by the price variables; and that investment is weakly affected by these price variables, implying that investment depends on a host of other variables beyond macro-stability.

Several national and international assessments are now available on the varied experience of stabilisation and its economic and social impacts. In most of these accounts, the essential issue appears to be not with why stabilise, but with *how to manage stabilisation*. It is amply clear that stabilisation is a continuous process, and that there is no one-size-fits-all policy package to provide any quick fixes to macroeconomic imbalance of individual countries. Stabilisation measures, as with any macroeconomic policy decision, also carry risks and costs. Hence a prudent management of stabilisation would require a thorough consensus on when and how benefits would outweigh economic and social costs, and how the latter can be mitigated to contain a decline in income and employment entitlement of the poor, and any possible outbreak of social unrest.

Table 4.5 Growth and stability indices: regression estimates with panel data

Independent variables	Dependent variable: PCGR estimated coefficient				
	(1)	(2)	(3)	(4)	(5)
Constant	2.254^b	2.397^b	1.467^b	1.871^b	-15.026^b
IGDR					5.608^b
INFL	-0.001^a			-0.002^b	
BGDR		0.038		0.050	
CADR			-0.157^b	-0.187^b	
Observations	354	296	360	283	303
R^2	0.159	0.071	0.134	0.188	0.367

Notes:
GLS estimation is used to obtain estimated coefficients, assuming same slope and intercept for all the cross-section units and White heteroskedasticty consistent standard errors. Coefficients are statistically significant at ^{a}10 per cent, ^{b}1 per cent.
Definition of the variables: PCGR: per capita real GDP growth rate (per cent annual, based on constant 1995 USD); IGDR: Gross domestic investment (per cent of GDP, logarithms of); INFL: inflation, consumer price index (per cent annual); BGDR: budget deficit, overall including grants (per cent of GDP); CADR: current account deficit (per cent of GDP). The sample used 20 countries, and covered the period 1980–99.

Sources: WDI (2001), CD-ROM; World Bank, IFS-IMF, (2001), CD-ROM

Stability is not an end in itself. Rather it creates the enabling environment for growth. Thus, for example, macroeconomic stability, the guiding principle of Chile's economic polices, ushered in the longest growth cycle in the country's history, and reduced poverty and unemployment substantially. A stable fiscal and current account balance was matched by policies to encourage savings and investment, boost productivity and exports, attract external capital but discourage short-term capital inflows.

It is not that decision-makers are unaware that stability is only a precondition, albeit a significant one, of growth, and that growth can be hindered by a number of structural constraints and infrastructural handicaps. The essential caution in respect of stabilisation is rather on the establishment of the appropriate degree of the measures, the time adjustments needed and the sequencing of policies. It is equally important that policies do not excessively conflict; for example, among those that reduce fiscal deficit and the ones needed to create a fiscal space for critical public expenditures. A further caution is that stability, quickly attained through rapid compression of development expenditures and imports, cannot be sustained unless there is a resumption of investment and growth. As the lessons of experience tell us, macroeconomic stability is needed for growth to take place, but then growth is also needed to sustain stability, especially in economies with vast poverty and underemployment.

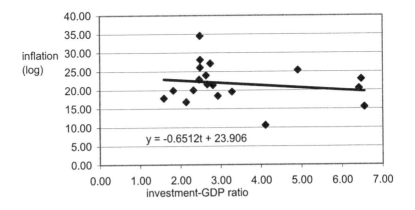

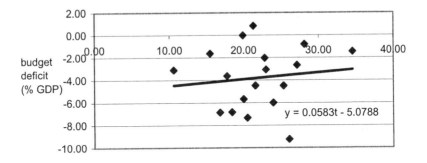

Notes:
Logarithms of inflation used to take care of large volatility in their values. Investment figure includes both private and public investment, and budget deficit figures include grants.
Trend line is estimated by the equation Y= a + bt.

Sources: World Development Indicators (2001); World Bank dataset

Figure 4.2 Investment, inflation and budget deficit: cross-country scatter

Table 4.6 Savings and investment, 1980–99 (annual growth rate)

	Savings	Investment
Bangladesh	4.69[c]	−0.19
Barbados	−1.35[c]	−4.59[c]
Bolivia	−3.30[c]	−0.19
Brazil	−0.73[b]	−0.11
Bulgaria	−7.65[c]	−7.57[c]
Chile	3.79[c]	3.20[c]
Egypt, Arab Republic	−1.12[c]	−3.83[c]
Hungary	−1.55[b]	−1.64[c]
Indonesia	0.12	0.90[c]
Kenya	−3.15[b]	−2.76[c]
Nepal	1.88[c]	1.55[c]
Pakistan	3.39[c]	−1.20[c]
Peru	−2.86[c]	−1.51[a]
Philippines	−2.40[c]	−0.26
Sri Lanka	2.26[c]	−4.54[c]
Tanzania	[d]	[d]
Thailand	2.64[c]	2.48[c]
Uganda	4.89	7.06[c]
Ukraine	−5.41[c]	n.a.
Zimbabwe	0.44	1.51[a]

Notes:
[a] level of significance at 0.10 per cent level
[b] level of significance at 0.05 per cent level
[c] level of significance at 0.01 per cent level
[d] dropped from analysis owing to insufficient number years of data
n.a.: not available

Sources: WDI (2001); World Bank dataset

Furthermore, markets even if 'forced' into a state of stability are inherently vulnerable, not simply to domestic policy distortions, but also to external factors, namely terms of trade shocks, short-term capital flows and so on. This is when the 'visible' hand of the government may be necessary, and other growth-related policies come into play. The East Asian success is better understood when both the roles of the market and the public interventions are factored in toward explaining how higher investments and growth were achieved (Amsden 1989).

POST-WASHINGTON CONSENSUS: THE PRSP MODEL?

Disenchantment with the 'Washington Consensus' (WC) surfaced and gathered momentum during the 1990s, and major protests across countries were staged against the WB and IMF. The disenchantment was not only with respect to the WC prescription failing to enable countries to return to a sustained growth path, but also with alleged *widening of income inequality*, both within countries and between countries (Cornia 1999). The WC was quickly relegated, and Stiglitz (1998) and others called for the need to develop a post-Washington Consensus (Bird 2001). While there has been a general acceptance of moving beyond the WC, the ideas of post-WC are yet to be articulated. The basic shifts in consideration of the WB/IMF may be summed up as follows. The post-Washington Consensus is more accommodating on the key role of the governments, especially in adopting *counter-cyclical* policies, if and when warranted, and the issues of governance, wider participation and social equity. These must be discussed and 'owned' by the country concerned, and hence IMF/WB lending will be taken in greater confidence and legitimacy (Islam 2001; Bird 2001). With respect to external shocks, and externally driven financial crisis, macro-policy must be designed to contain 'speculation' and possibly regulate short-term speculative capital flows. All this is hardly surprising, in that these are simply an acceptance of what went wrong in the understanding of the build-up to the Asian financial crisis, and how IMF prescriptions, with the bias of a pro-cyclical stance to rectitude, became suspect (South Korea and Malaysia, for example, took a more pragmatic stand, introducing controls on short-term loans).

With alleged lack of sustained growth and poverty alleviation, with respect to the WC, the IMF/WB sought rectitude in *poverty* as the new over-arching theme. The Poverty Reduction Strategy Papers (PRSPs) came quickly into currency.[9] In point of fact, the Bretton Woods institutions defined the new locus of their concessional lending strategy as critically dependent on country-owned, participation-based PRSPs, and initiated the process, especially for those countries that qualified for debt relief consideration under the Heavily Indebted Poor Countries (HIPC) initiative. The PRSPs would then define the poverty-focused development agenda of the individual country, and it would be drawn up through active participation of the national stakeholders.[10]

The WB/IMF now appears to be in a curious situation. Previously, under the WC macro model, the policy prescriptions were clear and simple (focused on controlling inflation, and fiscal and external deficits) and their impact relatively easy to monitor (although increasingly other areas of adjustments and micro-stability were added to the dimensions of conditionality; compare Bird 2001). Although in the recent period various modifications were attempted on 'one-size-fits-all', the inherent macro-advocacy was the same. With the emergence of PRSPs, and the transfer of their 'ownership' to the individual countries, the WB/IMF do not seem to have a unique macro model yet! While inner tensions prevail within the WB, between the 'finance' and the 'development' agents ('civil society' agents, as Kanbur (2001) termed them), the WC's macro stance has certainly become diluted.

> 'Black and white' has been replaced by 'grey'. 'Definites' have been replaced by 'maybes'. (Bird 2001)

The preparation of PRSPs is in progress at the individual country levels, and it will require some time before experiences on individual country macro-planning designs and outcomes are synthesised. The WB has recently put together a *Sourcebook for Poverty Reduction Strategies*, containing a host of themes and chapters, to serve as 'guidelines' for designing various economics and social policies, including macro-policy framework at the country level.

The macro chapter, 'Macroeconomic policy and poverty reduction' (Ames et al. 2001), provides broad guidelines as follows:

- 'economic growth is the single most important factor influencing poverty, and macroeconomic stability is essential for high and sustainable rates of growth';
- 'macroeconomic stability by itself, however, does not ensure high rates of economic growth'; other key *structural* measures are necessary!
- 'growth alone is not sufficient for poverty reduction. Growth associated with progressive distributional change will have a greater impact on poverty than growth which leaves distribution unchanged';
- 'to safeguard macroeconomic stability, the government budget, including the country's poverty reduction strategies, must be financed in a sustainable, non-inflationary manner';
- 'except in cases where macroeconomic imbalances are severe, there will usually be some scope for flexibility in setting short-term macroeconomic targets'.

In some sense, there are some fundamental concessions being forwarded, compared with the WC stance: that macro-stability *per se* will not deliver 'magic' solutions; that *equity-sensitive* measures are needed alongside *growth* measures for maximum poverty impact; that short-term macro targets can be flexibly designed, provided macroeconomic elements are in balance!

That macroeconomic stability is a strong precondition for growth is not at dispute, but one has to carefully weigh the *means* and the *ends* of the economic levers used. A critical contention of the 'stabilisation' protagonists (WB/IMF) over the 1980s and 1990s has been that price stability through stringent monetary policies, and reduction of fiscal and current account deficits, would bring efficiency and create the climate of sustained investment growth. In most countries, growth has been inadequate, and poverty and unemployment remain persistently high. While this so-called Washington Consensus is now widely derogated, it should be clearly understood why it is so. Severe inflation is still bad; severe deficits must still be avoided. Policy-planners did not have a hold (conditionality, less government, and so on) on how severe was severe. Consequently, while some price stability was attained, they faced a rather constricted fiscal and import space (in the absence of any rapid increases in tax revenues or export earnings) to manoeuvre on development expenditures or targeted poverty programmes. In their evolving PRSP guidelines, WB/IMF do now concede that 'There is no unique set of thresholds for each macroeconomic variable between stability and instability' (World Bank 2001).

The above position accommodates a part of the concerns expressed by the WB critics, but still remains unhelpful in understanding how the *same* 'stabilisation' concerns would interact in a wider development and political economy context, which the WB's *Sourcebook* is trying to espouse. The fetishism about price stability and fiscal austerity still remains strong. These elements do restrict the planning 'space' for a policy-planner facing an era of declining concessional foreign loans and of competitive FDIs.

Thus a post-Washington Consensus has not yet crystallised. A focus, let alone the macro-policy focus, is yet to emerge. What has evolved so far is that a national 'ownership' of a country development agenda is being underscored, thus conceding that one size does not fit all. So far as the PRSP process (en route to a post-Washington Consensus!) is concerned, several worries still remain. The preliminary experience with the preparation of PRSPs and interim-PRSPs suggests that, first, while there still remains (and quite rightly) a strict insistence by WB/IMF on 'getting prices right' for macroeconomic stability, there is very little discourse on how the economic levers (fiscal, monetary and exchange rate policies) are to be designed to bring about such stability. A significant concern is on how the *macro-strategy* will blend with the *development agenda* which a country is being asked to design.[11] Otherwise, the poverty strategy in the PRSP will not constitute a strategy, but a series of programmes, project and social sector 'add-ons'.[12] Second, in the absence of the scope for formulating *alternative* macro models to address poverty reduction, the developing countries may very well confront a double jeopardy; they may *de facto* face a 'stabilisation' conditionality and a 'poverty' conditionality, in the event that a country achieves neither the macro targets nor the poverty targets. That would hardly enhance the credibility of the new PRSP process, as expressed in the emerging concerns.

The perception of a large section of people is that the PRSP is the traditional IMF and World Bank recipe for reforms which must be accepted in order to access their resources. The PRSP is seen as the sugar coating for the reforms process and may face the same fate as the earlier generation of unowned reforms. (*CPD Programme on Independent Review of Bangladesh's Development*, March 2002)

The focus needs re-orientation. The formulation of the macroeconomic policy framework must lie at the heart of the PRSP strategy; these two must not be seen as exercises independent of each other. A critical link will be on how the alternative macro-policy measures are drawn up to define the allocative and redistributive framework that would enhance employment and reduce poverty. In order to accommodate the goal of poverty reduction and full employment, one would need to rethink a degree of flexibilisation in the stabilisation standards and design alternative macroeconomic measures (especially in respect of fiscal, monetary and exchange rate policies) in the wider context of financing a development strategy that fosters investment, growth and employment and reduces poverty.

THREE ISSUES AND CONSIDERATIONS

Stable Markets; Stable Growth?

Our previous discussion seems to point out that most countries through a fairly strict stabilisation programme produced, by and large, a price discipline, and even where (as in some cases) they have not fully complied with the 'right' prices, the prices were possibly not 'too wrong', especially in the context of an ambivalence regarding what precisely are the right prices. In some other extreme cases, such as those observed during the Asian crisis and the Argentinian crisis, several domestic policy-induced and external shocks have rocked the price structure.

There was an implicit belief that the adoption of a stabilisation programme would (together with a range of structural adjustment programmes) help stabilise markets, which in turn would support the resumption of efficient and stable growth. The two decades of the stabilisation practice has shown that attempts to get prices right may not automatically stabilise markets (note the 'boom–bust' frequency in the financial markets in several countries), or stabilise growth (unless stabilised growth implied low growth equilibrium). Furthermore, constricted monetary and fiscal policy, focused largely on inflation control, in many instances dampened aggregate demand, and often affected vital public expenditures on infrastructure development and maintenance, social provisions, and so on. If the PRSPs were to tread the same macroeconomic route to 'getting prices right', questions will certainly re-emerge, regarding what is the real objective of macro-policy, and what precisely are we trying to stabilise: prices, markets or growth? Experience has shown that stability in one of these need not ensure the stability of the others in any automatic sense. Furthermore, as Ocampo (2002) emphasises, 'the consistency that ought to characterise macroeconomic policies should be based on a broad definition of stability that recognises that there is no single correlation between its alternative definitions and that significant trade-offs may be involved'.[13]

Slow and inadequate growth that has largely characterised the post-reform period (except during the first part of the 1990s, possibly coinciding with growth regeneration in the United States and some European Union countries) by itself has produced scepticism and protests. This has been fuelled by the boom–bust financial markets, and subsequent growth volatility, with enormous consequences in terms of lost income/ employment of the individual citizen, and of reduced assets by the individual enterprises. Stabilisation of prices as the overarching objective of current macroeconomic policy-making has become thoroughly suspect. What then is (are) the alternative(s)?

In free market economies, macro regimes, according to Tobin (1996), can be broadly classified as (i) those in which 'demand creates its own supply' (demand-managed approach to full-employment equilibrium) and (ii) those where 'supply creates its own demand' (supply-constraints to full-employment equilibrium). In the post-Second World War period, the macroeconomic objective was dominated by full employment and growth considerations (with sustainable external balances). Policies pursued thereafter witnessed growth dividends and full employment (or near full employment) in much of the industrialised world, and tangible growth in many other parts of the world (notably East Asia). This high growth period between 1950 and 1973, often dubbed the 'golden era', came to a halt during the 1980s after the two oil price shocks of 1973 and 1979. The Keynesian demand-management approach to macroeconomic policies came to be relegated, and often put into disrepute, when inflation targeting became the dominant macro-policy concern. (One may note that in the Keynesian framework inflation control depended more on microeconomic and labour market policies.[14]) Tobin, himself taking a neo-Keynesian stance, argued (ostensibly in the context of industrialised countries, especially the United States) that over time economies keep moving from one regime to the other. During the past two decades, in the developing countries as well as the developed, there was a major, pervasive policy shift towards the second regime, inspired by alleged 'government failures' of the previous decades, and entailing a series of 'contractionary' policies and market liberalisation measures.

Today, given alleged 'new market failures', there is a call in the more recent literature for a return to Keynesian demand management, the paradigm that characterised the growth/development strategies of the 1950s–70s: the role of the government in particular.[15] 'Government intervention is at least sometimes (many would argue frequently) desirable to stabilise the level of economic activity' (Greenwald and Stiglitz 1993).

Would this again be a simple moving from one economic regime to the other, as Tobin argued? Even in demand-management regimes, the Keynesians are divided (see literature on old and new Keynesians; for example Greenwald and Stiglitz 1993). There are obviously the middle-ground practitioners who view that during the 1950s–70s the framework of a demand-managed economy was held hostage by governments, while the more recent 'price stabilisation' macro-policy was held hostage to speculation, crony capitalism and 'short-termish dashes'. Given now the benefit of hindsight, and half a century of varied experiences, many practitioners have sought to search for a 'third-way' macroeconomic framework. Gordon Brown, the United Kingdom Chancellor of the Exchequer, in a recent keynote address to the Royal Economic Society (Brown 2001), has taken such a position, where he advocates the need for a *long-term growth strategy*, although strongly cautioning that 'stability' is a precondition for growth in Europe and the United Kingdom. (The European Union and the United Kingdom situations have some contextual differences, especially where the European Union has to deal with one currency, and a Central Bank, but twelve different fiscal regimes and labour markets; compare Allsopp 2002.) Indeed Brown (2001) calls for a 'modern Keynesian' approach (his third way!) to sustain and enhance employment through stability and growth, and focuses on the continuous blend of both *macroeconomic* and *microeconomic* measures, as well as R&D, to simultaneously increase productivity and sustain stability, without one or the other being solely charged with inflation targeting or employment generation.[16]

The developing countries as well may require a 'third-way' blend of macroeconomic and microeconomic measures (labour policies in particular) to reach long-term growth and employment targets. An essential precondition, as earlier contended, is the enhancement in the levels of *investment*. The East Asian economies achieved more than 30 per cent investment–GDP ratios. This was as much facilitated by macro-stability as by public interventions in incentive structures, and physical and social infrastructures. High savings-investment rates, among other factors, together with a relatively egalitarian growth, helped these economies to achieve full employment and structural transformation, namely *a movement of labour to higher productivity sectors.* Such achievements will be less forthcoming when stabilisation *per se* tends to return a low growth, and even a declining effective demand, and when *rates* of investment show declining trends (Table 4.6).

In the case of developing countries, which are far-distanced from a full-employment economy, the 'stability' and 'growth' perspectives would need to be addressed somewhat differently (from, for example, the European Union's 'Stability and Growth Pact' (SGP)). In the developing countries, every policy-planner would almost unanimously agree on the need for macro-stability! Moreover, there are strong analytical considerations behind the need for prudent fiscal, monetary and exchange rate policies (Lora and Olivera 1998). It is important to understand why and to what extent (i) economic reforms, especially stabilisation policies, could not attain the goals (of price stability, deficit reduction, and so on) which these policies were set to attain; (ii) why these policies, in trying to establish price efficiency, failed to resume sustained investment and growth, and in many country cases ended in a so-called stabilisation trap.

The need for stability in markets, as stated earlier, is hardly in dispute. The end and vital consideration, however, is on how to foster stable growth in the long run.

Centrality of Employment; Productive Employment

The practice and experience of macroeconomic policy-planning during the past half-century, by both the developed and the developing countries, has produced a reasonable knowledge base from which the individual countries could now draw pragmatic lessons, on which policies are likely to work better in the given economic and social circumstances of the country. It is also well known that during the immediate post-war decades, several (of the developed) countries moved along a demand-managed policy towards a full-employment state; thereafter, sustaining or stabilising employment at near full-employment levels needed modification in the economic levers that were first used to obtain such employment levels. *The Economic Survey of Europe 1949*, prepared under Gunner Myrdal, contained a separate section on the 'Level of effective demand', a theme which has now been relegated to priorities of inflation targeting. A 'third-way' macroeconomic framework, for example, as contained in Brown (2001), is essentially an effort towards fine-tuning the balance of demand and supply-side considerations for near full-employment economies (European Commission 2001). The social institutions in the individual country would possibly determine the kind of 'third way' forward, relevant to that particular country.

The developing countries, which are confronted with vast surplus labour and low productivity, are also deeply caught in distributive tensions and economic and social insecurity. No wonder that now the multilateral organisations and the donor community have decided unanimously to focus on poverty targeting for which a renewed, re-focused development strategy was indispensable.[17] A return to the goal of full, productive and freely chosen employment is emerging as an imperative.[18]

Dudley Seers, the architect of ILO's Colombia employment report, provides a positive spin on the need for placing employment as a central objective of development. He came to this conclusion when he worked out that, given the growth–employment relationship at that time, Colombia would have required to grow at 14 per cent for 15 years at stretch to absorb the five million unemployed. Thus he maintained, 'What a development plan needs to concentrate on is first an employment target and then – to achieve the target – not so much the pace as the process of growth' (Seers 1971).

Given the state of world poverty and unemployment, and low growth in individual countries (and at the global level), many in recent years as well have emphasised the significance of employment as a central goal. Godfrey (1991), in his analysis of Asian economies, emphasised 'labour shortage' as the aim of economic planning. In fact, Bruton (2001) identifies 'sustained labour demand' as a primary macro objective. The macro question he asks is, 'To what extent and in what way can considerations of aggregate demand and, to a lesser extent, aggregate supply contribute to the development process?', and he states further that 'strong demand presence, a demand pressure that presses firmly against supply of all resources, especially labour, is a major advantage in achieving the development objective.'

Such an employment-focused development objective had been advocated earlier by many notable economists. Chakravarty (1987), for example, argued that 'employment-oriented planning' was 'of great analytical and practical significance for many developing countries'. He maintained, without completely refuting the basic logic of standard growth theories, that 'getting fixated on the most rapid accumulation of physical capital may not provide the most appropriate strategy during the transition from a labour-surplus stage to a situation where easily available labour has been fully deployed in productive pursuits' (ibid.).

In this context, ILO's convention 122 on the goal of full employment provides a significant *economic* and *social* foundation. According to this convention, employment is both an economic and a social objective (note the links of employment to equity, poverty alleviation and a basic income protection).

   The above possibly presupposes employment generation as essentially *formal sector (FS) job growth*, which is more likely to provide the necessary nexus for initiating formal employment relationships and institutions, in protecting basic rights of workers and employers. In the advanced economies, the bulk of the employment–population ratio is characterised as such (for example 80–90 per cent of total employment in the United Kingdom, the United States, France and Japan is wage employment). In contrast, the formal sector job growth in the developing countries is dismally low (largely between 10 and 30 per cent), with near stagnancy in manufacturing employment and fast proliferation in informal sector jobs (see Figure 4.3). In the developing countries, the informal sector has grown out of proportion, precisely because of the lack of demand for labour in the formal sector; and it is in the informal sector that one naturally tends to observe maximum decent work deficits.

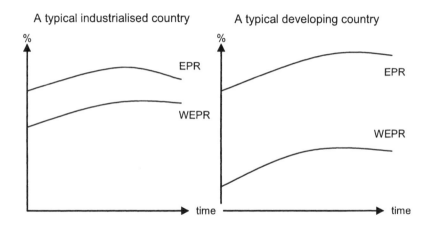

Figure 4.3 Employment–population ratio (EPR) and wage employment (%, EPR)

   In the developing countries, the lack of, or slow growth in, FS jobs is possibly one of the greatest failures of development in the past half-century. This calls for a serious rethinking on the new development agenda that needs to underpin structural changes, increase in labour demand and shifts in labour demand to higher productivity sectors through future industrialisation and trade, and other sectoral policies. The paradigms during the 1950s and 1960s on structural transformation and the so-called Lewisian turning points in development through, *inter alia*, labour market tightening are meaningfully re-emerging.[19] The notion of sustained FS job growth (as part of an employment strategy) can, in the ultimate analysis, be a significant cornerstone in the promotion of decent work.

Macroeconomic Environment; Environment for Macro-policy

That there is the need for a stable macroeconomic environment for stable growth and employment generation has never been in dispute. During the past two decades, in particular, and under the conditional lending programmes of the WB/IMF, policy-makers have assiduously tried to reach 'given' macroeconomic targets, using economic levers that were more in tune with 'short-termish dashes' than with longer-term objectives.[20] The sanctity of such an environment came under increasing scrutiny when first, such environment failed to show any growth dynamics; and, second, the policies (such as public expenditure cuts and import controls) by which such an environment was brought about were themselves found to be adversely affecting aggregate demand, and consequently individual incomes and employment.

Several analysts and empirical researchers have thus questioned the 'sufficiency conditions' of the following, even if they are found 'necessary':

- *getting prices right will enable stabilisation.* Several studies have shown how inflation control has as much to do with orthodox anti-inflationary macro-instruments as structural and institutional policies.[21]
- *stability will usher in growth.* Although Fischer (1993) emphasises a strong negative relationship between inflation and growth, there are other studies which show that the evidence is mixed (see the section, 'Post-Washington Consensus: the PRSP model). In fact, there has been very little focus on how far an economy could afford an inflationary pressure in the process of growth and employment generation. The WB's *Sourcebook* cites low-inflation economies as those having less than 20 per cent inflation rate.
- *growth will lead to employment generation.* Here, the *pattern*, hence the design, of growth needs to be factored in. Employment is neither automatic nor cost-free. The growth–productivity–employment relationship needs to be examined, and understood well. The equation on employment growth and productivity growth has to be reviewed in a correct perspective, especially taking into consideration economic and social constraints facing the individual country.[22]

All these imply that the macro-policy framework needs to be supported by a number of other policies, microeconomic and institutional. This would further imply that a *country-specific* approach was needed to understanding the efficiency of macro-policies. Even within a country, given the variety of constraints (formal–informal sector divide in the labour force; social groups, institutions and bargaining regulations), it would be only natural to draw up *alternative macro-scenarios*, taking into account the tolerable *range* (instead of points) of fiscal, monetary and exchange rate targets. The range and alternative scenario concepts would allow an individual country degrees of freedom in planning under various constraints (which may be broadly defined as the *environment* for effective playing out of the macroeconomic policies).

In respect of another crucial dimension of the 'environment', it would be significant and expedient to identify the ingredients of a labour market policy, and the labour market institutions that would help support an employment-friendly macroeconomic policy framework.

This would necessarily require addressing issues of governance, social dialogue and social compacts to enable a better effectiveness of the impact of macro-policies. In fact, for a country to attain stable growth and steady investment levels, there must be a conducive legal and social infrastructure, with well-defined accountability and responsibilities of employees, workers and the government, that would support policy reforms (see box titled 'Barbados: protocols and partnerships on critical economic and social policy decisions' on how the tripartite partners in Barbados so ingenuously handled hard macro choices in the early 1990s).

CONSENSUS ON MACROECONOMIC FRAMEWORK: BY WHOM, FOR WHOM?

Some of the issues and ideas discussed above tend to appear at once common-sensical and highly debatable. There is a long history to these debates, and at times they have been confined to academic and ideological warfare. In the real world of policy-making, the issue of macro regime is complex, and not simply guided by demand *or* supply constraints. That is because there is no unique 'technology' of macroeconomic designs, especially when country-specific structures and institutions play such an enormous role in their implementation and effectiveness. Economic populism, whether as a lobby for free markets or strong governments, can be misleading. During the past two decades, as part of the structural adjustment programmes, every developing country has been strictly advised by WB/IMF to cut fiscal deficits and to reduce the size of the government and public expenditure. This obviously conflates the need for fiscal balance with what the roles and functions of a government should be in a particular economic and social setting.[23] The designing and formulation of macroeconomic policies cannot be disembedded from the overall economic, social and political context of a country's development process.

Barbados: protocols and partnerships on critical economic and social policy decisions

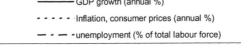
——— GDP growth (annual %)
- - - - - Inflation, consumer prices (annual %)
— - — - unemployment (% of total labour force)

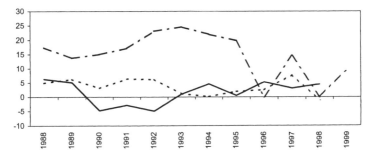

Source: World Bank (2000), *World Development Indicators*

In the wake of massive resentment, both by workers' and employers' groups, and public protests against the proposed structural adjustment programme (SAP) in 1991, a process of mediation and renewed cooperation among the social partners was initiated by civil society representatives, predominantly the church leadership. The workers felt that the SAP proposal would entail a heavy social price and an uneven burden on the poorer workers. The process evolved into what is known as the first protocol, 'The protocol for the implementation of a prices and incomes policy, 1993–95'. This tripartite agreement was primarily designed to conduct a truly collective effort to get the economy out of the crisis, but through various pre-emptive measures to minimise layoffs and social hardships. Thus the parties agreed to avoid the IMF prescription of a devaluation; to focus on competitiveness and productivity; to accept wage freezes until wage increases could be effected through productivity gains; to consider retrenchment as a last resort, and after ensuring at least one earner of a family retains his/her job, and so on. The agreement fostered a national resolve to overcome the economic crisis, and indeed helped the political process to implement difficult economic decisions to achieve stability and resumption of growth.

The success of the first protocol was followed by the second, 'The protocol for the implementation of a prices and incomes policy, 1995–97', which, against the backdrop of a moderate growth success, sought to deepen the role of and broaden the agenda of social dialogue to effect better articulation of macroeconomic and labour market policies. The parties moved away from 'wage freezes' to 'wage restraints', such that Barbados sustained its international competitiveness through higher productivity. Performance-related pay and incentives were introduced. The third protocol, 'The protocol for the implementation of a social partnership, 1998–2000', sought to consolidate the perceived gains from partnerships in economic and social development, especially in an era of globalisation; to maintain a peaceful industrial climate; and to reduce income disparities through employment promotion and other measures of social inclusion.

It is interesting to note that the three protocols, covering the period 1993–2000, are associated with (i) an average annual economic growth rate of 4 per cent; (ii) an inflation rate of close to 2 per cent; (iii) a decline in unemployment from nearly 22 per cent in 1994 to 9.8 per cent in 1998.

The Barbados model of 'social compacts' has become a major point of reference for the entire Caribbean region.

Source: Muqtada, M. (2001), 'A global agenda for employment: review of national perspectives', mimeo; a modified version is quoted in ILO, *Global Employment Agenda*, 2003.

And, as we all know, there are several stakeholders in this process, representing the population and interest groups. It is the consensus and commitment of these stakeholders that are vital in the design and implementation of a macroeconomic reform package.

From the analysis and diagnosis of policy issues in the previous sections, the following seem to emerge, as possible *considerations* in the design of a macroeconomic policy framework.

1. *A macroeconomic policy framework must support, and be designed according to, the economic and social objective pursued.* The neoliberal macroeconomic objective of 'getting prices right' over the past two decades perhaps attained some degree of price discipline, but certainly failed to show what this stabilisation meant for growth and employment.[24] The latter, in many instances, contracted. A return to the goal of full employment and decent work provides an alternative long-term objective.[25] Such an objective needs to be cast in a long-term framework of sustained investment and growth.

2. *The goal of full employment and decent work raises considerations of economic and social values, simultaneously.* Such an objective is broad-based, and is in conformity with the emerging global order towards *integrated* economic and social progress, underpinned by global campaigns against poverty (together with other millennium goals) and breach of human rights. If the social malaise and negative social indicators are seen to be linked to, and emanating from, the economic order, it is not enough to strive simply to mitigate these negative social effects. It is necessary to address the *disease* (lack of remunerative employment, social protection, and so on) alongside the provision for treatment of the *symptoms* (targeted poverty programmes, food stamps, and so on). It is worth noting that varying the fiscal and budgetary instruments could be guided as much by social considerations as economic ones.

3. *Growth is needed (not only for employment but also) for sustaining macroeconomic stability, inasmuch as stability is needed for growth.* Given that there has been a significant contraction in global output, and low and inadequate economic growth in most of the individual countries, with consequences of pervasive poverty and unemployment, there exist emphatic considerations to seek measures, at the national and international levels, towards national and global output expansion. As noted earlier, it is extremely difficult for countries to sustain stability, brought about largely through contractionary monetary and fiscal policies, if growth and employment generation do not resume quickly. This is particularly worrisome for countries facing mass unemployment and poverty. The global output contraction over the past two decades may

not have been as 'deep' as during the Great Depression of the 1930s, but its prolonged tenure certainly calls for a re-think on accommodating under-consumption and demand management approaches to restoring full employment. An employment-centred growth strategy would require a reconsideration of Keynesian demand-management policies, alongside price stability considerations. Over the past 20 years, there appears to have been a disconnect between these approaches.

4. *The effectiveness of a macro-policy will depend both on markets and prudent public interventions.* It is evident that different countries are differently placed in the trajectory towards full employment (also following different paths, for example, the United States, Japan, the European Union) and hence the economic levers (conforming to resource positions, employment elasticities, institutional structures) will have to be varyingly applied. The market must continue to play a dominant role, for otherwise the economy will not have 'a rational system of economic calculations' (Khan and Muqtada 1997). But the real problem lies elsewhere, namely whether a non-intervention, 'deterministic' macro approach will automatically deliver a full-employment output level. Removing distortions and supply constraints may ensure an equilibrium (of aggregate supply and aggregative demand), but this could easily coexist with substantial unemployment. This is what Keynes said, in explaining the Great Depression: that economies under stresses of contractionary policies could run into a state of under-consumption, and that demand-management policies would be needed to boost consumption, employment, income and output. It appears that this would entail a degree of government intervention, the degree of such intervention depending on the GNP gap (difference between actual and potential GNP) and whether the incidences of poverty and unemployment are big or small. Moreover, 'Keynesian macroeconomics has one immense advantage over its old and new classical rivals: it can explain, and they cannot, the main repeatedly observed characteristics of business fluctuations' (Tobin 1996).

5. *The formulation of a macroeconomic policy framework will necessarily have to be pragmatic and country-specific.* 'One size fits all' cannot be a sensible approach. It is imperative that macro-policy design at the individual country level takes into account whether, and to what extent, the economy is *supply-constrained* and/or *demand-constrained*. It is equally important to understand whether *pro-cyclical* and/or *anti-cyclical* economic levers would best ease these constraints, for that particular economy at that particular point in time. Policy priorities would be better identified in such a pragmatic approach, one that could act between 'balancing prices' and balancing growth and employment. This would in

all likelihood be tantamount to each individual country drawing up its own unique 'third way' macro framework, focused on growth and employment.

6. *A macroeconomic policy framework must set macro-targets that are feasible, and are flexible within bounds of alternative growth and employment scenarios.* Accommodating a 'range' in price stability (that is, a modified definition of 'distortion') is a positive stance that is emerging in the PRSP guidelines of the WB and IMF. Previously, lending conditionalities based on achieving precise 'point' macro-targets, in rather 'short-termish dashes', left very little room for manoeuvre, and little scope for damage control. The point to note here is that there are several variations on any macroeconomic theme (being increasingly recognised by WB/IMF). A useful guide is on identifying the *toleration limits* (of inflation and fiscal deficits), and drawing up *alternative* scenarios of getting/keeping the labour force fully employed.

7. *In macro-planning, the links between long-term macro objectives (namely employment and growth) and short-term macro-instruments need to be understood, and factored in.* Macroeconomic policies can have immediate repercussions (budget and import compressions, devaluations, and so on), but such 'short-termish dashes' must be weighed against the long-term policy perspectives on growth and employment (Brown 2001). The nuances of macroeconomic policy-making would thus lie in balancing the market's allocative efficiency (without making a fetish of it) and the incentives to growth and employment. Thus, for instance, a moderate degree of inflation (hitherto unacceptable to the WB/IMF) could be tolerated if the exchange rate could be used flexibly, or if concessional loans were available, or if expenditure switching were acceptable. Similarly, public investments in many developing countries have been shown to encourage private investment (infrastructures, and so on), but if, in the process, public sector borrowing is extensive, it will also tend to 'crowd out' private investment.

8. *For the developing countries, in particular, macro-policies and instruments need to be critically related to 'financing development'.* For the developing countries, especially those facing a 'stabilisation trap', surplus labour and poverty, room for manoeuvre perhaps will have to come through a prudent use of the monetary and fiscal levers, and a degree of focused government intervention to boost investment and employment generation. In fact, a *fiscal master plan* could be devised, linked to the broader objective of financing development. Such a fiscal objective, instead of concentrating on easy (but often disastrous) modes of cutting down public expenditure, ought to focus on (i) rationalising public expenditure (infrastructure, skills, housing), (ii) support to private sector investment; (iii) targeting poverty reduction and social goals; (iv)

aggressive resource mobilisation. A mildly expansionary fiscal policy may entail a degree of inflation, but, so long as it is monitored closely as simply a 'recovery' inflation, it can in fact be conducive to reducing unemployment and idle capacity. For the LDCs, there may be a need for external support for 'creating' a fiscal space, through concessional loans, FDIs, debt reduction programmes, and so on.

9. *An appropriate environment for macroeconomic policy is as critical as the establishment of the macro-policy environment itself.*[26] Such an environment requires more than what is called for in the WB's structural adjustment programmes (SAPs) in order to support the effective implementation of stabilisation policies. The broader environment is related to issues of governance (Banuri 1990), and institutions and regulations, especially when macro choices require decisions on trade-offs. Whether it is a question of devaluation, wage-moderation or social protection, there has to be consensus on shared responsibilities, and transparency. Democratic institutions, such as tripartism, when appropriately developed (as in many European Union and Scandinavian countries, Australia, and so on) reflect, even in conflict, trends in economic and social progress. In developing countries, with the formal sector accounting for, in most cases, less than 20 per cent of the employed labour force, such a democratic representation and environment is weak.

A FINAL REMARK: A COORDINATED GLOBAL EMPLOYMENT STRATEGY

As we noted at the outset, global growth and productive employment sharply contracted during the past two decades, especially when compared with the golden era of 1950–73. Many individual countries registered such a scenario, including the European Union, Japan and, in the recent period, the United States. Fetishism, almost all around the globe, with 'getting prices right' and restructuring have in fact shrunk markets. More than twenty years of inadequate and fluctuating growth, combined with growing inequality, translated into pervasive poverty, insecurity and social exclusion. 'Essentially it means that for the first time in two generations, failures on the demand side of the economy – insufficient private spending to make use of the available productive capacity – have become the clear and present limitation on prosperity for a large part of the world' (Krugman 1999).

An appropriate stimulus needs to be sought, both globally and at the country level, in order to increase productive employment. It must be an imperative now to look beyond price stability, and to call for global alliances on a coordinated strategy for stable growth and employment. Some of the recent signals for a global stimulus, with calls for a greater flow of concessional aid to the developing countries, debt reductions and re-scheduling, and market access for exports from the developing world, are encouraging. These would constitute a significant support to the stimulus required, indeed a support to the individual country's right to development. The real stimulus, however, would have to come first from within, namely national efforts and commitment to growth, full employment and decent work.[27] International support, governance and monitoring can then be devised to complement and coordinate such national efforts.

For the developing countries, especially those confronted with a large labour surplus, the designing and implementation of macro-policies within a full-employment and decent work framework is more than an economic proposition. It is possibly the most significant way to give effect to the country's commitments to uphold the economic and human rights of the individual.[28] Such a policy stance and commitment at the national level could provide building blocks for the international campaign on, and support for reaching, the millennial goals, given close linkages between employment, poverty and other social goals. A country's right to development and an individual's right to decent work would, then, underpin and reinforce the rationale for coordinated global employment strategy.

ACKNOWLEDGEMENTS

A previous version of the views contained in the chapter was discussed at an informal meeting of the Employment and Development group, set up by the Employment Strategy Department of the ILO. This version has taken into account many helpful remarks and suggestions from the participants, in particular from Rashid Amjad, Peter Auer and Ajit Ghose. Statistical assistance and useful research suggestions from Sudip Ranjan Basu, and data and web search assistance from Anne Drougard, are gratefully acknowledged. Needless to say, the author remains responsible for any errors and critical omissions.

NOTES

1. The author is currently the Chief of the Employment Policies Unit in the Employment Strategy Department of the ILO. The views expressed in this chapter are the author's own, and do not necessarily represent those of the ILO.

2. This is a sample that the author has selected for further empirical work. It contains nine countries where the ILO has recently conducted in-depth country employment policy reviews (CEPRs), which the author has coordinated.

3. UNCTAD (2002: 24) states that 'the proportion of the total population living on less than $1 a day rose from 51 per cent in the three years before the adoption of a programme (Enhanced Structural Adjustment Facility) to 52 per cent in the first three years after and 53 per cent in the next three years'.

4 The tripartite conclusions of the ILO Committee on employment, 1996, contained emphatic considerations of policies, for developed and developing countries, towards full employment.

5. The recent scandals in the US corporate world are sending shock waves among investors, and the ordinary citizens whose small but life-times' savings have been lured into a maze of fraudulent accounting practices. 'I think we need a philosophy for capitalism. A new philosophy. I call it decent capitalism' (Charles Handy, keynote speech, ILO's Second Enterprise Forum, 1999).

6. See, among others, Fischer (1993) and several studies by the staff of the IMF, in Bredenkamp and Schadler (1999).

7. The IMF staff study (Bredenkamp and Schadler 1999, p. 133), in explaining the determinants of growth (Chapter 5), subsumes variables used by Fischer, and introduces several other price and non-price variables. Nearly 994 observations, and 13 explanatory variables, return a R^2 of 0.22! *Investment* does not feature among these. Japan's prolonged low growth in recent years, despite near-zero real rates of interest, points to the need for considering various other explanatory factors.

8. See Ocampo (2002).

9. The UNDP has already embarked on a regional programme entitled 'The macroeconomics of poverty reduction'.

10. In other low- and middle-income countries, such as Egypt, the WB is undertaking 'Social and structural policy' reviews, predominantly focused on poverty alleviation.

11. Such a concern is being expressed at the country level PRSP preparation. See, for example, CPD (2002).

12. Ocampo (2002).

13. Ocampo (2002).

14. Brown (2001).

15. See Malinvaud et al. (1997).

16. Brown (2001).

17. Cf. Meier and Stiglitz (2001); Ocampo (2002).

18. See ILO's Convention 122.

19. See Meier and Stiglitz (2001) for a historical account of these development debates. Also see Bruton (2001).

20. Brown (2001).

21. See, for example Banuri (1990), and several WIDER studies on the subject. Some of the results are summarised in Taylor (1988).

22. While e + p = o (that is employment growth *plus* productivity growth is *equal to* output growth), both e and p can be positive if o is sufficiently high (Verdoorn's law).

23. For instance, the Scandinavian economies where public expenditure is relatively very high (40–50 per cent of GDP) would have to re-set their social and institutional settings if they were to follow the WB/IMF prescription.

24. 'The fact of the matter is that unemployment is not a phantasm, modern societies need ways of dealing with it, and the self-regulating market economy has not done so.' See Stiglitz's foreword to Polanyi (2002).

25. See ILO's Convention 122 on the goal of full employment; and ILO (1999) for an exposition of 'decent work'.

26. Greenwald and Stiglitz (1993).

27. For the developing country, it may be pointed out that a commitment to full employment, and achieving it, requires a full utilisation of its labour resources, given the current rate of capital formation, and need not be guided by any pre-determined per capita income levels. Japan, South Korea and Taiwan–China achieved near full employment in the late 1960s and early 1970s; subsequently, these countries undertook policies to move towards a higher productivity frontier. See Oshima (1987).
28. This is especially in the manner 'full employment' goal is defined by ILO's Convention 122.

REFERENCES

Allsopp, C. (2002), 'The future of macroeconomic policy in the European Union', Discussion Paper No. 7, Bank of England.
Ames, B., W. Brown, S. Devarajan and A. Izquierdo (2001), 'Macroeconomic policy and poverty reduction', in *Sourcebook for Poverty Reduction Strategies*, Washington, DC: World Bank.
Amsden, A. (1989), *Asia's Next Giant: South Korea and Late Industrialization*, New York: Oxford University Press.
Balassa, B. (1982), *Development Strategies in Semi-industrializing Economies*, Baltimore: Johns Hopkins University Press.
Banuri, T.J. (1990), *Economic Liberalization: No Panacea*, Oxford: Clarendon Press.
Bhagwati, J. and T.N. Srinivasan (1983), 'Trade policy and development', in R. Dornbusch and J.A. Frankel (eds), *International Economic Policy Theory and Evidence*, Baltimore: John Hopkins University Press.
Bird, G. (2001), 'What happened to the Washington Consensus?', *World Economics*, **2** (4).
Bredenkamp, H. and S. Schadler (eds) (1999), *Economic Adjustment and Reforms in Low-income Countries*, Washington, DC: IMF.
Brown, G. (2001), 'The conditions for high and stable growth and employment', *The Economic Journal*, 111, May.
Bruton, H.J. (2001), *On the Search for Well-being*, Ann Arbor: University of Michigan Press.
Chakravarty, S. (1987), *Logic of Employment-oriented Planning in Developing Countries*, G.L. Mehta Lecture, Madras.
Cornia, G.A. (1999), 'Liberalization, globalization and income distribution', Working Paper No. 157, UNU/WIDER.
CPD (Centre for Policy Dialogue) (2002a), *State of Bangladesh Economy on the Eve of the Development Forum 2002*, Dhaka, Bangladesh.
CPD (Centre for Policy Dialogue) (2002b), *CPD Programme on Independent review of Bangladesh's Development*, Dhaka, Bangladesh: CPD.
European Commission (2001), 'The EU Economy 2001 Review', *European Economy*, **73**.
Fischer, S. (1993), 'The role of macroeconomic factors in growth', *Journal of Monetary Economics*, 32.
Geest, W. van der and Rolph van der Hoeven (eds) (1999), *Adjustment, Employment and Missing Institutions in Africa*, in association with James Currey, Geneva: ILO.
Godfrey, M. (1991), 'Labour shortage as an aim of employment strategy: an overview of trends and prospects in developing Asia', in ILO-ARTEP, *Employment and Labour Market Interventions*, New Delhi.

Greenwald, B. and J. Stiglitz (1993), 'New and old Keynesians', *Journal of Economic Perspectives*, **7** (1).
ILO (1996–97), *National Policies in a Global Context*, World Employment Report, Geneva: ILO.
ILO (1999), *Decent Work*, Report of the Director-General of the 87th session of the International Labour Conference, Geneva.
ILO (2001), *Reducing Decent Work Deficit – A Global Challenge*, Report of the Director-General for the 89th session of the International Labour Conference, Geneva.
ILO (2003), *Global Employment Agenda*, Geneva: ILO.
Islam, I. (2001), 'The East Asian crisis and the Bretton Woods institutions: the demise of the "Washington Consensus?"', mimeo, Brisbane: Griffith University.
Kalecki, M. (1972), *Selected Essays on the Economic Growth of the Socialist and Mixed Economies*, Cambridge: Cambridge University Press.
Kanbur, R. (2001), 'Economic policy, distribution and poverty: the nature of disagreements', *World Development*, **29** (6).
Khan, A.R. and M. Muqtada (eds) (1997), *Employment Expansion and Macroeconomic Stability under Increasing Globalization*, London: Macmillan Press Ltd and New York: St Martin's Press.
Krueger, A.O. (1992), 'Policy lessons from development experience since the second world war', paper presented at the first ADB Conference on Development Economics, Manila.
Krugman, P. (1999), *The Return of Depression Economics*, NY: W.W. Norton and Company.
Lewis, A. (1970), 'Summary: the causes of unemployment in Less Developed Countries and some research topics', *International Labour Review*, **101** (5).
Little, I.M.D et al. (1993), *Boom, Crisis and Adjustment: The Macroeconomic Experience of Developing Countries*, World Bank and Oxford University Press.
Lora, E. and M. Olivera (1998), 'Macro policy and employment problems in Latin America', Working Paper 372, Cartagena: Inter-American Development Bank.
Malinvaud, E. et al. (1997), *Development Strategy and Management of the Market Economy*, vol. 1, Oxford: Oxford University Press.
Meier, G.M. and J.E. Stiglitz (2001), *Frontiers of Development Economics: the Future in Perspective*, World Bank, New York: Oxford University Press.
Ocampo, J.A. (2002), 'Rethinking the development agenda', *Cambridge Journal of Economics*, **26**.
Oshima, H.T. (1987), *Economic Growth in Monsoon Asia*, University of Tokyo Press.
Polanyi, K. (2002), *The Great Transformation*, Boston: Beacon Press.
Seers, D. (1971), 'The Colombian employment programme', in W. Galenson, selected *Essays on Employment*, Geneva: ILO.
Sen, A.K. (1983), 'Development: which way now?', *Economic Journal*, 93, December.
Stiglitz, J. (1998), *More instruments and broader goals: moving towards the post-Washington Consensus*, WIDER Annual Lecture.
Taylor, L. (1988), *Varieties of Stabilization Experiences: Towards Sensible Macroeconomics in the Third World*, Oxford: Clarendon Press.
Tobin, J. (1996), *Full Employment and Growth: Further Keynesian essays on policy*, Cheltenham, UK and Brookfield, USA: Edward Elgar.
UNCTAD (2002), *The Least Developed Countries Report 2002*, New York and Geneva: United Nations.

Wade, R. (1990), *Governing the Market: Economic Theory and the Role of the Government in East Asian Industrialization*, Princeton, NJ: Princeton University Press.

World Bank (2001a), *Sourcebook for Poverty Reduction Strategies*, Washington, DC: World Bank.

World Bank (2001b), *World Development Indicators*, Washington, DC: World Bank.

APPENDIX

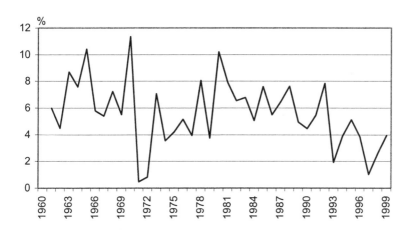

Source: World Bank (2001), WDI CD-ROM.

(a) Pakistan

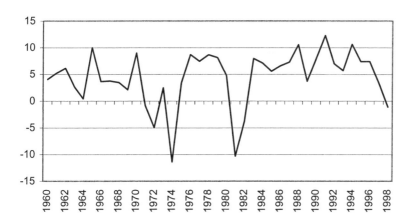

Source: World Bank (2001), WDI CD-ROM.

(b) Chile

Debates on globalisation

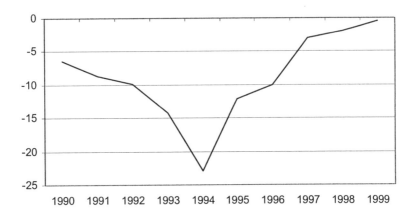

Source: World Bank (2001), WDI CD-ROM.

(c) Ukraine

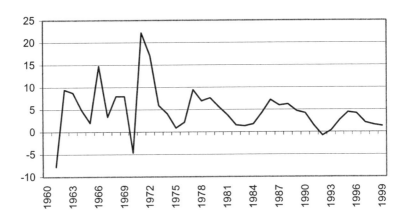

Source: World Bank (2001), WDI CD-ROM.

(d) Kenya

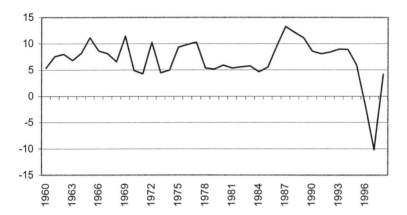

Source: World Bank (2001) WDI CD-ROM

(e) Thailand

Figure 4A.1   Growth fluctuations: GDP growth rate (annual %)

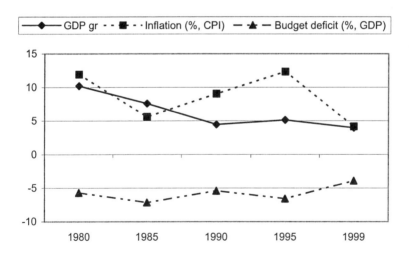

Source: World Bank (2001), WDI CD-ROM

(a) Pakistan

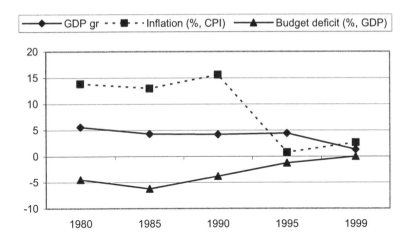

Source: World Bank (2001), WDI CD-ROM

(b) Kenya

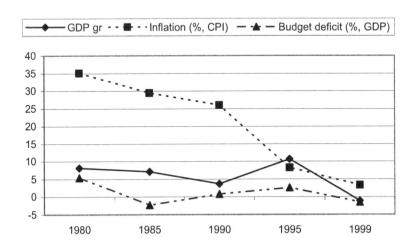

Source: World Bank (2001), WDI CD-ROM

(c) Chile

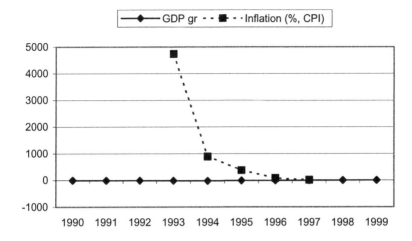

Source: World Bank (2001), WDI CD-ROM

(d) Ukraine

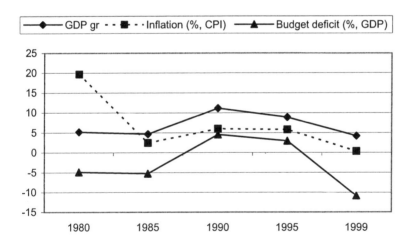

Source: World Bank (2001), WDI CD-ROM

(e) Thailand

Figure 4A.2   Growth rate and stability

5. Foreign direct investment policy and economic development

Bernie Bishop

INTRODUCTION

Developing countries have traditionally used a range of restrictive policy measures to ensure that foreign direct investment (FDI) plays a positive role in their economic development. Specific policy measures have included local content rules, joint venture and technology transfer requirements, limitations on investment in certain sectors of the economy and a screening process to implement them.

In recent years these restrictive policies have faced increasing criticism. The underlying basis of much of this criticism is that, because of the rapid globalisation occurring in many industries, there is increasing competition among countries for FDI so that they are not left out of global production networks. Accordingly developing countries need to liberalise by removing all of the traditional restrictions if they are to continue to attract FDI and gain the advantages that it has to offer.

The argument in this chapter is that it cannot be assumed that doing away with all restrictions will automatically lead to benefits from FDI. One of the major benefits for developing countries from FDI is the contribution that it can make to the development of local firms and industries (Borenstein et al. 1998; UNCTAD 2003). This contribution arises through local firms learning about the product or process technology of the foreign firm or the management and marketing techniques that the foreign firm employs. Learning and diffusion of the knowledge gained takes place in a variety of ways. These include the training of employees who later move to work in local firms; training of suppliers in product, process or design technology; and local firms imitating what their foreign competitors are doing to improve productivity. Thus, over time, local firms themselves will become competitive not only with their foreign counterparts but also in the wider international setting.

On the other hand, it is possible that, rather than learning from foreign firms, local firms may be driven out of business by the superior competitive advantages that foreign firms possess. This may lead to serious economic and social dislocation within the host state. While it can be argued that over time the incoming foreign investment will lead to new opportunities for local entrepreneurs, there can be quite a lengthy period of adjustment within the industry. In addition, despite potential improvements in productivity within the industry because of the foreign direct investment, it is possible that levels of both direct and indirect employment may never reach those that existed before the entry of the foreign firms.

Whether or not foreign investment plays a constructive role in the development of local forms and industries depends to a significant extent on the capability of local firms to learn from their foreign counterparts. Thus, if local firms do not have the capability to learn from foreign firms, there may be a case for continuing to impose restrictions on FDI to attempt to keep it out of those sectors where it has the potential for major dislocation, while at the same time encouraging foreign investors to impart their knowledge to locals in those sectors where there is the capability for learning to occur. This is not to say that restrictions should remain in place indefinitely. Economies such as Korea and Taiwan have shown that restrictions need to be removed as the economy matures so that the competitive advantages to be derived from FDI can be gained. There is increasing evidence that general education levels are the most appropriate indicator of capabilities to benefit from FDI. Until a developing economy has the resources to achieve a reasonable level of general education some continuation of restrictive measures towards FDI may therefore be warranted.

This chapter begins by reviewing the traditional restrictive measures that have been used by developing countries and the rationale for them. Next it canvasses the major strands of criticism that have been directed at these policy measures. Finally it proceeds to examine the question whether these criticisms are justified and whether action should be taken to remove them.

DEVELOPING COUNTRY POLICIES TOWARDS FDI

Local Content Rules

The objective of local content rules is to encourage foreign investors to source some of their raw materials, components and services from local firms, thereby contributing to the development of those local firms, and industries. Such development occurs through foreign investors training local suppliers in order to bring them up to international standards. However, as will be noted below, local content rules are criticised on the grounds that they lead to higher prices for domestic goods because inputs are not supplied at the most competitive rates. In order to run local content policies effectively, it is therefore necessary to protect foreign investors and others who produce final goods from competing imports. Thus critics argue that local content rules prevent domestic firms from ever becoming truly competitive in the international market place. Local content rules were proscribed by the Trade Related Investment Measures (TRIMs) agreement negotiated under the Uruguay Round but there have been recent moves by some developing countries to have this decision reconsidered.

Joint Venture and Technology Transfer Requirements

The economic development rationale for joint venture policies and the technology transfer requirements that often accompany them is similar to local content rules. Developing countries hope that joint venture requirements will result in local joint venture partners learning from the superior production processes and management and marketing techniques of the foreign investor. Further it is hoped that the advanced know-how will not only benefit the joint venture partner but also help upgrade supplier capabilities. Over time, as employees leave the joint venture they will take the knowledge gained with them and in that way the knowledge will be diffused throughout the industry. Yet, as will be noted later, there are several serious criticisms of joint venture policies to the effect that, if they do not deter investors altogether, they will most likely result in outdated technologies being utilised. It is argued that foreign investors will be unlikely to bring in their latest technology if there is a requirement that this be given away to local firms who may become competitors (Moran 1998, 1999).

Sectoral Restrictions

In addition to joint venture requirements developing countries often have a list of industries where foreign investment is 'restricted' or 'prohibited'. Sometimes the reasons cited for this are national security or protection of public order, health and safety and so on. However, in many cases the real reason is that it is felt that local firms in those industries would not be able to withstand the competition from foreign entrants. Thus there is a fear on the part of developing countries that if those industries were opened local firms would disappear or be crowded out. This would be compounded if joint venture requirements and controls over mergers and acquisitions were simultaneously abolished. A possible result is that, in the absence of effective implementation of competition laws, some sectors could become dominated by just a few foreign firms, leading not only to the adverse consequences of oligopolies or monopolies but also to the possibility of political manipulation.

Screening

Most developing countries have screening agencies in place in order to enforce their policies towards foreign investment. Typically these agencies are placed at a high level within the bureaucracy, being part of a powerful trade and industry ministry or part of the prime minister's department. Their function is to approve all or certain classes of foreign investment with a view to ensuring that there is a national benefit. While the exact nature of the national benefit is often left unspecified, it is clear, for developing countries at least, that this involves the development of local industry capability.

Screening agencies are often attacked on the grounds that they act politically, rather than on economic grounds, and that they cause unnecessary bureaucratic hurdles for foreign investors. To counter the latter criticism many developing countries have attempted to establish their investment agencies as one-stop shops to prevent investors having to go through the screening agency as a first step and then to a range of government departments responsible for the various permits and licences that may be needed. However the one-stop shop concept rarely works in practice, as it is difficult for one central agency to have the necessary expertise to assess investment applications across the entire range of industry categories and therefore some reference to other agencies is inevitably necessary (Sader 2002).

There is a view that screening agencies should gradually disappear. For example, a World Bank Study (IFC and FIAS 1997) suggested that screening agencies should transform into investment promotion agencies and, while acknowledging the difficulties of such a changed role, outlined some cases where this has been partially achieved. It discussed the new role for investment agencies in terms of image building, investment generation and investor servicing (ibid., pp. 49–50). Certainly this approach has merits from the investor point of view. However from the point of view of developing countries it means a loss of the ability to monitor foreign investment and its impact. Again developing countries are unlikely to abandon this lightly. A good example is China. While China agreed to remove its local content policies and relax its joint venture requirements upon entry to the WTO, the issue of investment approval was not negotiable.

CRITICISMS OF RESTRICTIVE POLICIES

The first line of criticism directed against these policies is that they amount simply to protection for local industries and that such protectionism can only be harmful to the economy because of its tendency to breed inefficiency. A study by the OECD (1998) is a good example of this line of criticism. The study undertook a review of the restrictions that existed in Argentina, Brazil, Chile, Indonesia, Malaysia and the Philippines. It divided restrictions into the categories of screening requirements, sectoral prohibitions, local content rules and other performance requirements, land-ownership restrictions, expatriate employment, requirements for technology transfer and the role of the state in the economy that might restrict FDI opportunities.

The study noted that all countries continued to have sectoral restrictions applying to some industries, with these being most pronounced in the services sector. It suggested that the real reason for sectoral restrictions was to protect domestic industries despite developing countries' often-stated position that the restrictions remain in place for national security reasons. It made particular mention of restrictions in finance sectors and argued that the restrictions that were in place in Asian countries at the time may well have been partly responsible for the Asian crisis because of the lack of competition in the financial sector.

The study grouped local content rules and other performance requirements under the heading of trade restrictions and noted that these too are simply protective devices. It argued that the main disadvantage arising from such restrictions is that, rather than benefiting local industry, they principally benefit foreign investors. The reasoning here is that FDI firms move in behind the protective wall, resulting in large profits that they transfer back to their shareholders in developed economies.

Moran's work on FDI policy (1998, 1999) also adopts this line of criticism, particularly in relation to local content rules. He argues (1999, pp. 45–6) that local content rules are simply infant industry measures and have the effect of raising costs and prices in the host economy, thereby detracting from the development of internationally competitive firms.

Yet, while there is some validity in these arguments, policy-makers in developing economies are well aware of the dangers and may be able to avoid them. For example, a detailed study of two major corporations in Shanghai – Shanghai VW and Shanghai Bell – has shown that careful use of local content rules can be successful in helping to develop local industry (Li and Yeung 1999). In addition Sun's study (1998) of the automobile industry and the electronics industry in China found that local content rules had assisted the development of both industries, pointing out the dramatic increase in local content that had occurred during the evolution of those industries. However others disagree that local content rules have been beneficial on an economy-wide basis, arguing that, while local content requirements might have developed local supplier industries, this was at the expense of efficiency in costs of production and competitiveness (Xia and Lu 2001). In setting out the evidence for and against local content rules UNCTAD (2001, p. 169) suggests that the effectiveness of local content rules has been much debated but that some studies have shown that they have contributed to the development of supplier industries in Korea, Taiwan, Brazil, Mexico and Thailand. Thus there is no consensus as to whether there is any justification for the abolition of local content rules because of their supposedly harmful protective nature.

A second line of criticism directed at restrictive FDI policy measures is that they actually inhibit technology transfer and hence the development of local firms and industries rather than promoting this. Thomsen's study (1999) is a useful example here. The author's principal argument is that the Asian crisis should have provided the impetus for developing countries in South East Asia to eliminate barriers to foreign investment in domestic market oriented sectors. It identified restrictions as screening, limits on foreign equity, negative lists and land-ownership.

The author's major argument proceeded along the following lines. He suggested that FDI in South East Asia may have propelled export growth but not necessarily economic development. He said that exports have been limited to a small number of products and sectors and that they have been produced in foreign enclaves for the most part. Thus there is low value-added as well as a poor record of technology transfer. In addition, because foreign investors import most of their components for quality reasons, there have been relatively few linkages with local firms. The record of technology transfer in ASEAN has also not been good, despite some studies showing some level of staff training and training of local suppliers. He argued that the record of technology transfer has been disappointing, because there is low absorptive capacity in local firms, and that foreign investors have been confined to enclaves. While he noted that the restrictive policies had the intention of developing indigenous capabilities, he suggested that those policies actually deter foreign investment (and hence limit the possible learning effect), particularly in domestic market oriented sectors.

The solution proposed was to open up the domestic market to foreign investment. It was assumed that this would lead to greater competitive pressure for domestic firms and this in turn would lead to greater levels of technology transfer. The author cited Reuber's work (1973) to make the case that technology transfer is greater in domestic market oriented investment than in export oriented investment.

This study acknowledged that developing countries aim to utilise foreign investment to build up local firms and industries. However, it did not canvass the possible adverse effects of a sudden opening of these industries to foreign competition. In addition, while it is noted that levels of technology transfer in export oriented industries have been low because of low absorptive capacity, no argument is advanced to show that the level of absorptive capacity in domestic market oriented industries is any better. Thus the conclusion that an opening of these industries to foreign investment will necessarily lead to higher levels of technology transfer because of competition can be questioned.

Moran's work (1998, 1999) also criticises restrictive foreign investment policies on the grounds that they inhibit technology transfer. He argues that when local content requirements (for example) are used there are weak incentives for firms to upgrade technology or maintain the highest standards of quality because there is no competition from suppliers or other producers in the international market place. He also suggests that mandatory joint venture requirements result in foreign investors utilising older technology because of their fear of losing cutting edge technology to joint venture partners. He claims that there is no evidence that joint venture or technology transfer requirements result in more linkages to the local economy, improved market access or technological upgrading of local firms than do wholly owned operations (1999, p. 47). He argues that where these have been in place there has been a lag in technology acquisition, an absence of advanced management processes, and few linkages with local firms. Moran's principal argument is that FDI contributes most to development when it is export oriented and integrated into the global operations of parent companies. When this occurs, the highest level of technology is used, better linkage outcomes result and sophisticated management and marketing techniques are introduced to the host economy. Some examples from Mexico and Malaysia are cited to show how dynamic internationally competitive subsidiaries have led to linkages in a number of industries including automobiles, petrochemicals and electronics (ibid., pp. 42–4).

Nonetheless many developing countries continue to insist on some form of joint venture requirement in many industry sectors and there is some evidence that this has resulted in technology transfer. Sun (1998) argues that part of the reason for foreign investment leading to an increase in domestic investment in China has been because of the joint venture policy. He argues that joint ventures have provided local partners with the financial and physical resources for other projects and that the learning that occurred provided local joint venture partners with investment opportunities in new products. Athukorala and Menon (1995) refer to the role that joint ventures have played in furnishing Malaysian counterparts with international marketing knowledge.

Doner and Ramsay (1993) argue that Thai firms in the textile industry have been strengthened as a result of their joint venture relationships. In his study of technology transfer by Japanese investors in South East Asia, Urata (1995) found that there was a correlation between a high level of local participation and the transfer of more advanced technologies. He explained this by arguing that, in joint ventures with a high degree of local participation, local partners are able to pressure their foreign counterparts for more advanced knowledge.

Again there is no consensus that joint venture requirements and other restrictive measures necessarily deter technology transfer and the development of local firms and industries. It can be argued that policy-makers in developing countries attempt to use technology transfer and joint venture requirements only in industries where they know that there is sufficient absorptive capacity and where there is the likelihood that such restrictions might promote technology transfer and local industry development. They are well aware that joint ventures will not be acceptable to foreign investors in some sectors (particularly high technology projects) and for this reason do not always have a blanket joint venture policy.

A third line of criticism follows from the protectionist argument. It is that restrictive foreign investment policy measures suffer from the same rent-seeking problems as all industry policy initiatives and that they should therefore be removed. The argument here is that measures such as local content rules and joint venture requirements provide policy-makers with an opportunity to reward supporters by giving them a chance to capture some of the profits from the incoming FDI. It is suggested that there is a tendency to pressure foreign investors to use particular suppliers or particular joint venture partners who may have good connections to the host government. While there is no doubt that some rent seeking occurs, it can be avoided to a significant degree if the bureaucracy is able to be insulated from such demands. It can be argued that this occurred in the implementation of both Korea and Taiwan's restrictive investment policies during the earlier stages of their economic development (Bishop 1997).

IS THERE ANY JUSTIFICATION FOR MAINTAINING RESTRICTIVE MEASURES?

There are two compelling reasons why restrictive measures might need to be kept in place by developing economies for some time to come. The first is to guard against the possible negative effects of crowding out. The second is to attempt to ensure that FDI leads to the growth and development of local firms and industries.

Turning first to the issue of crowding out, the danger here is that a sudden opening of all sectors to foreign investment may lead to local firms being driven out of business. This may have serious consequences for employment and social stability in the host state. Because of this, host countries wish to keep some sectors off limits to foreign investors or at least have joint venture requirements in those sectors.

There is some evidence that a fear of crowding out may be justified. Bloomstrom and Kokko (1997) acknowledge that crowding out of local investors is a real possibility in developing countries. They suggest that there is a large risk that, rather than making local firms competitive, MNCs will crowd them out. They also point out that there is a possibility that MNCs lead to industry concentration in developing countries, noting however that this does not always have adverse effects. The OECD (2002) also acknowledges that the effect of FDI in increasing industry concentration is stronger in developing countries than for developed economies.

Unfortunately econometric analysis at the aggregate level offers little resolution of the crowding-out issue. An UNCTAD study (1999, pp. 189–93) found that in the majority of cases FDI could not be seen to have had either a crowding-out or a crowding-in effect. Similarly, a more recent study by Research Information Systems for Non-Aligned and Developing Countries (Kumar and Pradhan 2002) found that for most countries in the survey there was a neutral effect. Interestingly, both studies found that Korea and Thailand had demonstrated a crowding-in effect. Both of these countries have had a history of actively pursuing policies restricting investment in certain sectors of the economy. Korea has only recently liberalised its foreign investment policies while Thailand still has restrictions in many sectors.

On the other hand, the UNCTAD study found a crowding-out effect in Chile and several other Central American countries, while the RIS study found a crowding-out effect in Singapore and the Philippines. UNCTAD notes that sudden liberalisation may lead to adverse consequences and that this has occurred in some Latin American countries when capital-intensive production methods were used by incoming TNCs resulting in a negative effect on employment (1999, p. 213). It is suggested that a gradual pace of liberalisation may be necessary to allow domestic capabilities to develop (ibid., p. 252). In a review of the various studies noted above, UNCTAD (2003, p. 105) suggests that the issue has not yet been settled. It seems therefore that developing counties are likely to continue to impose some restrictive measures.

As noted above, the second argument for the maintenance of restrictive measures is to ensure that FDI leads to the growth of domestic firms and industries. Other than in very small economies, it is unlikely that sufficient amounts of FDI can be attracted for it to act as the main engine of growth. Its main role is to act as a catalyst for the development of domestic firms and industries. There is a growing body of evidence to suggest that developing countries might need to keep some restrictive policy measures in place until there is sufficient capability throughout the entire economy for local firms to be able to compete with and learn from incoming foreign investors.

In its 1999 *World Investment Report*, UNCTAD suggested that the impact of FDI on development depends on the extent to which it plays a role in building local industry (ibid., p. 322). Throughout the report reference was made to the importance of the capability of domestic industries in determining whether FDI will play a positive role in economic development. For example, when discussing technology transfer the report noted that the best way to improve linkages is to raise the capabilities of local suppliers (ibid., p. 212) and that government can improve technology transfer with better domestic skills, capabilities, supplier networks and infrastructure (ibid., p. 210). It said that governments in developing countries need to strengthen national learning systems as happened in the Asian NICs if they want to get the best out of FDI (ibid., p. 198). It cautioned that in the absence of domestic capability FDI can have a negative impact on domestic technological deepening, because local firms that might otherwise have developed technology on their own to serve the local market will no longer be motivated to do so if a TNC moves in. The report noted that countries such as Korea and Brazil that restricted TNC entry in some sectors went on to develop an indigenous technological capability, whereas countries such as Thailand and Mexico that allowed highly advanced TNCs to enter freely in some sectors did not develop an indigenous technological capability in those industries (ibid., p. 214). Bloomstrom and Kokko (1997) cite some studies that show productivity has been improved at the aggregate level as a result of FDI but caution that where there is a large gap in technology levels between foreign and local firms this is unlikely to occur.

In their study of spillovers arising through worker mobility, Fosfuri et al. (2001) also noted that a low level of technological capability in domestic firms reduces the potential for spillovers. While Sjoholm (1999) found that there were some spillovers from foreign investors to local Indonesian firms despite a technology gap, he acknowledged that 'at a certain level the gap may be so large that it will be impossible for domestic firms to absorb foreign technologies with their existing experience, educational level and technological knowledge' (ibid., p. 71).

If we turn to the more micro-level studies there is ample evidence that low levels of local capability or absorptive capacity inhibit learning by local firms. A study by Capanelli (1998) of the electronics industry in Malaysia suggested that there is a relatively low level of capability among local firms to supply inputs and that a policy of supporting 'indigenous technological progress which stresses the formation of human capital and financial assistance to firms would greatly promote the gradual upgrading of locally owned input makers to higher technological levels' (ibid., p. 222). An earlier study of 11 firms in the electronics industry by Salleh (1995) also found disappointing levels of local content in the electronics industry due, in part, to low levels of capability of local industry. A study by Chen of the semi-conductor industry in Malaysia concluded that a major difficulty with integrating local firms into the production cycle was the 'severe dearth of educated human resources' (Chen 1998, p. 146). Saad's review (1995) of the impact of FDI in Indonesia suggests that there had been limited technology transfer with the main constraint being limited absorptive capacity in local firms due to, amongst other things, low levels of education in technical areas. A study of foreign investment in China's special economic zones also pointed out that low skill levels in the workforce and the lack of institutional infrastructure such as research institutes were inhibiting technology development in local firms (Wu 1999, p. 100).

In each chapter of UNCTAD's 1999 report there was some attention to appropriate government policies towards FDI for upgrading capabilities. It seems clear that the authors of the report have some sympathy with the developing country position of utilising policy instruments (such as those mentioned earlier) to ensure that FDI has a positive developmental impact. The report noted that developing countries cannot expect that their technological base will be transformed simply through an open-door policy to FDI (ibid., pp. 219, 317) and that a passive laissez-faire approach towards FDI may not be sufficient for development purposes (ibid., p. 325). The report noted that there may be a role for government in selecting those TNCs that will contribute most to the development process (ibid., p. 183). This of course requires some form of screening process. Further the report suggested that there may be a case for protecting some industries from FDI to allow learning to take place, as happened in countries such as Korea and Taiwan. It noted that, while this is essentially an infant industry argument, it might be valid provided that local firms have the potential to become competitive and provided that this does not take so long that the social costs outweigh the social benefits (ibid., p. 320). This implies some sectoral restrictions on FDI. The report also noted that traditional policies such as local content rules and technology transfer requirements, when used in the context of upgrading capabilities, may be beneficial (ibid., p. 323).

The development experience of economies such as Taiwan tends to lend weight to the argument that restrictive policies towards FDI can be successfully used to promote local industry development. An APEC study (1997) shows that Taiwan's restrictive policies towards FDI were successful in ensuring that FDI played a positive role in the development of various industries principally by ensuring that local industry had the capability to compete with foreign investors before liberalisation occurred. This study contains some very useful sectoral case studies of semiconductors, retail trade, telecommunications and finance.

The study traced the development of Taiwan's semiconductor industry from the first foreign investment in electronic goods in the export processing zones established in the late 1960s. It showed how the active involvement in industry development by research institutions sponsored by the government, the enforcement of technology transfer and joint venture requirements on foreign investors, the training of local engineers, the use of technology-licensing agreements and the recruitment of skilled overseas Taiwanese to return to Taiwan enabled the Taiwanese electronic industry to become competitive to the point where foreign firms felt that it was in their interest to establish semiconductor fabrication plants in Taiwan because, if they did not, locals would soon have the knowledge to do so. Quite clearly this case study demonstrated that the development of local industry capability was essential in order for the host economy to gain the most out of FDI.

A similar pattern emerges in the study of the retail sector. In order to develop large-scale supermarkets in Taiwan, foreign investors were encouraged to enter into joint ventures with locals. In this way both the Dutch chain 'Macro' and the French 'Carrefour' entered into joint venture with local partners. The study suggested that local partners learnt both managerial techniques and the technical aspects of establishing a large-scale supermarket from the more experienced foreign firms. This knowledge was soon diffused throughout the retail sector in Taiwan.

In the telecommunications and finance sectors foreign investment has been used to improve the overall competitiveness of these industries. However the report notes that liberalisation of telecommunications only commenced in 1996 and was spread over several years. It was clear that at this time there was sufficient capability in the local industry for local firms to be able to compete for licences with foreign investors. It could be argued that Taiwan's gradual liberalisation of the banking sector is also aimed at ensuring that locals are not crowded out of the market.

It can therefore be argued, both on the basis of individual industry level studies in various countries and on the basis of the development experience of countries such as Taiwan, that some restrictive policies might be necessary during the process of building local capability. Further, there seems to be a growing consensus that education levels are the most important factor in determining whether local firms have the capability to learn from FDI and, by implication, whether FDI can benefit the development process.

The OECD's recent study (2002) goes much further than previous OECD work in acknowledging that the capability of domestic firms and industries is important. This study suggests that the greatest potential for technology transfer from FDI is via suppliers. It admits that, for FDI to have a positive and long-term impact on the business sector in the host country, the technology gap between the foreign firm and local firms must not be too large. It recognises that investment in education is crucial not only in maximising the attraction of FDI in the first place but also in ensuring that it results in positive spillovers. It also notes that, while some positive effects are occurring because those who work for multinational companies are being trained by them, there is weaker evidence that this knowledge is being diffused throughout the economy. It suggests that the general level of education is vital if this is to occur.

A more specific study of intra-firm technology transfer between Japanese parent companies and their overseas affiliates also found that educational levels in host countries is an important determinant of intra-firm technology transfer (Urata and Kawai 2000). The authors say 'that these findings suggest that upgrading educational attainment and particularly promoting skills such as engineering would have a high rate of return' (ibid., p. 70).

A study by Borenstein et al. (1998) sheds some light on what level of education might be indicative of a sufficiently high level of local capability to benefit from FDI. They argued that the main contribution of foreign direct investment to economic growth arises through its role in stimulating technological progress rather than simply acting as a supplier of capital. They found that, for foreign investment to have a positive influence on growth, an average level of 0.5 years of secondary schooling is necessary in the male population of working age. Below this, FDI did not have any effect on growth. Thus the study demonstrates that without a reasonable general educational and skill level foreign investment might not make a positive contribution to either economic growth or development.

UNCTAD's 1999 *World Development Report* has also noted the necessity of building domestic capability in order to gain positive developmental outcomes from FDI. This has been discussed above. However, an additional point needs to be made here. UNCTAD (1999, p. 222) point out that not too many developing countries are in a position to create the domestic capabilities required in the near future. They discuss efforts that were previously made in the negotiation of a code of conduct for TNCs to impart some obligation on developed countries to assist developing countries in this regard. They note also that under the WTO TRIPs agreement developed countries are also supposed to play this role.

The arguments raised above have implications for liberalisation. The issue is whether liberalisation should proceed without first building up the capability of local firms with both general policies such as raising the general education level and more specific policies to upgrade skills. While it can be argued that the specific restrictive policies outlined above will only be effective if there is a certain level of domestic capability, developing countries may be of the view that by having such policies in place they can be selective about FDI and ensure that it is matched with existing capabilities. This would not be possible in a liberalised environment. Thus, although there are pitfalls in pursuing the traditional types of policies towards FDI, it seems likely that developing countries will be unwilling to abandon them until they are convinced that a more liberal approach will benefit local industry development.

CONCLUSION

There are a number of conclusions that can be drawn from the discussion above.

First, while there are sound theoretical arguments to advance the cause of liberalisation of FDI policy, many criticisms of restrictive policies fail to recognise that traditional policies towards FDI have been successful in developing local industry in some countries and in some sectors. The cases of Korea and Taiwan stand out here. However, there is also evidence from China and some South East Asian countries.

Second, insufficient attention is paid to the need to build local industry capability prior to the removal of restrictions. A number of the studies mentioned above have drawn attention to the possibility of crowding out and the need for technological capabilities of local firms to be sufficiently competitive with foreign investors if there is to be a benefit. Avoiding crowding out and creating competitive local firms can only occur through building local capabilities. There is a growing consensus that raising local capabilities occurs best by raising general education levels.

Third, the issue of investment liberalisation is firmly on the WTO agenda in the Doha Round. It seems unlikely that much headway will be made with this issue until there is a greater recognition by developed countries that developing countries need assistance to enhance education levels to improve capabilities either prior to or, at the very least, in conjunction with the liberalisation process.

REFERENCES

APEC Economic Committee (1997), *The Impact of Investment Liberalisation in APEC*, Singapore: APEC Secretariat.

Athukorala, P. and J. Menon (1995), 'Developing with foreign investment: Malaysia', *Australian Economic Review*, January–March, 9–22.

Bishop, B. (1997), *Foreign Direct Investment in Korea; The Role of the State*, London: Ashgate.

Bloomstrom, M. and A. Kokko (1997), 'The impact of foreign investment on host countries: a review of the empirical evidence', Paper No. 1745, Washington, DC: International Trade Division, International Economics Department, World Bank.

Borenstein, E., J. De Gregorio and J. Lee (1998), 'How does foreign direct investment affect economic growth?', *Journal of International Economics*, **45**, 115–35.

Capanelli G. (1998), 'Technology transfer from Japanese consumer electronic films via buyer–supplier relations', in K. Jomo, G. Felker and R. Rasiah (eds), *Industrial Technology Development in Malaysia – Industry and Firm Studies*, London: Routledge, pp. 191–231.

Chen, G. (1998), 'The semiconductor industry in Malaysia', in K. Jomo, G. Felker and R. Rasiah (eds), *Industrial Technology Development in Malaysia – Industry and Firm Studies*, London: Routledge, pp. 125–50.

Doner, R. and A. Ramsay (1993), 'Postimperialism and development in Thailand', *World Development*, **21** (5), 691–704.

Fosfuri, A., M. Motta and T. Ronde (2001), 'Foreign direct investment and spillovers through workers' mobility', *Journal of International Economics*, **53** (1), 205–22.

IFC (International Finance Corporation) and FIAS (Foreign Investment Advisory Service) (1997), *Foreign Direct Investment: Lessons of Experience*, Washington.

Kumar, N. and J. Pradhan (2002), *FDI, Externalities and Economic Growth in Developing Countries*, Delhi: Research Information Systems for Non-Aligned and Developing Countries.

Li, X. and Y. Yeung (1999), 'Inter-firm linkages and regional impact of transnational corporations: comparing case studies from Shanghai, China', *Human Geography*, **81** (3), 61–73.

Moran, T. (1998), *Foreign Direct Investment and Development*, Washington, DC: Institute for International Economics.

Moran, T. (1999), 'Foreign direct investment and development – a reassessment of the evidence and policy implications', paper at OECD Conference on the Role of International Investment in Development, OECD, Paris, 20–21 September.

OECD (1998), *Foreign Direct Investment and Economic Development – Lessons from Six Emerging Economies*, Paris: OECD.

OECD (2002), *Foreign Direct Investment for Development – Maximising Benefits, Minimising Costs*, Paris: OECD.

Reuber, G. (ed.) (1973), *Private Foreign Investment in Development*, Oxford: Clarendon Press.

Saad, I. (1995), 'FDI, structural change and deregulation in Indonesia', in *The New Wave of Foreign Direct Investment in Asia*, Singapore: Nomura Research Institute and Institute of South East Asian Studies, pp. 197–221.

Sader, F. (2002),'Administering private investment: necessary, but dangerous', APEC Seminar on Investments, 'One Stop Shop', Lima, Peru, 26–27 February.

Salleh, I. (1995), 'Foreign direct investment and technology transfer in the Malaysian electronics industry', in *The New Wave of Foreign Direct Investment in Asia*, Singapore: Nomura Research Institute and Institute of South East Asian Studies, pp. 133–60.

Sjoholm, F. (1999), 'Technology gap, competition and spillovers from foreign direct investment; evidence from establishment data', *The Journal of Development Studies*, **36** (1), 53–73.

Sun, H. (1998), *Foreign Investment and Economic Development in China 1979–1996*, Aldershot: Ashgate Press.

Thomsen, S. (1999), 'Southeast Asia: the role of foreign direct investment policies in development', Working Paper on International Investment, Paris: Directorate for Financial, Fiscal and Enterprise Affairs, OECD.

UNCTAD (United Nations Conference on Trade and Development) (1999), *World Investment Report 1999: Foreign Direct Investment and the Challenge of Development*, New York and Geneva: United Nations.

UNCTAD (United Nations Conference on Trade and Development) (2001), *World Investment Report 2001: Promoting Linkages*, New York and Geneva: United Nations.

UNCTAD (United Nations Conference on Trade and Development) (2003), *World Investment Report 2003: FDI Policies for Development: National and International Perspectives*, New York and Geneva: United Nations.

Urata, S. (1995), 'Japanese foreign direct investment and technology transfer in Asia', paper presented at the conference, Does Ownership Matter? Japanese Multinationals in Asia, Massachusetts Institute of Technology, 20–21 September.

Urata, S. and H. Kawai (2000), 'Intrafirm technology transfer by Japanese manufacturing firms in East Asia', in T. Ito and A. Krueger (eds), *The Role of Foreign Direct Investment in East Asia's Economic Development*, Chicago: University of Chicago Press, pp. 49–79.

Wu, W. (1999), *Pioneering Economic Reform in China's Special Economic Zones*, Aldershot: Ashgate.

Xia, Y. and Y. Lu (2001), 'FDI and host country linkages: assessing the effectiveness and development impact of the policy measures: the case of the automobile industry in China', paper prepared for the UNCTAD Secretariat, Geneva.

PART II

Globalisation in the Asia-Pacific region:
selected case studies

6. Changing China's political economy: uniting and dividing impacts of globalisation

Leong H. Liew

INTRODUCTION

China's market reform and integration into the global economy has been a resounding success. China's official estimates show that its economy grew at an annual rate of 9.7 per cent between 1978 and 1998 (Lardy 2002, p. 12) and at an annual rate of 7.7 per cent between 1998 and 2002 (NBSC 2003, p. 27).[1] Between 1995 and 2000 China received 40 per cent of the foreign direct investment flows into Asia and in the 1990s it outperformed most of its Asian neighbours in export growth (CSRC 2002, Ch. 5).

Globalisation has delivered high economic growth, and many non-economic benefits that are indirectly derived from this economic growth, to China. However, the economic benefits have not been distributed equally and non-economic outcomes are not all positive. As a result, globalisation divides as much as it unites China. This chapter examines how the direct and indirect economic impacts of globalisation are both uniting and dividing China. I argue that the impressive increase in the size of China's economy – a result of its success in market reform and integration into the global economy – has contributed to a growth in national confidence and a positive feeling of being 'Chinese'. The rise in national confidence from economic success is accompanied by developments in an instrument of globalisation: the Internet, which is facilitating public discourse on social problems and further development of civil society in China, which marketisation has given space to develop. Democracy has yet to follow the political liberalisation that has accompanied China's market reform. Nevertheless, the growth in civil society in China is beginning to make national and local governments more accountable. The market creates the political space necessary for civil society to develop, but it also facilitates official accountability. It restrains the predatory instincts of local governments because of their need to make their local environment attractive to factors of production to promote local development.

Outcomes of globalisation are not all positive. Globalisation is Janus-faced. There is now a backlash in industrialised countries against globalisation, owing to loss of jobs in labour-intensive sectors in these countries as a result of competition from unskilled-labour-abundant countries like China. China's labour-intensive industries gain from globalisation, but China does not have a comparative advantage in capital-intensive heavy industries and agriculture, and jobs in these sectors and in state-owned enterprises (SOEs) are being lost as China opens its domestic economy to foreign competition. So far job losses in China have not undermined China's engagement with the global economy, but it is becoming increasingly clear that the massive reduction in poverty as a result of this engagement has not prevented widening inequality in incomes and status as China's economic structure adjusts to increased internal and external competition.

Growing income inequalities are a great challenge to China's central government. It continues to face challenges to its rule in Tibet and Xinjiang, and ethnic and regional income inequalities are exacerbating ethnic tensions in these provinces, which weaken national unity. The central government has implemented polices to moderate income inequalities and reduce the threat posed by secessionist movements, but some of these policies have turned out to be counterproductive and have inflamed, not calmed, ethnic tensions.

GLOBALISATION AND CHINESE NATIONALISM

Depending on whether purchasing power calculations are used, China now has the second or third largest economy in the world after the United States and perhaps Japan. In 2002 China ranked fifth in world merchandise exports (5 per cent of the total) and sixth in merchandise imports (6 per cent of the total). China now buys 31 per cent of Asia's exports compared with the 10 per cent bought by Japan, which absorbed 20 per cent of the region's exports a decade ago (Keliher 2004). In just over 20 years of economic reform, China has replaced Japan as the engine of growth for Asia.

It is not just the rapid increase in the size of China's economy that impresses. Economic growth in China has reduced significantly the numbers of its citizens living in poverty. In 1978 60 per cent of China's population were living below the international poverty standard (World Bank 1997a, p. 3), but by 1996 the number of people living below the absolute poverty line had fallen to less than 6 per cent of the population (World Bank 1997b, p. 2). Some scholars like Stiglitz (2002, pp. 180–94) saw China's economic reform as a policy challenge to the IMF/World Bank. China's approach to economic reform differs from the approach prescribed by the IMF/World Bank, but China's reform has produced outcomes better than outcomes of reform in countries in the Commonwealth of Independent States, which have followed more closely the IMF/World Bank prescription of economic reform.[2]

China's impressive post-Mao economic performance and growing significance in the global economy – achieved following the 'Chinese way' – have helped to reverse attitudes among China's citizens to the 'backwardness of Chinese culture' (Liew and Smith 2004, p. 7). China is now courted as an influential member of the international community, admired by some nations but feared by others, generating a cottage industry of academic discourse over whether China should be contained or engaged. Beijing's success in winning the bid to stage the 2008 Olympics highlights China's importance as an emerging and confident international player. Gone now is the anxiety about 'Chinese ways' among many Chinese cultural leaders, as evidenced by the wave of Chinese literary and cinematic products capturing both art-house and mainstream audiences around the world. Ben Hillman (2004, p. 82) describes this phenomenon as 'a renewed celebration of Chineseness'. For Hillman, this form of Chinese nationalism, like all forms of cultural nationalism, is a positive force. They create a sense of community and link the past to the future, providing a sense of direction for the nation as a whole.

GLOBALISATION AND CIVIL SOCIETY

Globalisation implies marketisation of the domestic economy, which has loosened the hold that the state has over the individual. The number and diversity of civic groups in China have increased dramatically in response to loosening state controls (Pei 1998, p. 291). Between 1979 and 1992 the number of these associations that are organised nationally grew by an average of 48 per cent a year. The growth of these associations at the provincial and municipal levels was even higher. In the eight provinces and the cities examined by Pei, the annual growth rates averaged 56 and 86 per cent respectively. Pei's data show that the distribution of national, provincial and municipal civic associations changed significantly between 1978 and 1992, reflecting the depoliticisation of Chinese society in that period. In 1978 about half the national, provincial and municipal associations surveyed were involved in the natural sciences, technology and engineering. These associations were involved in 'politically safe' areas and their over-representation before the reform period is to be expected. The share of this type of association fell in the course of reform – to about 20 per cent of the total in 1992. Meanwhile, academic associations involved in the social sciences, humanities and management studies rose significantly to about a quarter of the total. Even more dramatic was the growth in professional and managerial associations and business and trade associations. From being less than 5 per cent of those surveyed in 1978, they had become about a third of the total in 1992.

The Internet, a symbol and tool of the age of globalisation, is helping to promote civil society in China. The Internet has created a new virtual community and has improved the effectiveness of existing civic organisations, reducing further the reach of the state. It fosters debate and problem articulation in ways that were inconceivable before the Internet was available (Yang 2003, p. 454). The many spontaneous expressions of indignation on the Internet at the 1999 US bombing of the Chinese embassy in Belgrade and the 2001 US spy plane incident, from ordinary Chinese, are good examples of the power of the Internet in facilitating expressions of non-state-sponsored nationalism. Within hours of the Chinese people learning of the two incidents, the Internet was frantic with fervently nationalist discussions (Liew and Smith 2004, p. 13).

The Internet has made it difficult for authorities to hide 'bad news'. A 1999 report circulated on the Internet on how official mismanagement of Henan's blood collection and transfusion service caused the spread of AIDS to large numbers of people in the province contributed to greater public awareness of AIDS and official culpability (Yang 2003, p. 464), which have finally led to official recognition of the seriousness of the AIDS problem and action at the national level. In sum, the Internet is bringing people together more easily and providing new ways of organising collective action. This promotes a vigorous civil society that checks abuse of official power and controls corruption, generating legitimacy and political stability, which promotes unity.

GLOBALISATION AND LOCAL DEVELOPMENT

Globalisation restrains the hands of local governments and promotes local development in China. According to Wei (2002, p. 5), the more open a region in China, the higher is its economic growth, and rural areas that are more open experience faster reductions in poverty. Baumol (1990) makes a distinction between productive and unproductive entrepreneurship. In his view, productive entrepreneurship creates wealth, and unproductive entrepreneurship merely redistributes wealth. Property rights are one of the 'rules of the game' that determine whether a society encourages productive or unproductive entrepreneurship. When private property rights are encroached upon or are inadequately protected, entrepreneurs concentrate their efforts on protecting their existing wealth and redistributing other people's wealth, and neglect production. Baumol illustrated his argument with examples from feudal China. He explained that official positions were highly coveted in feudal China because weak legal protection of property rights allowed imperial officials to depredate the general population. Wealth gained through productive entrepreneurship could easily be lost to the predatory actions of officials. The consequence of this, according to Baumol, was low levels of productive investment and economic development.

Olson (1993) contrasted the behaviour of roving predators with that of stationary bandits to illustrate the importance of secure private property rights for economic growth. He speculated on life in a locality where anarchy reigns. In that kind of society, uncoordinated theft by roving bandits destroys the incentive to produce, making the local population and bandits worse off as a result. The incentive to produce is improved, according to Olson, if the bandit chief makes a commitment to the locality by establishing himself or herself as a warlord. Uncoordinated theft is replaced by organised theft. A secure warlord will have the incentive to provide security and other public goods that will stimulate economic activity. An insecure warlord with temporary tenure will have no incentive to provide public goods that complement other inputs in production. Instead, productive assets will either be confiscated or be left to run down.

Olson's distinction between organised and uncoordinated theft is an important one when one deals with the question of economic reform and transition. Administrative decentralisation lowers entry barriers into the corruption market, which was monopolised previously by the central state. Murphy et al. (1992) argued that decentralised corruption, where many state agents of various levels are able to extract bribes by obstructing trade where before only one or a small number could do so, increases economic inefficiency. In China local governments have been accused of using their new powers as a result of administrative devolution to act in predatory ways. They are accused of levying illegal taxes on enterprises and, in some instances, the forced recruitment of labour for local government projects. However, local village-township enterprises have flourished and localities prospered despite these types of behaviour. This suggests that the predatory behaviour has not been 'excessive', to the point where entrepreneurial activity is extinguished. According to Montinola et al. (1995), it is competition between local governments, an outcome of 'market-preserving federalism',[3] that explains why the predatory behaviour of local governments has not been 'excessive'. With fiscal decentralisation, the amount of resources available to local governments depends critically on local economic performance, which is closely linked to the level of local investment. Unlike roving warlords, stationary autocrats have the incentive to provide conditions that are conducive to economic growth (Olson 1993). In the words of Montinola et al., regions have 'to provide a hospitable environment' for factors of production, lest they move elsewhere. Thus the growing openness of China's economy increases the bargaining power of owners of factors of production vis-à-vis local governments. Globalisation gives factors of production increasing choice, which acts as a brake on the predatory tendencies of local governments and promotes local development and poverty reduction.

GLOBALISATION AND SOCIAL DIVISIONS

Agriculture and SOEs are clear losers as a result of China's marketisation and engagement with the global economy. As trade protection is lifted in China with WTO membership, China's southern provinces will increasingly find it cheaper to import agricultural commodities like wheat, soybeans and vegetable oils rather than buying them from farmers in the north-east (Oxan 2000, p. 13). Post-WTO entry incomes of village residents were projected in a Chinese Academy of Social Sciences (CASS) study to fall by 2.1 per cent and rental price of agricultural land by 18.4 per cent. In addition, agriculture was forecasted to lose 10 million jobs as a result of WTO entry (Li et al. 2000, p. 70).

The unemployment as a result of the lifting of trade barriers is mainly structural, caused by China's consumers and producers adapting to the convergence of domestic and international prices, and is balanced by the growth in employment in sectors where China enjoys comparative advantage. However, globalisation also requires the reduction of surplus labour in SOEs. The resulting unemployment is a legacy of China's centrally planned economy and is largely systemic and is not automatically ameliorated by increased employment in the private sector. In the 1990s 50 million rural workers left farming, many leaving to seek jobs in urban areas (Brooks and Tao 2003, p. 12), and from 1989 to 2001 reform of SOEs reduced urban employment by about 40 million. Despite these reductions in employment, there are still about 150 million surplus workers in the rural sector and 10–11 million in SOEs (Brooks and Tao 2003, p. 3).

China's private sector is increasingly called upon to create new employment for surplus labour released from agriculture and SOEs and new entrants into the labour force. China took serious steps towards ownership reform only after 10 years of economic reform. Once the Party gave the green light to private ownership in the 1990s, the growth of private enterprises took off, as can be seen in Table 6.1.

Table 6.1 Development of private enterprises

Year	Number (000)	Annual growth (%)	Employees (10 000)	Annual growth (%)	Registered capital (100 million yuan)	Annual growth (%)
1989	91		164		84	
1990	98	7.7	170	3.7	95	13.1
1991	108	10.2	184	8.2	123	29.5
1992	140	29.6	232	26.1	221	79.7
1993	238	70.0	373	60.8	681	208.1
1994	432	81.5	648	73.7	1448	112.6
1995	655	51.6	956	47.5	2622	81.1
1996	819	25.0	1171	22.5	3752	43.1
1997	961	17.3	1349	15.2	5140	37.0
1998	1201	25.0	1701	26.1	7000	36.2
Nov. 1999	1486	23.7	1901	11.8		

Source: Yan (2002, p. 194)

The rapid growth in private enterprise has hastened the deregulation of the labour market. This has contributed significantly to employment generation but at the cost of substantial widening in income inequality. The World Bank estimated that China's Gini coefficient increased from 0.29 in the 1980s to 0.39 in the 1990s, transforming China from one of the world's most equal countries (in terms of income) before reform to one in the middle of world rankings by the 1990s (World Bank 1997a, p. 2). In another study, Wang et al. (2002) estimated China's post-reform Gini coefficient to be as high as 0.49. China's entry into the WTO is destined to widen inequality further (Zhai and Li 2002). As income inequality increased, so has inequality of access to public goods such as health (World Bank 1997b) and education (Solinger 1999, pp. 266–9). The latter is the result of China's weakening of its pre-reform commitments to state-guaranteed social rights (Wong 2004, p. 170) and has resulted in China not improving its Human Development Index (HDI) world ranking of 96 since 1975 despite its spectacular economic growth (UNDP 2002). Take illiteracy rates – one of the sub-sets of indicators that are used to calculate the HDI – for example. Provincial rates of illiteracy and semi-illiteracy in China range from a low of 1.3, 1.6 and 1.7 per cent of population in Beijing, Liaoning and Tianjin to a high of 24.8, 32.2 and 61.7 per cent in Gansu, Qinghai and Tibet (Yang and Zhang 2001, pp. 227–8).

The significant change in income distribution has produced a profound shift in China's people's perceptions of the relative status of social groups. Table 6.2 shows the outcome of a survey of how members of different social strata evaluate their social standing, carried out by China's Academy of Social Sciences (Lu 2002) in three cities (Shenzhen, Hefei, Hanchuan) and one county (Zhenning). Two observations from the data are particularly interesting. First, even casual and unemployed workers rank themselves higher than peasants and, second, political and civic (P&C) leaders do not rank themselves first in three of the four places surveyed. In Shenzhen, the city in China's southern Guangdong Province specially built as part of a special economic zone at the beginning of reform, and Hefei, the capital of Anhui Province, private entrepreneurs rank themselves higher than P&C leaders rank themselves. In Hefei P&C leaders rank themselves below what managers, professional and technical (P&T) staff and even non-professional white-collar staff rank themselves, and in Zhenning P&C leaders rank themselves below P&T staff but above private entrepreneurs. What the survey clearly indicates is that market reform in China has in less than a generation re-established more or less the pre-revolution social hierarchy.

Table 6.2   Social standing (self-evaluation)

Social stratum	Social standing (max. 10 pts)			
	Shenzhen	Hefei	Hanchuan	Zhenning
Political and civic leaders	6.8	5.4	5.5	4.7
Managers	6.4	5.6	4.9	n.a.
Private entrepreneurs	7.1	6.0	4.0	4.0
Professional and technical staff	6.2	5.7	5.1	5.4
Non-professional white-collar	5.6	5.5	4.7	4.3
Small business owners	5.8	4.7	4.4	4.2
Service workers	4.9	5.1	4.0	4.6
Production workers	5.3	4.8	4.4	3.8
Peasants	n.a.	n.a.	3.8	3.7
Casual workers/unemployed	5.7	5.2	4.1	4.3
Average	5.7	5.2	4.2	3.9

Source: Lu (2002, p. 32)

GLOBALISATION AND ETHNIC SEPARATISM

Ethnic minority areas, in common with other areas of China, have enjoyed economic benefits derived from the marketisation and globalisation of China's economy. However, the benefits have not been shared equally across China and many minority areas have fallen behind. Marketisation and globalisation have led to growing inequalities between and within domestic regions. Markets tend to reward factors of production according to their economic contribution, and ownership of assets and productivity of factors of production vary considerably across domestic regions and population.

Table 6.3 shows the comparative economic performance in the first 20 years of economic reform for China nationally, five autonomous national-minority regions in China that have provincial status, and the most economically successful province, Guangdong. While the standard of living of Guangdong has leaped way ahead of the national average, the standard of living of the five national-minority provinces has remained behind the national average, and in three of these provinces – Tibet, Ningxia and Neimenggu – it has fallen further behind. Tibet and Ningxia, in particular, have performed badly in relative terms. In 1978 Tibet's per capita GDP was 98.9 per cent of the national average, but by 1998 it had fallen to 58.4 per cent. Ningxia's per capita GDP was a respectable 97.6 per cent of the national average in 1978 but by 1998 had dropped to 66.8 per cent. These national-minority provinces have managed to achieve respectable economic growth rates since 1978 but have fallen further behind economic growth in the rest of the nation because of their poorer resource endowments and geographical locations that markets penalise.

In national-minority regions, aggregated regional economic data may not always give a complete picture of local welfare. Take Xinjiang as an example. Xinjiang appears to be an economic success and an exception to the economic performance of most hinterland provinces. Its GDP and per capita GDP growth between 1978 and 1998 were above the national averages, with per capita GDP increasing from 82.6 per cent to 97.4 per cent of the national average over this period. One might expect that this economic success would contribute positively to the closer integration of Xinjiang into the People's Republic. However, closer examination of these data indicating Xinjiang's recent GDP growth casts doubts on this positive evaluation. When Xinjiang's GDP figures are decomposed into expenditure components, we see not only that economic growth in this province through the 1990s was driven primarily by investment but also that state units were responsible for most of this investment – more so than for investments nationally and for almost all other provinces (see Table 6.4). In 1998 state units' share of investment in fixed assets was 81.3 per cent in Xinjiang[4] and the 1996 and 1997 shares are similar. This means that at least 60 per cent or more of Xinjiang's GDP was attributable to government final consumption and investment by state units, compared with about 33 per cent nationally. Xinjiang's GDP is more dependent on government consumption and investment than even Tibet's.[5]

Table 6.3 *National and provincial GDP (1978 and 1998)*

	National[a]	Guangdong	Tibet	Xinjiang	Ningxia	Neimenggu	Guangxi
GDP (100 million yuan)							
1978	3 624.1	185.9	6.7	39.1	13.0	58.0	75.9
1998	79 395.7	7 919.1	91.2	1 116.7	227.5	1 192.3	1 903.0
GDP per capita (yuan)							
1978	379	369	375	313	370	317	225
1998	6 392	11 143	3 736	6 229	4 270	5 069	4 076
Share of national GDP (%)							
1978	100.0	5.1	0.2	1.1	0.4	1.6	2.1
1998	100.0	10.0	0.1	1.4	0.3	1.5	2.4
Ratio of provincial per capita GDP to national per capita GDP (%)							
1978	100.0	97.4	98.9	82.6	97.6	83.6	59.4
1998	100.0	174.3	58.4	97.4	66.8	79.3	63.8
Av. annual GDP growth (78–98)[b]	9.7	14.0	8.8	10.6	8.6	c	c
Av. annual per capita GDP growth (78–98)[b]	8.3	12.0	6.9	8.6	6.3	c	c

Notes:
[a]National means Mainland China, excluding Hong Kong
[b]Author's calculations from NBS data
[c]Not reported because calculations, which are based on real GDP and real GDP per capita indices data, give inconsistent results.

Source: NBS (1999) and author's calculations

Table 6.4 National and provincial compositions of GDP (%)

National	GDP	Household consumption	Government consumption	Investment	Net exports[a]
1993	100.0	45.5	13.0	43.5	−2.0
1994	100.0	45.1	12.7	40.9	1.3
1995	100.0	46.1	11.4	40.8	1.7
1996	100.0	47.1	11.5	39.3	2.1
1997	100.0	46.5	11.6	38.0	3.8
1998	100.0	46.2	11.9	38.1	3.8

Xinjiang	GDP	Household consumption	Government consumption	Investment	Net exports
1993	100.0	45.2	14.3	70.4	−29.9
1994	100.0	41.7	14.0	72.4	−28.1
1995	100.0	45.3	15.0	68.0	−28.3
1996	100.0	46.4	17.1	52.7	−16.2
1997	100.0	44.3	16.7	53.8	−14.8
1998	100.0	44.1	16.6	61.4	−22.1

Tibet	GDP	Household consumption	Government consumption	Investment	Net exports
1993	100.0	48.9	13.8	37.3	0.0
1994	100.0	54.9	15.2	49.3	−19.4
1995	100.0	40.4	12.9	46.7	−0.1
1996	100.0	46.7	14.2	40.9	−1.8
1997	100.0	45.2	15.3	39.7	−0.2
1998	100.0	41.6	16.3	39.1	3.1[b]

Guangdong	GDP	Household consumption	Government consumption	Investment	Net exports
1993	100.0	42.3	10.8	45.2	1.7
1994	100.0	44.5	9.6	43.9	2.0
1995	100.0	45.1	10.5	41.5	2.8
1996	100.0	44.5	11.0	41.7	2.7
1997	100.0	43.4	12.8	37.4	6.4
1998	100.0	42.1	13.2	38.5	6.2

Notes:
[a] Aggregate exports (overseas exports and exports to the rest of Mainland China) less aggregate imports (from overseas and the rest of Mainland China)
[b] This figure is likely to be incorrect (see Note 5).

Source: Author's calculations using data in NBS (1999)

Xinjiang is a poor, net importing province. It is highly dependent on state fiscal subsidies and loans, although less so than Tibet. This is indicated in

Table 6.5, which displays the sectoral compositions of the current account identity of Xinjiang, Tibet and Guangdong. The identity states that

$$(T - G) + (S - I) \equiv (X - M) + R,$$

where

$(T - G)$ = provincial government revenue – provincial government expenditure,
$(S - I)$ = non-provincial government saving – non-provincial government investment,
$(X - M)$ = net exports (domestic and overseas), and
R = central fiscal transfers.

Guangdong, in contrast to Xinjiang and Tibet, is a net exporting province and, as Table 6.5 shows, makes a significant contribution to national saving, even though its provincial government receives net positive fiscal transfers from the centre.

Table 6.5   Current account identity

1998 % GDP	Local revenue– Local expenditure $(T - G)$	Net transfers (R)	Saving- investment $(S - I)$	Net exports $(X - M)$
Xinjiang	−7.2	7.0	−7.8	−22.1
Tibet	−45.5	45.8	94.3	3.1
Guangdong	−2.3	2.1	10.7	6.2

Source: Author's calculations using data in NBS (1999) and Table 11.2 of Wang (2004)

Xinjiang's high level of dependency on the state for economic growth is foremost a result of the continuing dominance of state units in the local economy's ownership structure. In 1998 66.1 per cent of gross industrial output was produced by state-owned industrial enterprises in Xinjiang, compared with 10.5 per cent in Guangdong and 28.8 per cent in Guangxi, the other national-minority province that has improved its relative economic position (NBS 1999, pp. 603, 629, 879). But this by itself is an inadequate explanation because Tibet's economy is just as dependent on state production as Xinjiang's; Tibet's state-owned units produced 65.5 per cent of the province's industrial output in 1998 (NBS 1999, p. 757). The reason for Xinjiang's extraordinary dependence on the state sector is found not on the production side but on the demand side. Instead of production by state-owned units, it is the investment demand by state-owned units that explains the dependence. This demand is explained by the large state investments in the oil and gas industries and cotton production, the state policy of promoting Han migration to Xinjiang, and large state infrastructure projects that aim to integrate the Han and non-Han areas within Xinjiang and to integrate Xinjiang with the rest of China.

Political reasons explain the extraordinary contribution of state investment to Xinjiang's GDP. China's national leadership see large-scale state investment as a multi-purpose tool for managing separatist leanings of the province's strong ethnic population. The investment serves, first, to temper and control separatist tendencies in Xinjiang – which have been given room to express themselves as globalisation has provided opportunities for Xinjiang's ethnic population to re-establish ties with fellow ethnics just across the border from China – and, second, to narrow the massive economic gap between the poor west and the prosperous south and eastern coastal regions, a gap that inflames these separatist tendencies. State investment stimulates the local economy and creates jobs for the Han immigrants from elsewhere in China, whose inbound move the government encourages to dilute the strong ethnic component of the province's population that is increasingly inclined to separatism.[6] In the former Premier Zhu Rongji's 2000 government report he outlined plans to develop western China, focusing on the development of highways, railways and telecommunications. This, he reported, was aimed at strengthening the unity of nationalities (*jiaqiang minzu tuanjie*), maintaining social stability (*weihu shehui wending*) and consolidating national borders (*gonggu bianfang*) (RMRB 2000, p. 2) – the political intent of integrating minorities for more cohesive nationhood was made quite clear. On his inspection tour of the region in the same year, Zhu called for the creation of a 'rock-hard' stronghold in Xinjiang to thwart separatists (Reuters 2000).

However, in attempting to control separatist movements in Xinjiang through massive state investment into the region, Beijing is contributing to the problem through an inappropriate choice of investments. Beijing has selected two industries to be the black (*hei*) (oil) and white (*bai*) (cotton) pillars (*zhizhu*) for developing Xinjiang through exploiting the province's natural resources (Dai 1999, p. 102). According to Dai, Xinjiang is one of China's five largest oil field bases and China's largest cotton producer. Since oil and gas production are capital-intensive activities, they are less effective for the central government's job-creation mission than labour-intensive cotton production. Cotton production is especially targeted to generate jobs for incoming Han immigrants because it uses labour-intensive technology. Cotton production in Xinjiang increased 25.5 times between 1978 and 1998, when about 40 per cent of Xinjiang's cotton was produced on farms managed by the Xinjiang New Construction Corporation (*Xinjiang xinjian gongsi*), better known by its former name, Xinjiang Production and Construction Corps

(XPCC) (*Xinjiang shengchan jianshe bingtuan*). XPCC is a centrally funded paramilitary-cum-production unit, directly responsible to the State Council, which has been used traditionally to promote Han migration into Xinjiang (Becquelin 2000, p. 78). Thus politics rather than economics are responsible for the impressive growth of cotton production in Xinjiang.

Yet cotton production in Xinjiang is riven with tensions. First, the politics and economics of cotton production are in ever deeper conflict with each other. While political interests propel cotton production for job creation for immigrant Han people in line with the central government's national integration imperative, economic interests seek to curb this production, which is increasingly unprofitable. Xinjiang's cotton is competitive against other domestic suppliers in price and quality, but is not competitive against overseas imports (Du 2000, p. 251) and so is being hit particularly hard by China's entry into the WTO. A study by China's Academy of Social Sciences forecasting developments in the cotton industry after China entered the WTO projected a nationwide 12.6 per cent fall in production, with a corresponding decline in employment of 22.6 per cent (Li et al. 2000, p. 75).

Second, Xinjiang is not suited to cotton production. The crucial factor here is water, which is likely to be the deciding factor in halting Xinjiang's cotton production. Cotton production requires vast amounts of water, which Xinjiang, in the nation's very dry north-west, does not have. Worsening water pollution, greater demand and unequal geographic distribution make water an increasingly scarce and precious resource nationwide, and therefore increasingly contentious. Nowhere is this felt more acutely than in Xinjiang, whose average precipitation is about one-ninth of the south-east's level (Economy 1999). Becquelin (2000, p. 84) detailed how competition between agricultural projects in Xinjiang has led to desertification, since irrigating a new project upstream cuts off the flow of water downstream. By the late 1990s, desertification afflicted 53 of Xinjiang's 87 districts. And worsening the environmental impact of cotton production is the excessive use of fertilisers and pesticides that government subsidies encourage. Fertilisers pollute ground water and rivers, causing other biological imbalances, and while pesticides have eradicated some pests they have caused other pests to flourish (Zheng and Qian 1998, pp. 219–20).

Third, there is inevitable tension within the Xinjiang population. The central government's cotton policy is highly unpopular among the Uighurs and other ethnic minorities in Xinjiang, who deeply resent the dilution of the minority population in Xinjiang, which this policy seeks to promote. Competition for water and other resources between the ethnic population and Han immigrants is worsening social relations between these people, as is competition for jobs in the state sector, as ethnic and Han workers contend for the remaining jobs in reformed SOEs and state bureaucracies.

Like the 'white' cotton pillar, the 'black' oil pillar of the central government's strategy for Xinjiang is also far from successful in promoting national integration. But the similarities go no further. The oil industry is profit making and exists largely because of market economics. Using capital-intensive technology, this industry generates few jobs, which are largely for skilled labour and so exclude the predominantly low-skilled ethnic minorities. Ethnic minorities generally resent Han immigrants taking an unfair proportion of the oil jobs, since the remuneration and status of these jobs are higher than for most other employment in the province.

But, without the government-promoted cotton and oil industries, what alternatives does Xinjiang have for surviving economically in a market economy? This province has neither the factor endowments, nor favourable location that would enable it to flourish in a market economy in the absence of state intervention. Light manufacturing using labour-intensive technology could soak up the abundant supply of low-skilled labour in Xinjiang. However Xinjiang is far from the coast and Guangdong, through which most of China's light industrial goods are exported, and the necessary transport infrastructure for linking Xinjiang to the south and the coast is poor. Xinjiang is not attractive to overseas Chinese investments, partly because it lacks the family connections and familiar language that help to lower business transaction costs and make Fujian and Guangdong the favourite destinations of many overseas Chinese investors. Rising production costs in the south and along the coast are driving many factories inland but, largely because of the poor transport infrastructure and distance, the north-west continues to be unattractive to most producers of export oriented light manufacturing goods.

The one type of enterprise that has been attracted to Xinjiang is the 'dirty industries'. Local officials, eager for outside investments and with very few options, are allowing these enterprises to relocate to Xinjiang from the prosperous eastern regions with little regulation. In a survey of 936 such enterprises in August 2000, 404 (43 per cent) failed to meet national environmental standards (AFP 2000). The benefits that these enterprises bring to Xinjiang through employment opportunities are negated by their detrimental effects, including ill health of the population and the adverse effect of water pollution on agriculture. Since indigenous agriculture will suffer some of this adverse effect, relocation of 'dirty industries' to Xinjiang is also likely to inflame ethnic tensions if allowed to continue without stringent environmental safeguards. Nevertheless, imposing these safeguards would make Xinjiang no longer attractive for enterprises attempting to evade environmental safeguards and would leave Xinjiang with even fewer employment opportunities.

CONCLUSION

Globalisation in China has two faces. This chapter argues that globalisation divides as well as unites China. China's engagement with the global economy has increased the size of its economy, measured according to purchasing power, to make it the world's largest after the United States. This has elevated China's position in the world and has ignited a new sense of pride among its citizens and increased their sense of community. Political liberalisation that has followed economic liberalisation and the development of the Internet have encouraged the growth of civil society in China. A vibrant civil society with assistance from the restraining hand of the market on local governments in China will make governments more accountable and in the long run promote political stability and unity.

Unfortunately globalisation is Janus-faced. Globalisation has promoted strong economic growth that has made a huge dent on poverty rates in China. However, the reduction in poverty has been accompanied by significant widening of income and social inequalities. These inequalities encourage ethnic separatist movements and official efforts to moderate regional income inequalities and control ethnic separatist movements have proven counterproductive and may threaten national unity.

NOTES

1. There are doubts over the reliability of China's official statistics. Annual growth rates may have been overestimated by up to 2 per cent, but, even if growth rates are lower by 2 per cent, China's economic growth in the reform period remains very impressive and ranks comfortably among the world's ten fastest growing economies (Lardy 2002, p. 12; World Bank 1997a, p. 3).
2. However, Sachs and Woo (2000) argued that China's strategy is the result of conditions that are unique to China and therefore cannot always be adopted by other transition countries.
3. According to Montinola et al. (1995, p. 55), 'market-preserving federalism' has the following five characteristics: there is an explicit division of powers between a hierarchy of governments, local governments have primary authority over local economies, the national government can ensure free trade in goods and factors across local government boundaries, all governments have hard budget constraints, and the division of authority between different levels of governments cannot be altered arbitrarily.
4. Calculated from data in NBS (1999). This compared with 93.7 per cent in Tibet, 44.1 per cent in Guangdong and 54.1 per cent nationally.
5. Some figures for Tibet are incorrect. If Tibet's value of net exports for 1998 is correct, then according to data of fiscal transfers from the Centre to Tibet the excess of non-provincial government's saving over its investment must be over 90 per cent of provincial GDP (Table 6.5), which cannot possibly be correct. Most investment in Tibet is undertaken by the state. Thus the error most probably lies in undervaluing household consumption and overvaluing non-provincial government saving. Local government expenditures include

subsidies granted to households and are therefore not equivalent to government consumption and investment. This means that the statement that Xinjiang's GDP is more dependent on government consumption and investment than Tibet's is not invalidated by the error in the data. Thanks to Wang Shaoguang for pointing out the inconsistency in Tibet's fiscal data and data on net exports.

6.   The Xinjiang Uighurs Autonomous Region has a population of about 17.2 million, of whom 47.7 per cent (8 million) are Uighurs, 38.4 per cent (6.6 million) are Han, 7.4 per cent (1.3 million) are Kazaks, and 4.5 per cent (0.8 million) are Hui (XW 1998, p. 9).

REFERENCES

AFP (2000), 'Xinjiang draws China's heavy polluting firms', *The Straits Times Interactive*, 26 September, available at wysiwyg://12/http://straitstimes.asia1.com.sg/asia/ea2_0926.html, accessed 27 September.

Baumol, William (1990), 'Entrepreneurship: productive, unproductive, and destructive', *Journal of Political Economy*, **98** (5), 893–921.

Becquelin, Nicolas (2000), 'Xinjiang in the nineties', *The China Journal*, 44, 65–92.

Brooks, Ray and Ran Tao (2003), 'China's labour market performance and challenges', IMF Working Paper, WP/03/210.

China Security Review Commission (CSRC) (2002), *Report to the Congress of the US: The National Security Implications of the Economic Relationship between the United States and China*, July.

Dai, Xiaoming (1999), *Zhongyang yu difang guangxi* (Centre–Local Relations), Beijing: Zhongguo minzhu fazhi chubanshe.

Du Lingchang (2000), 'Xinjiang nongxuye fazhan zhanlue' (Strategy for developing Xinjiang's agriculture and husbandry), in Ye Lianxin and Tu Minzhu (eds), *Zhongguo nongcun fazhan yanji baogao 1* (China's Rural Development Report 1), Beijing: Shehui kexue wenjian chubanshe.

Economy, Elizabeth (1999), 'The case study of China: reforms and resources: the implications for state capacity in the PRC', Occasional Paper, Project on Environment Scarcities, State Capacity, and Civil Violence, Cambridge: American Academy of Arts and Sciences and the University of Toronto.

Hillman, Ben (2004), 'Chinese nationalism and the Belgrade embassy bombing', in Leong H. Liew and Shaoguang Wang (eds), *Nationalism, Democracy and National Integration in China*, London: RoutledgeCurzon.

Keliher, Macabe (2004), 'Replacing US in Asian export market', *Asia Times*, 11 February, available at www.atimes.com/atimes/China/FB11Ado.1.html, accessed 17 May.

Lardy, Nicholas (2002), *Integrating China into the Global Economy*, Washington, DC: Brookings Institution Press.

Li Shantong, Zhai Fan and Xu Lin (2000), 'Jiaru shijie maoyi zuzhi dui Zhongguo de yingxiang' (Impact on China from entry into the WTO) in Yu Yongding, Zheng Bingwen and Song Hong (eds), *Zhongguo 'rushi' yanjiu baogao: jinru WTO de Zhongguo chanye* (Research Report on China's Entry into the WTO: Impact on China's Industries), Beijing: Shehui kexue wenjian chubanshe, pp. 35–84.

Liew, Leong H. and Doug Smith (2004), 'The nexus between nationalism, democracy and national integration', in Leong H. Liew and Shaoguang Wang (eds), *Nationalism, Democracy and National Integration in China*, London: RoutledgeCurzon.

Lu Xueyi (ed.) (2002), *Dangdai Zhongguo Shehui Jiecang Yanjiu Baogao* (Research Report on Social Stratification in Contemporary China), Beijing: Shehui kexue wenxian chubanshe.

Montinola, Gabriella, Yingyi Qian and Barry Weingast (1995), 'Federalism, Chinese style: the political basis for economic success in China', *World Politics*, 48, 50–81.

Murphy, Kevin, Andrei Shleifer and Robert W. Vishny (1992), 'The transition to a market economy: pitfalls of partial reform', *Quarterly Journal of Economics*, **107** (3): 889–920.

NBS (National Bureau of Statistics) (1999), *Comprehensive Statistical Data and Materials of 50 Years of New China*, Beijing: China Statistics Press.

NBSC (National Bureau of Statistics of China) (2003), *China Statistical Yearbook 2003*, Beijing: China Statistics Press.

Olson, Mancur (1993), 'Dictatorship, democracy, and development', *American Political Science Review*, **87** (3), 567–76.

Oxan (Oxford Analytica) (2000), 'China at the gates of the World Trade Organization', *Transition*, **11** (2), 13–14.

Pei, Minxin (1998), 'Chinese civic associations: an empirical analysis', *Modern China,* **24** (3), 285–318.

Reuters (2000), 'China denies ethnic tension exists in Xinjiang', MSNBC, available at http://famulus.msnbc.com/FamulusIntl/reuters09-26-020408asp?reg=PACRIM.

RMRB (*Renmin ribao*) (2000), 'Zhu Rongji Zongli zai jiujie quanguo renda sanci huiyi shang de zhengfu gongzuo baogao (zhai deng)' (Excerpts of Premier Zhu Rongji's Government Work Report at the Third Plenum, Ninth National People's Congress), 6 March, pp. 2–3.

Sachs, Jeffrey and Wing Thye Woo (2000), 'Understanding China's economic performance', *Journal of Policy Reform*, **4** (1).

Solinger, Dorothy (1999), *Contesting Citizenship in Urban China*, Berkeley: University of California Press.

Stiglitz, Joseph E. (2002), *Globalization and its Discontents*, New York: W.W. Norton and Co.

UNDP (2002), *Human Development Report*, available at http://hdr.undp.org/reports/global/2002/ en.

Wang, Shaoguang (2004), 'The price of national unity: the politics of fiscal transfer in China', in Leong H. Liew and Shaoguang Wang (eds), *Nationalism, Democracy and National Integration in China*, London: RoutledgeCurzon.

Wang, Shaoguang, Angang Hu and Yuanzhu Ding (2002), 'Laize shehui bumanzhe de yanzhong jinggao: Zhongguo shehui bu wending de zhuangkuang diaocha yu fenxi' (Warning from society's disaffected: investigation and analysis into China's social instability), *Zhanlue yu guanli* (Strategy and Management), (3), 26–33.

Wei, Shang-Jin (2002), 'Is globalization good for the poor in China?', *Finance & Development*, **39** (3), available at www.imf.org/external/pubs/ft/fandd/2002/09/wei.html.

Wong, Linda (2004), 'Market reforms, globalization and social justice in China', *Journal of Contemporary China*, **13** (38), 151–72.

World Bank (1997a), *China 2020*, Washington, DC: The World Bank.

World Bank (1997b), *China 2020: Sharing Rising Incomes*, Washington, DC: The World Bank.

WTO (2004), *International Trade Statistics 2003*, Geneva: WTO.

XW (Xinjiang Weiwuer zizhiqu difangzhi bianzuan weiyuanhui) (1998), *Xinjiang nianjian* (Xinjiang's yearbook), Ulumuqi: Xinjiang renmin chubanshe.

Yan, Zhimin (ed.) (2002), *Zhongguo xian jieduan jieji jieceng yanjiu* (Research on Class and Social Stratification in Contemporary China), Beijing: Zhongguo zhongyang dangxiao chubanshe.

Yang, Fangjiang and Zumin Zhang, (2001), *Zhejiang nongcun jumin shenghuo jingji fenxi* (Economic Analysis of the Livelihood of Zhejiang's Village Residents), Hangzhou: Zhejiang renmin chubanshe.

Yang, Guobin (2003), 'The internet and civil society in China: a preliminary assessment', *Journal of Contemporary China*, **12** (36), 453–76.

Zhai, Fan and Shantong Li (2002), 'The impact of WTO accession on income disparity in China', in Mary-Françoise Renard (ed.), *China and its Regions: Economic Growth and Reform in Chinese Provinces*, Cheltenham, UK and Northampton, MA, USA: Edward Elgar.

Zheng, Yisheng and Yihong Qian (1998), *Shendu youhuan: dangdai Zhongguo de kechixu fazhan wenti* (Grave Concerns: Problems of Sustainable Development for China), Beijing: Jinri Zhongguo chubanshe.

7. The 'new economy' and India's integration into the global market: the case of the silk industry

Moazzem Hossain and Clarisse Didelon

INTRODUCTION

The dynamism of global telecommunications markets is widely attributed to rapid technological development and an increasingly liberal policy environment. Over the past decade, a large number of Asian economies, including India, have also embarked on reform paths and witnessed significant expansion of their telecommunications networks and tremendous improvements in quality of services. To achieve these, choices have been made regarding the privatisation of state-owned telecommunications operators, the introduction of competition, the opening of markets to foreign investment and the establishment of pro-competitive regulations. While there is growing consensus that each of these elements is desirable, there are few countries that have immediately gone all the way on all fronts.

The Indian economy embraced an economic reform agenda in 1990 when the nation's current account deficit hit an all-time low, with a foreign exchange reserve worth only three months' imports. However, Rodrik and Subramanian (2004) argue that the reform process began even a decade earlier, in 1980, when the late Prime Minister Rajib Gandhi introduced a domestic business reform.

This resulted in Indian authorities coming to a realisation that development of an effective and efficient telecommunications sector is a key to the growing international competitiveness of the country. The government launched several reform measures in telecommunications in the past decade. Since 1991 the telecommunications sector has expanded exponentially as a result of these measures. In 1972 the country had only a million telephone lines; by 1996 it had more than 14 million, by 2000 more than 25 million and by June 2002 more than 41 million (NASSCOM 2002; Kathuria 2000; World Bank 1995). In this chapter an attempt is made, firstly, to investigate the emergence of the 'new economy' out of the expanded and modern telecommunications network over the last ten years. Secondly, the chapter attempts to demonstrate from a field survey how the silk industry in India progressed by embracing the services of the new economy sector.

EMERGENCE OF THE 'NEW ECONOMY'

> Our aim is to make India an IT super powerhouse. Our objective is to create entrepreneurs and employment and ultimately make a sustainable contribution to the growth of the Indian economy. (NASSCOM 2002)

These are the words of the President of the New Delhi based National Association of Software and Service Companies (NASSCOM). It appears that there is some truth in this claim. It is well known in the macroeconomics literature that the Indian economy has been experiencing a current account (CA) deficit for the last three decades. However, the economy has turned the corner, and now there is a sign of having a sustainable surplus in the future, including an impressive growth rate in GDP (6 per cent and over per annum). This is mainly driven by the establishment of a business-service sector that helped the economy to enter into more and more service exports. Telecommunications infrastructure building and the provision of IT services to the outside world made an overwhelming contribution in establishing the business-service (so-called new economy) sector in India.

In particular, the 'new economy' has emerged out of two major forces: growth in technology and innovation of knowledge-based goods and services, and globalisation of economic activity. The main drivers of these forces are information and communications technology (ICT), and foreign direct investment (FDI) in IT/software services and new IT-enabled (ITE) services. In other words, the new economy mainly comprises two elements of the information technology sector: IT/software services and IT-enabled services (see more detail in Hossain 2003). Between 2001 and 2002, these two elements contributed to the exports of about US$7.68 billion, with a rapid growth in IT/software (18 per cent) and in ITE services (68 per cent). These two elements so far have created more than 400 000 jobs for the Indian economy, with an accumulated wealth of US$20 billion. It is now widely accepted that the new economy is mainly driven by the domestically grown enterprises. In IT services, the Indian companies hold a 78 per cent share and the multinational companies (MNCs) hold the rest. Among the ITE service companies, a 55 per cent share is held by the domestic firms and the rest by the MNCs. In terms of total market share in values, the Indian companies hold three-quarters, as against one-quarter held by the MNCs. The major export destinations in the new economy sector are the Americas (63 per cent) and Europe (26 per cent) (Hossain 2003).

The New Economy: Export Opportunities

Export opportunities have been getting larger and larger with the new economy products over time. Table 7.1 presents the export growth rate between 1996 and 2001 in IT/software services. It appears that the total growth of exports with the IT services increased sixfold and the domestic market had a threefold expansion. The ratio of IT/software exports to total exports has been increasing continuously. This has increased from less than 14 per cent of the total exports in 2001 to 16.5 per cent in 2002 (Table 7.2). It will soon become a contributor to total exports by one-fifth. Export opportunities within the new economy sector have also been changing over time. The ITE services export share of total IT services exports has been increasing constantly since 1999. Table 7.3 shows that the ITE services export share was 14 per cent in 1999 and this reached 19 per cent in 2002. It has been projected that the ITES contribution will soon become one-quarter of the total exports of IT services. By any measure, these demonstrate a strong achievement by the sector within a short period of time.

Table 7.1 New economy: export opportunities (US$ million)

Year	Software/IT exports	Domestic software market
1996–97	1100	730
1998–99	2600	1560
2000–01	6217	2160
2002–03*	9500	2700

Note: * = projections

Source: NASSCOM (2002)

Table 7.2 Software exports to total exports (%)

Items	2001	2002	2003*
Software exports	13.80	16.50	18.60
Other exports	86.20	83.50	81.40

Note: * = projections

Source: NASSCOM (2002)

Table 7.3 ITES exports to IT exports (%)

Year	ITE services	IT services
1999–00	14.0	86.0
2000–01	14.5	85.5
2001–02	19.0	81.0
2002–03*	24.0	76.0

Note: * = projections

Source: NASSCOM (2002)

How was this possible? Table 7.4 demonstrates that the Indian IT industry has been occupying a major share of the global ITES and Business Process Outsourcing (BPO) segments of the industry. Currently India occupies an increasing global share of all key segments of the industry. For example, shares in 2002 for contact/call centres was 4.5 per cent, for back office operations 30 per cent, transcription and translation services 7.5 per cent, content development services 20 per cent and other services 17 per cent and this share has been increasing sustainably.

Table 7.4 Key segments of global ITES/BPO

Item	Contact/ call centre operations (1)	Back office (2)	Transcription and translation (3)	Content development services (4)	Other (5)
Global market size ($million, 2002)	8600	2000	425	2200	250
Indian market size ($million, 2002)	380 (4.5)	600 (30)	32 (7.5)	440 (20)	43 (17)
Minimum invest.	$3000–$10000	$1–2.5m.	$0.5m.	$10m.	$10–15m.

Source: NASSCOM (2002)

There are many factors behind the success of the Indian IT enterprises. Most importantly, English language skills give India a major competitive and technological edge over other nations (Einhorn 2003). Secondly, more and more MNCs are shifting their services to countries such as India, which can offer professional workers at low cost (Hussain 2003), and thirdly, India gains from job shift from more developed nations (Raghunathan 2003). For example, US banks and financial service companies are leading the way in outsourcing to India. It is widely believed that the US companies have saved more than $6 billion in the past four years by outsourcing procedures.

A list of major innovative activities by several MNCs currently operating in India is provided below:

- GE Medical in Bangalore has developed a high-resolution imaging machine for use in cardiac surgery and a portable ultrasound scanner as part of the company's global supply chain.
- Whirlpool's laboratory in Pune in the western state of Maharashtra is developing air conditioners and refrigerators.
- Intel's Bangalore facility has produced more than 50 new designs for semiconductors, telecommunications switching equipment and routers, and has also set up a new laboratory to help develop its next generation of microprocessors.
- Oracle's Bangalore facility develops customised software solutions and programmes for American companies.
- Hewlett Packard has developed prototypes of a small scanner that can scrutinise handwritten documents and letters and a simple computer for unskilled people.
- Aston Martin has contracted the design and development of the prototype of a new sports car to an Indian firm.
- Daimler Chrysler has a research centre that is working on applications in avionics and simulation and software development.

(Raghunathan 2003, p. 24)

The major factor for the job shift made by the above MNCs was cost. It is widely believed that wages of Indian engineers and PhD holders are ten times cheaper than wages of similarly skilled persons based in more developed countries such as the USA for the same services. The low wages/salaries have made the Indian services more attractive to the MNCs.

The Challenges Ahead

The emergence of the new economy as a separate identity in the Indian economy is no doubt a huge boost for generating additional export revenues to achieve a healthy current account balance. The sector, however, is not immune from challenges that may arise in the future. In the present globalisation era, there is always a threat of competition from other developing countries such as China and South East Asian nations. In this section, an investigation on future challenges is attempted. Before identifying the challenges and the weaknesses of the Indian economy against its competitors, let us summarise the strengths gained by India so far:

- Telecommunications technology and expanding teledensity are found to be the major driver of the emerging new economy sector. Indian Union and state capital cities where the IT and ITE services industry is based have teledensity of 14 per 100 against the all-India density of only 3 per 100. The subscribers for the fixed line network have increased eightfold since 1991, while cellular phones have increased 30-fold since 1997.
- The IT and ITE service industry has contributed over $25 billion to the country's foreign exchange reserve of $70 billion. The industry is poised to achieve $50 billion exports in 2008.
- All this has created a healthy current account balance for India in recent times. After almost a quarter of a century of current account deficit, the nation achieved a surplus in 2001. Presently, the economy has foreign currency reserves to the value of a year's imports as against a reserve of one month's imports in 1991.

The major challenges for the industry have been debated by two world experts on outsourcing and BPO issues, Corbett (2003) and Roxenburgh (2003). According to these authors, the following are the most important challenges that need to be addressed to keep the Indian IT and ITE services industry competitive:

- The political spectre of EU/US job losses: in the West, the loss of jobs due to outsourcing has been the major issue of disappointment for the trade union movement and ordinary workers.
- India's image problem worldwide in terms of social, religious and economic inequality and intolerance: the age-old system of caste and the constant rivalry between Hindus and Muslims have created an environment which cannot be considered business friendly.
- India's constant arms conflict, including prospects of a nuclear conflict with Pakistan, is not conducive to procuring a healthy political environment.
- The Indian government has been phasing out the tax incentives currently in place to the industry.
- The WTO are imposing a 'level playing field' strategy for member nations. In other words, they have a policy of having a completely open business and trade arrangement.
- Competitors from Ireland, China and South East Asia (the Philippines, Vietnam and Cambodia) are probable threats to India in the future.

(NASSCOM 2002)

With the achievements in information and telecommunications technology, and with the emerging new economy sector, the manufacturing and textile industry in India seems to be a relevant case where further improvement can be achieved through using these services. The rest of the chapter presents a case study of the silk industry in India and demonstrates how successful this industry is in embracing the new economy sector in order to make further progress in both domestic and international markets. This objective of the study has been achieved by conducting a survey of the Indian silk industry in 2002. Why silk? As in the case of the new economy sector, Bangalore is the home of the silk business in India. This survey is expected to demonstrate the extent of integration the silk industry has been enjoying with the domestic and international markets owing to the ready access to the new economy sector based in Bangalore.

THE SILK INDUSTRY OF INDIA

Silk Production and the Domestic Market Structure

Silk production is seen as one of the most ancient industries of India. Historical evidence suggests that silk weaving was introduced quite early in India, around 140 BC. However, its introduction was not as a result of sericulture, which was introduced far later, possibly at the beginning of the second millennium.

India produces four types of commercial silk. Three of them are called 'wild' silk, because the silkworms are not domesticated (Eri, Tasar and Muga silks), but the rest of the production (as in other parts of the world) is mainly represented by mulberry silk, because the silkworms are fed with mulberry leaves. South India, and particularly South Karnataka, is the main region where the mulberry silk production takes place, with more than 60 per cent of India's total production. Other silk producing states are Andhra Pradesh (22 per cent) and Tamil Nadu (5 per cent).

Sericulture is a domestic activity that takes place at household level in the villages, and six million people depend on it for a major part of their income (Guétat-Bernard 1994). Sericulture includes moriculture, that is, the cultivation of mulberry trees. Ninety-five per cent of cocoon producers are small farmers owning less than 4 hectares of land out of which 0.25 to 0.5 hectares are dedicated to mulberry cultivation.

When the cocoon is ready, the producer must sell it within ten days, before the pupa breaks the silk yarn. There are 43 regulated cocoon markets in Karnataka,[1] located in urban or semi-urban areas with a high concentration of reelers. Most Indian filatures are equipped with obsolete machines (like *charka*). The modern automatic reeling machines generally used in Japan and Korea are not suitable in Indian operations owing to the types of cocoon (the crossbreed multivoltine) available in mulberry sericulture.

To regulate the marketing of yarn, the Karnataka Government established a silk exchange in 1979 in Bangalore. But, more frequently, raw silk is bought by middlemen in the villages or small towns where it was reeled, and they sell it to weavers and master-weavers in Bangalore or other silk centres. By and large, power loom units are decentralised and operated from sheds of manufacturer-wholesalers or exporters in order to avoid the legal restriction of the Factories Act. Independent weaving is rare, largely because of a fragile financial base combined with lack of market information. It is precisely these factors that make the master-weaver traders strong, resulting in poor returns to the individual weavers as day workers or wage earners.

The final stage of the production of silk as a finished product occurs mainly in Bangalore, the capital of Karnataka. Firms are mainly located in the city in accordance with their range of activities. Twisting, weaving, dyeing and printing are done in the peripheries of south and west Bangalore, as well as near the premises of the wholesalers who employ day workers in the final production. Manufacturer-wholesalers are mainly located in two streets: the Avenue Road and the Jumma Masjid Road in the old part of the city. Exporters, who often control all the stages of production beginning with twisting, are located in residential areas that are clean and less crowded. In many weaving centres, exporters take over the role of merchant-distributors, and in some cases they also operate in the domestic market. Retailers are more often settled in two places: Mahatma Gandhi Road, a luxury and cosmopolitan suburb, and at the crossing of Chickpet Road and BVK Iyengar Road.

To assist producers at all stages and to assist exporters, a few supporting agencies have been established by the Union Government. The Central Silk Board (CSB) was established in 1949 and its head office is located in Bangalore. It has three major activities: research and development, seed maintenance and development of sericulture, and development of the silk industry. The Indian Silk Export Promotion Council, set up in 1983, has roles in relation to export promotion and acts as the registered authority on Indian silk exporters.

Global Market and Opportunities

Despite its aura of luxury and wealth, the production of silk is a highly labour-intensive, low capital-intensity industry ideally suited to the conditions of a labour-abundant economy (Sinha 1990). Not surprisingly, production has expanded rapidly in recent years in China and India and has declined in Japan and Korea (see Figure 7.1).

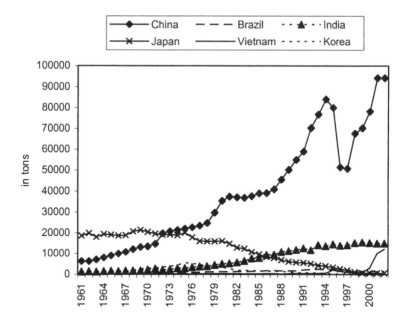

Figure 7.1   Production of raw silk and waste, 1961–2002

With 70 per cent of the world production, China is today the top silk-producing country. Other Asian countries produce almost exclusively for their own needs. It is interesting to note that, unlike many other labour-intensively produced luxury goods, a large proportion of silk is consumed by the country of origin. In the middle of the 1980s, Vietnam, a country that has a long tradition in sericulture and silk production, began a new programme of development of sericulture. Since this period its production has grown strongly.

India produces 15 000 tons of silk a year,[2] but the domestic market absorbs 20 000 tons, leading the importing nations of raw silk. In fact, 85 per cent of the Indian production is used for the domestic market. The huge domestic consumption is due to the demand for silk in weaving saris (the common female dress in India) and other traditional cloths. There are a number of silk centres in India that are famous for their particular style of weaving saris, or for their embroidery styles like Varanasi, Mysore and Kancheepuram. Silk exports from India are in the form of either fabrics or ready-made goods, as exports of raw silk and spun silk are not allowed. Largely the private traders handle the export of silk goods from India. Despite efforts undertaken by the government to improve quality, the Indian production does not generally reach the international quality standards because the stages of production are not modernised enough. So silk exporters from India are often expected to meet quality requests that do not apply to the Indian market. Indian production makes up only 5 per cent of the global silk trade.

The international silk trade is conducted in a number of forms including cocoons, reeled raw silk, silk yarn, fabrics, ready-made goods and waste silk. At the end of the 1980s a structural change took place in the silk market: overproduction in China led to the appearance of cheap finished products in Western markets that caused a certain image problem. Then in 1996 Chinese production fell by almost 40 per cent.

Only 25 per cent of the international production is for the global market. Silk is only 0.2 per cent of the volume of the world textile market, but its commercial value is far more important. After China, only Brazil is in a position to make a large part of its production available for the world market, mainly at the top end of the market. As Indian silk goods occupy the lowest price ranges in the world market, competition with sophisticated manufacturers in Western Europe, Japan and Korea is extremely limited. However it is expected that the quality and quantity of Indian silk will bring it into direct competition with China on the world market.

The main world importers of silk are the industrialised nations. These nations import raw products of silk, transform them into high value-added goods and export them at high prices. Major destinations of Indian silk exports are subdivided by the Central Silk Board into traditional and non-traditional markets on the basis of the importance of traditional silk products (such as saris) to their destinations from India. Traditional markets are mainly the UAE, Singapore and Hong Kong. The importance of the non-traditional markets (industrial nations) has continued to grow in relative terms.

A number of incentives and facilities are provided to Indian exporters by the government. These include import replenishment licences, custom duty exemptions and an advance-licensing scheme, whereby 140 per cent of the yarn requirement for export orders can be imported for export production. Most imports of yarn into India are under the replenishment and advance-licensing schemes. Duty-free machinery importation is allowed for 100 per cent export oriented units. For the purpose of obtaining those facilities, exporters must be registered with the Indian Silk Export Promotion Council and goods need to undergo reshipment inspection at the certification centres of the CSB. At present there are reported to be about 1500 exporters registered, amongst whom around 100 leading exporters have an annual export exceeding Rs 50 lakhs (more than $100 000).

E-COMMERCE (THE NEW ECONOMY) AND SILK FIRMS IN BANGALORE: A SURVEY

The Survey

India is in an unusual setting in which to analyse the communications revolution. While the new communications technologies of cable television, the Internet, satellites and telecommunications are impacting on Indian society in dramatic ways, the subcontinent is still mainly a developing region in which the majority of citizens depend on the bullock cart for transportation and selling labour for making a daily living (Singhal and Rogers 2000).

Under the present revolution in information and telecommunications technology and with the emerging new economy, the silk industry in India seems to be a relevant case where further improvement has been anticipated. This is an age-old industry (more than 200 years in Karnataka) and has been organised in a traditional way. As shown earlier, the first stage of production of silk relies on poor conditions at workplaces, particularly in the rural areas. The dramatic improvement in telecommunications in India is likely to play a major role in transforming the silk industry from backwardness. Activities such as software design, email and mobile phone services are expected to help the industry expand in both domestic and international markets. The selection of the silk industry here for examining the impact of the new economy sector is useful, particularly in the view of the industry's ever-increasing international links. The major objective of the survey, therefore, is to examine how the improved telecommunications network has been supporting the silk industry to achieve its commercial goals and the growth of business.

The survey was conducted during September–November 2002 on 76 silk firms located in Bangalore city. The selection of firms was random, and we mostly used the *Getit Yellow Pages* of Bangalore and the Internet for the interviews. The number of firms selected according to their respective production activity was established from their listing under 'Activities'.[3]

Information about the size, age and activities[4] of the firms was first collected. But the main part of the survey was the reconstitution of the social network. Following a hierarchical ascendant classification on the descriptive data the firms were divided into six groups:

- *Retailers*: These are small firms with fewer than ten employees. Their customers are exclusively private individuals from Bangalore, and the suppliers are mainly from Bangalore and South India.

- *Small wholesalers*: These have fewer than ten employees, with no production activity. Their suppliers are mainly from Bangalore, but their customers are from all over Southern and Northern India.
- *Twisters and medium manufacturer-wholesalers*: These firms have between 10 and 50 employees. They perform some activities in the first stages of production: twisting and weaving. Some of them have suppliers from foreign nations, but their customers are mainly from Bangalore.
- *Wholesaler-exporters*: These are mainly wholesalers, but also have a retail outlet. They are big firms (most of them have more than 50 employees), mainly wholesalers, with a few having export activity.
- *Exporter-wholesalers*: These are the firms having no production activity. All of them have customers in foreign countries but they also have some customers within South India and from other parts of India.
- *Exporters*: These are big firms (employing more than 50 people) and their customers are exclusively from foreign nations. All of them also perform twisting and weaving activities.

Types of Communication in Use

The survey in Bangalore allows us firstly to observe how various means of communication are used in relation to one another (according to the frequency of use).

Table 7.5 summarises the correlation between the frequency of usage of one means of communication and the frequency of usage of each other means of communication. For example, a '+' sign between fax and email means that, when fax is used very often,[5] email is used very often too. The '–' sign between meeting and email means that, when meeting is used often or very often, email is never used or used occasionally.

Table 7.5 Relationship between the frequencies of usage of means of communication

	Post	Phone	Mobile	Fax	Email
Meeting	+	+	+	?	–
Post	X	+	+	+	+
Phone	+	X	+	NS	NS
Mobile	+	+	X	+	?
Fax	+	NS	+	X	+

Notes:
? = it is hard to determine whether the relationship is positive or negative
X = no test was conducted
NS = non-significant relationship

Moreover, there is a correlation between the number of means of communication owned by firms and the frequency of their usage.[6] When a firm has all the means of communication, it uses them often or very often. When a firm has only two or three means of communication, it uses them occasionally or sometimes.

However, it was asked in what context the means of communication are used. The choice of a particular type of telecommunication service and the frequency of its use can be different according to the type of firm, the interlocutor and its localisation. Table 7.6 gives a synthetic view of the test results.[7] They show in which contexts each means of communication has been more frequently used.

Table 7.6 Context of usage of means of communication by the firms

	% of relationships in which the means is frequently used	Size of the firm	Activity of the firm	Kind of interlocutor	Location of interlocutor
Face-to-face meeting	57.5	Small/ medium	Retail/ wholesale	X	Local
Post	36.8	X	Wholesale/ export	Customer	National/ international
Phone	67.2	Medium/ big	Wholesale	X	Regional
Mobile phone	26.7	Big	Wholesale	X	Local
Fax	23.3	Big	Export	Customer	International
E-mail	20.7	Big	Export	Customer	International

Note: X = non-significant above 5%

It is observed that face-to-face meetings rate second as a means of communication after phone conversations. This demonstrates that firms really need to meet their interlocutor before engaging in a business activity. They need to meet to evaluate the risks of the transaction; the risk of not been paid by a customer or the risk of receiving materials of a quality that does not match their requirements. They also use face-to-face meetings to build the climate of confidence necessary in commencing trade.

In some cases of relationships, when the customer or the suppliers are located in foreign countries, fax and email are the more often used means of communication.

It has been observed that the use of means of telecommunication mainly depends on the size of the firms and the distance of the interlocutors. The type of interlocutor has no significant relation with the choice of a particular means of communication.

Use of the Internet

The Internet directly serves the area of electronic commerce. There are a number of definitions of electronic commerce (Mann 2000). For example, if all the financial and commercial transactions are taking place electronically, this may be regarded as electronic commerce. Other electronic commerce takes place over the Internet, usually through a buyer visiting the seller's website and making a transaction on the Internet. The latter is the more recent one and seems to be promising to some authors (Bloor 2000), mainly in regard to small business in developing countries. But the evidence of real benefits is still anecdotal, and the obstacles to affordable access remain formidable (Goldstein and O'Connor 2000).

There are two major kinds of electronic commerce: B to B, meaning business to business and involving only firms; and B to C, business to consumers, involving firms and private individuals. B-to-B transactions account for as much as 80–90 per cent of global electronic commerce, and the greatest volume of e-commerce is located in the United States and in Europe.

Participation in e-commerce by the silk-producers and merchants is currently limited owing to a variety of factors such as lack of infrastructure and awareness, high cost of Internet connectivity and inadequate skilled human resources. Effective use of electronic commerce requires profound transformation in the organisation of the firm, a change that not all Indian silk-producers are ready to undertake (Moodley 2002). In Bangalore 24 out of 74 firms surveyed had websites in 2002. Most of them were wholesalers or exporters. However, only four were in websites to make electronic transactions, and they were in the retailer category.

According to the sellers, the Internet marketplace is very attractive because, no matter how small the firm, they can sell their products all over the world. They do not need to make capital investment to open up a shop or a showroom (Raipuria 2000). This seems to be the reason that businesses in Bangalore set up websites. For the buyers, electronic commerce is convenient too, because the buyers can explore new products all over the world and compare prices (Chkhichaku 1999). But are the websites in silk businesses really used for trade? It has been suggested in the survey that the Web was not very useful.

There is an interesting difference between what people who create a website expect from it and the way the websites are actually used by those who consult them. Websites are used by firms in order to check what is available on their competitor's site. Moreover, it is very difficult to sell silk on the Web because textiles and silks are products people need to touch. They must feel the texture before buying (Ternisien et al. 2001).

One of the biggest problems for Internet transactions is the security of money transfer. It is difficult for firms from developing countries to create the climate of confidence that is necessary for electronic commerce (Goldstein and O'Connor 2001). For Indian businesses it is even more difficult. The Internet is not often used in India for commercial transactions because credit card transfers are not perceived as secured and because credit cards are not used universally: only five million people had credit cards in India in 2002, and the average spent per card per month was only Rs 1000.

CONCLUSIONS

The Indian economy has achieved phenomenal progress in the area of telecommunications services over the last ten years. Modernisation of telecommunications technology and the establishment of telecommunications infrastructure have paved the way for developing the new economy sector comprising mainly IT and ITE services. The new economy has been successful in competing in the global market and has been the major driver in creating and attracting new export markets. At present export earnings out of this sector have hit US$10 billion, and this amount will represent one-fifth of the total within a very short period of time. It is expected that in 2008 exports from the new economy sector will reach US$50 billion. It appears that, in recent years, the new economy has been a major factor in turning the age-old current account deficit into surplus.

Has this been equally reflected in the domestic market? The case study on India's silk industry presented in the second part of this chapter provides a disappointing result. It demonstrates that this industry is yet to embrace fully the services provided by the new economy sector. The results show that only a few large firms use the services of modern telecommunications networks such as mobile phones, fax and the Internet. It can safely be said that, while India was successful in internationalising the new economy within a short period of time, it has failed to provide the same services to all types of domestic export-led firms. It appears that the new economy's benefit has yet to trickle down to the local level. Some analysts (Khan 2004; Waslekar 2004) strongly suggest that the 2004 general election was won by the opposition owing not only to their popularity but also to the predecessor's failure to bring fruits of the new-economy-led growth to the doorsteps of the millions of poor. It has been recognised that the middle class has been so far enjoying the benefits from the new economy boom.

NOTES

1. Those cocoon markets were established in 1959 by the government to protect producers against middlemen. Despite those markets, the majority of the production is still sold by middlemen in the traditional production area, whereas in areas closer to markets all the production is sold in markets.
2. India is the second largest producer after China, but one of the biggest importers.
3. Unfortunately it was impossible to escape from biases in terms of selecting small-scale firms engaging in twisting and weaving activities. These firms are not listed in the Yellow Pages.
4. The firms generally perform multi-activities. Some both are exporters and perform production activities such as twisting, weaving, printing and tailoring.
5. In the survey the choice options for frequency were 'never', 'occasionally', 'sometimes', 'often', 'very often'.
6. This relationship is the result of a Principal Component Analysis.
7. These were Chi² tests, used to evaluate the relationship between the frequency of use of one particular means of communication and the data that described the firms (size, activity, kind of interlocutors and their location).

REFERENCES

Bloor, R. (2000), *The Electronic B@zaar: From the Silk Road to the E-Road.* London: Nicholas Brealey Publishing.

Chkhichaku, A. (1999), *Le Commerce Electronique: Concepts et Réalité*, Mémoire de Licence en Sciences Economiques, Université Cadi Ayyad, Marrakech.

Corbett, M. (2003), 'Outsource India', paper presented to the NASSCOM Conference on Outsourcing and BPO, Chennai, 26 January.

Einhorn, B. (2003), 'English gives India tech edge', *The Australian Financial Review*, 7 July.

Goldstein, A. and G. O'Connor (2000), 'E-commerce for development: prospects and policy issues', OECD Development Centre, Technical Paper No. 164.

Goldstein, A. and G. O'Connor (2001), 'Janvier, Entre Charybbe et Scylla. Centre de Développement', available at www.observateurocde.org/news/printpage.php/aid/501/Entre_Charybbe_et_Scylla.html.

Guétat-Bernard, Hélène (1994), 'Emplois ruraux non-agricoles: enjeux d'une diversification et réalité dans ce secteur d'emplois: l'exemple du Sud-Karnataka', thèse sous la direction d'Ignacy Sachs et Jean Racine.

Hossain, M. (2003), 'Globalisation and the growth of India's "new economy"', Third International Convention of Asia Scholars, ICAS and National University of Singapore, 19–22 August, available at www.icas.org.

Hussain, Z. (2003), 'MNCs eye brains and bottom line', *The Straits Times*, Singapore, 23 August.

Kathuria, R. (2000), 'Telecom policy reforms in India', *Global Business Review*, 1 (2), 301–26.

Khan, S. (2004), 'A dynasty re-vitalized: Sonia Gandhi damns predictions with stunning win', *The Independent*, London, 18 May.

Mann, C.L. (2000), 'Electronic commerce in developing countries: issues for domestic policy and WTO negotiations', available at: www.ile.com/publications.

Moodley, S. (2002), 'Connecting to global markets in the Internet age: the case of South African wooden furniture producers', *Development Southern Africa*, **19** (5), December.

NASSCOM (2002), *IT Enabled Services: Background and Reference Resource,* New Delhi: National Association of Software and Service Companies.

Raghunathan, V.K. (2003), 'India gains from job shift', *The Strait Times*, Singapore, 23 August.

Raipuria, K. (2000), 'Electronic commerce: opportunities for Indian exports', *Economical and Political Weekly,* **35** (35–36), September.

Rodrik, D. and A. Subramanian (2004), 'From "Hindu growth" to productivity surge: the mystery of the Indian growth transition' (draft), D. Rodrik personal website.

Roxenburgh (2003), 'The BRO phenomenon: an opportunity for Indian outsourcing vendors?', paper presented in the NASSCOM Conference on Outsourcing and BPO, Chennai, 21 January.

Singhal, A. and E. Rogers (2000), *India's Communication Revolution from Bullock Carts to Cyber Marts*, New Delhi: Sage Publications.

Sinha, S. (1990), *The Development of Indian Silk: A Wealth of Opportunities,* London: Intermediate Technology Publications.

Ternisien, M., G. Chantome and A.-F. Diguet (2001), 'Le commerce électronique interentreprises: son impact dans le secteur textile-habillement', France: Ministère de l'Economie, des Finances et de l'Industrie, December.

Waslekar, S. (2004), 'India's crisis of values', *The Globalist*, 13 May.

World Bank (1995), 'Economic development in India: achievements and Challenges', a world bank country study, Washington, DC.

8. Globalisation, poverty and disparities: the case of Sri Lanka

Jayatilleke S. Bandara and Athula Naranpanawa

Globalisation is no longer an option, it is a fact. Developing countries have either to learn to manage it far more skilfully, or simply drown in the global cross currents. (Mahbub ul Haq)

INTRODUCTION

Globalisation has been one of the most debated topics in recent years. The concept of globalisation is complex and it means different things to different people. Many observers, however, agree that it involves increases in trade and capital flows, information and human mobility across geographical boundaries (see for example, Masson 2001; Bhalla 1998). As Stiglitz (2002, p. 9) states 'fundamentally, it is the closer integration of the countries and peoples of the world which has been brought about by the enormous reduction of costs of transportation and communication, and the breaking down of artificial barriers to the flows of goods, services, capital, knowledge, and (to a lesser extent) people across borders'.

Many trade and development economists, policy-makers and policy analysts around the world believe that globalisation (particularly trade liberalisation) promotes growth and reduces poverty. There exists a large body of theoretical and empirical literature on how trade liberalisation helps to promote growth and reduce poverty. The critics of globalisation, sometimes known as anti-globalisers, argue that developing countries' integration into the world economy makes the poor poorer and the rich richer in developing countries. The most common criticism of globalisation is that it increases poverty and inequality. Much of the research related to the link between openness, growth and poverty has been based on cross-country regression. Using this approach, Dollar and Kraay (2001a, 2001b) have examined the link between trade, growth and poverty. Their results have fuelled the debate further. Lubker et al. (2002, p. 556) have summarised the findings of the Dollar and Kraay research project as follows:

(i)   on average across countries and over time, growth is distribution neutral; thus
(ii) any factor which increases the growth rate is good for the poor;
(iii) World Bank and IMF policy packages increase the growth rate; therefore
(iv) these policy packages should be the core of poverty reduction strategies.

The results of Dollar and Kraay's research have been subjected to severe criticism on the basis of methodology, data and definitions. According to critical studies by Lubker et al. (2002, p. 256), Wei (2002, p. 26), Wade (2002), Ravallion (2001) and Chen and Ravallion (2004), the main problems of Dollar and Kraay's research are:

1. the empirical work being based on theoretically unsound equations;
2. the use of flawed data;
3. inappropriately defined policy variables and not testing them in a consistent manner;
4. the inability to compare the income and inequality owing to differences in definitions of key variables and methods of data collection;
5. the differences in culture and institutions that may influence growth or inequality.

In particular, Wade (2002) is very critical about the poverty data published by the World Bank.

These weaknesses of cross-country studies have led to a need for providing evidence from case studies. Systematic case studies related to individual countries will at least complement cross-country studies such as the study by Dollar and Kraay. As Chen and Ravallion (2004, p. 30) argue, 'aggregate inequality or poverty may not change with trade reform even though there are gainers and losers at all levels of living'. They further argue that policy analysis that simply averages across diversities may miss important matters which are critical to the policy debate. Using China as a case study, they have shown that the impact of trade liberalisation on multi-dimensional aspects of poverty, such as access to human and physical infrastructure and geographical disparities, is important in the developing economy setting.

Sri Lanka constitutes a very good case study for a number of reasons. Firstly (and most importantly), many development and trade economists regard Sri Lanka as a well-known outlier among developing countries.

When it regained independence from the British in 1948 it was regarded as one of Asia's rich and promising nations. Until recently it was often regarded as a role model for a third world democratic welfare state. Since the Second World War, successive governments in Sri Lanka have given priority to universal provision of education, health care and securing a minimum level of consumption for all citizens. According to a recent World Bank report, 'it was one of the first developing countries to understand the multi-dimensional nature of poverty, and has strongly emphasised policies aimed at promoting free health and education as early as the 1930s' (World Bank 2000, p. 27). There was extraordinary progress in education, health care and nutrition in Sri Lanka between the 1940s and the 1960s and Sri Lanka became an exception among developing countries (see Anand and Kambur 1991; Isenman 1980; Sen 1981; Streeten 1979). By the 1960s, Sri Lanka's human development indicators had improved to a status almost similar to those of the developed countries and the fastest growing countries in South East Asia. The country became the third-world welfare model because of its early emphasis on satisfying basic needs, the astonishing success of its welfare programmes and deep-rooted parliamentary democracy.

As pointed out by Easterly and Pritchett (1993, p. 39), 'in the early 1960s, a group of distinguished World Bank economists forecasted a per capita growth rate for Sri Lanka that would exceed Taiwan's over the period 1962–76'. The former Singaporean Prime Minister who visited Sri Lanka in 1979 'expressed the view that Sri Lanka could overtake by 1990 the level of development achieved by Singapore up to 1979 if she resolved the ethnic crisis' (quoted in Kelegama 2000, p. 1489). None of these predictions about Sri Lanka materialised. Although Sri Lanka has continued the globalisation process for nearly a quarter of a century without much policy interruption, its image as a model of development and democracy has been rapidly and severely tarnished over the 1980s and 1990s.

Secondly, while Sri Lanka was struggling to maintain sustainable economic growth with a high level of welfare and peace, East Asian countries were not only maintaining higher economic growth but also overtaking Sri Lanka's exceptional welfare indicators by the beginning of the new century. Although the per capita income level of countries such as Singapore, Malaysia and Korea was similar to Sri Lanka's in the 1960s, they achieved a per capita income level several times higher than that of Sri Lanka by the end of 1990s. They also managed to maintain political stability. In contrast, Sri Lanka has performed poorly over the past two decades and it is presently facing a huge economic and political crisis. In 2001 a negative GDP growth rate was recorded for the first time in the history of independent Sri Lanka, and a political solution to the ethnic problem is yet to be found.[1] Recently a number of studies have attempted to explain the reasons for Sri Lanka's tragic story of development under such titles as 'A tale of missed opportunities' (Snodgrass 1999), 'Sri Lanka: what went wrong' (Kelegama 2000) and 'Sri Lanka: recapturing missed opportunities' (World Bank 2000). According to these studies, Sri Lanka's underachievement and its economic crisis can be attributed to a two-decade war, economic policy mistakes, the welfare-oriented inward-looking policies implemented in the 1960s and 1970s, the large and inefficient public sector and poor governance.

Thirdly, Sri Lanka was the first country in South Asia to initiate far-reaching policy reforms to integrate into the world economy, as early as the late 1970s. It has completed a quarter-century of the globalisation process without much interruption (such as going back to a closed economy). Finally, Sri Lanka can be considered one of few developing countries which achieved a reasonable economic growth by integrating into the world economy, while waging a two-decade war against the separatist Liberation Tigers of Tamil Eelam (LTTE) in the north and east of the country.

The recent process of Sri Lanka's integration into the global economy began with the major policy reform package implemented in Sri Lanka from 1977. This policy package included trade liberalisation, incentives to foreign direct investment (FDI), privatisation, a reduction in the size of the public sector, and a reduction in welfare expenditure. The economic impact of these programmes on economic aggregates such as economic growth, employment, export orientation and industrialisation has been extensively investigated by a large number of studies (see, for example, Athukorala and Jayasuriya 1994; Athukorala and Rajapathirana 2000; Cuthbertson and Athukorala 1991). However, their impacts on income inequalities, poverty, regional disparities and other political, social and cultural dimensions have not received much attention. Any evaluation of the impacts of globalisation on the Sri Lankan economy ignoring these aspects would be misleading.

The main purpose of this chapter is, therefore, to investigate the impact of the opening up of the Sri Lankan economy on income inequality, poverty and regional disparities. The next section of this chapter is an overview of the process of Sri Lanka's integration into the world economy. The section 'Benefits of globalisation' summarises so-called 'gains' from globalisation to the Sri Lankan economy as highlighted in the literature. The impacts of globalisation on inequality and poverty are evaluated in the section 'Impact on inequality and poverty'. The exclusion and regional disparities are examined in the section 'exclusion and regional disparities'. The last section of the chapter contains concluding remarks.

HISTORICAL OVERVIEW OF THE GLOBALISATION PROCESS OF THE SRI LANKAN ECONOMY

As noted in the introduction, Sri Lanka was considered one of the most promising new nations among other newly independent developing nations when it gained independence from the British in 1948. Its trade policy regime is summarised in Table 8.1. There is a large body of literature which reviews and evaluates the history of trade policy in post-independence Sri Lanka. As can be seen from the table, the trade policy changes were associated with the swings in the political pendulum until 1977. Sri Lanka experienced periodic peaceful changes in government, and political power changed periodically between two major political parties, that is, the right-of-centre pro-Western market-oriented United National Party (UNP) and the left-of-centre Sri Lanka Freedom Party (SLFP), or coalitions of parties, until 1977. This trend has, however, changed after 1977, indicating that both major parties are now in favour of integration of the Sri Lankan economy into the global economy. In 1994 when the People's Alliance (left-of-centre coalition) came to power, as Athukorala and Rajapathirana (2000, p. 44) note, 'for the first time in the post-independence era, the change of government did not result in a shift in the basic trust of the national development policy'.

From 1948 to 1956 the first post-independence government (right-of-centre UNP) continued with colonial open economy based on plantation agriculture. More than 90 per cent of its export earnings came from three agricultural products (tea, rubber and coconut). As a newly independent nation, Sri Lanka committed to provide a wide range of welfare programmes including food subsidies, free education and health, and subsidised public transportation, while the enjoying benefits of the commodity boom after the Second World War and the Korean war under a post-colonial open economic policy. The economic boom, however, collapsed by 1952 and the government attempted to adjust prices of subsidised food, creating a political crisis in 1953 as a result of a civil disobedience campaign led by the left parties. These events led to the defeat of the UNP government and a change of government in 1956, creating long-lasting impacts on Sri Lanka's political and economic history. As Snodgrass (1999, p. 95) notes, 'the 1956 election was a watershed in which the *Mahajana Eksath Peramuna* (MEP), a coalition led by the Sri Lanka Freedom Party (SLFP), came to power after mobilising an engulfing wave of accumulated political, cultural and economic grievances'. This government change signalled the origin of a change in the political ethos in Sri Lanka, which led to significant changes in policy-making.

Table 8.1 Changes in policy regime: an historical overview

	Policy regime	Political regime	Average real economic growth (%)	Average per capita economic growth (%)
1948–56: Continuation of colonial globalised economy	1948–56: Continuation of open economy with 'populism'	Right-of-centre UNP government	3.2	0.6
1956–77: Closed economy with restrictions to globalisation	1956–60: Closing up with 'populism'	Left-of-centre SLFP government		
	1960–65: Continuation of closed economy	Left-of-centre SLFP government	2.5	0.0
	1965–70: Partial departure from the closed economy	Right-of-centre UNP government	7.8	5.5
	1970–77: Back to closed economy	Left-of-centre SLFP coalition government with left parties	4.0	2.4
1977 to date: Globalisation following the world trend	1977–89: Opening up – first phase	Right-of-centre UNP government	4.6	3.0
	1990–94: Opening up – second phase	Right-of-centre UNP government	5.3	4.1
	1995–2001: Continuation of open economy	Left-of-centre PA government	2.9	n.a.
	2002–04: Continuation of open economy	Right-of-centre UNF government	5.0	n.a.
	2004 to date: Continuation of open economy	Left-of-centre UPFA		

The political commitment of this left-of-centre government was to maintain consumer subsidies and extend direct government involvement in the production, services and trade sectors.

Adverse commodity prices coupled with an expansionary fiscal policy led to balance of payments deficits continuously from 1957. The policy response to the balance of payments problems in the late 1950s mainly relied on the imposition of import restrictions. This continued to be the major policy response until 1977. Details of the control regime (or closed economy, 1957–77) have been documented in various trade studies. In general, salient features of the control regime include:

1. the introduction of quantitative trade restrictions by replacing tariffs on most of the imported items;
2. the import tariff structure being highly differentiated according to the magnitude of competition with domestic import-substitutes;
3. exchange control restrictions on foreign investments;
4. direct government involvement in the production, services and trade sectors.

The left-of-centre governments which held power between 1956 and 1965 (with a brief interruption of a few months in 1960) and between 1970 and 1977 continued the closed economic policy.

The protection of import-substitution industries discriminated against exporting industries. The right-of-centre-government which came to power in 1965 favoured a gradual relaxation of controls on trade and exchange. The policy orientation during the period 1965–70 can be described as a partial move from the control regime towards export promotion. In November 1977 the Sri Lankan rupee was devalued by 20 per cent following the devaluation of the British pound. A dual exchange rate system was introduced to encourage exports. Despite attempts at partial liberalisation, the adverse balance of payments continued to worsen during the period 1966–70. A coalition of the SLFP and left-wing parties came to power in 1970 and its policy orientation favoured closed economic policies similar to those of previous left-of-centre governments. Immediate economic circumstances and their ideological leanings led to the abortion of partial liberalisation attempts of the previous government and reimposition of import and exchange controls.

Despite partial liberalisation towards the end of the 1960s, the policy regime during the period 1956–77 can be considered a 'controlled regime' with anti-globalisation policies. The entire period was politically dominated by left-of-centre governments except for a five-year interlude (1965–70). The growth performance was poor (see Table 8.1) and the unemployment rate increased. Many industries suffered from a severe under-utilisation problem. Investment was low. Foreign investments were discouraged by the regime. On the other hand, the postponement of the general election by two years, cuts in consumer subsidies, shortages of essential goods and the nationalisation of newspapers and some business undertakings turned public opinion against the government and created the political climate for the defeat of the left-of-centre government in 1977. This brought into power the pro-western, market-oriented right-of-centre government of the UNP with an overwhelming majority.

The economic policies of the newly elected government were said to be based on the experience of outward-oriented economies in South East Asia. Thus, in formulating new economic policies, the government considered newly industrialised South Asian countries, particularly Singapore, as models to be followed. In line with this political and economic stance, the government initiated a series of liberalisation measures centred on a more outward-oriented growth strategy which drastically altered the previous policy orientation. In November 1977 the UNP government announced this new open economic policy package including far-reaching changes in trade and exchange rate policies. Both the IMF and the World Bank provided generous support to these policy adjustments. Besides these institutions, western donor countries promised the UNP government support for the implementation of the new policy package. By implementing this package in 1977, Sri Lanka became the first country in South Asia to introduce a radical liberalisation process.

The central thrust of the reforms was aimed at the achievement of a less regulated, more market oriented open economy. The details of this policy package have been extensively documented in many recent studies (Cuthbertson and Athukorala 1991; Athukorala and Jayasuriya 1994; Athukorala and Rajapathirana 2000). The main components of the 1977 policy package can be summarised as follows. A tariff reform replaced most of the perverse quantitative restrictions with tariffs. The previous dual exchange rate system was abolished and the exchange rate was unified. Many exchange controls were removed and a large devaluation took place. Measures were taken to attract foreign direct investment. Steps were taken to remove price controls and food subsidies were restricted to the low-income groups. The government also initiated massive public sector investment programmes centred on three 'leading projects'. The largest project was the Mahaweli Development Project (a major irrigation and power project), which involved extensive construction activities. The second project was a housing construction programme and the third one was the setting up of the Greater Colombo Economic Commission (GCEC), which established the free trade zone (FTZ) in order to attract foreign investors.

The initial reform package of opening up the Sri Lankan economy and integrating into the world economy is known as the 'first phase' of liberalisation. The eruption of ethnic riots in 1983 and the escalation of civil war in the North East and the insurrection launched by the Janatha Vimuckthi Peramuna (JVP) or People's Liberation Front (a radical extreme-left movement in the south) during the period 1987–89 led Sri Lanka into political and social turmoil. Many observers believe that these events have been the main reasons for Sri Lanka's failure to achieve the full benefits of globalisation. Towards the end of the 1980s Sri Lanka was facing an increase in defence expenditure and growing budget and current account deficits. The flow of foreign direct investment declined. Under this macroeconomic environment, the government initiated the 'second phase' or second wave of liberalisation in June 1989 with the help of the World Bank and the IMF. As Athukorala and Rajapathirana (2000, p. 43) summarise, this package 'included an ambitious privatisation programme, further tariff cuts and simplification, the removal of exchange controls on current account transactions, commitment to a flexible exchange rate, and an initiative to cut the fiscal deficit'. This phase of reform continued in the 1990s and was regarded as the intensification of the reform programme introduced in 1977.

The People's Alliance (PA) government (a left-of-centre government) came to power in 1994 by defeating the UNP, which was in power for 17 years from 1977 to 1994. As noted at the beginning, the PA government committed to continue the previous government's open economic policy for the first time in the economic history of post-independence Sri Lanka. During the period of the PA government, 1994–2001, the North East war intensified and defence expenditure increased rapidly. A negative economic growth rate was recorded in 2001 for the first time after independence. However, the government maintained open economic policies. The United National Front (UNF) government led by the UNP and Tamil and Muslim minority parties came to power in December 2001 by promising to find a peaceful solution to the ethnic conflict and to maintain open economic policies. This regime was in power only for a brief period. In April 2004 the United People's Freedom Alliance (UPFA) led by the PA and JVP (left-of-centre alliance) came to power. This government is also continuing with open economic policies and the peace process. In fact, currently the opening up of the economy has become bipartisan policy in Sri Lanka. All in all, the period from 1977 to date can be considered the period of globalisation of the Sri Lankan economy. The reform process since 1977 has resulted in significant integration of the Sri Lankan economy into the world economy. Figure 8.1 shows the increased openness of the Sri Lankan economy after 1977 (total trade expressed as a percentage of GDP).

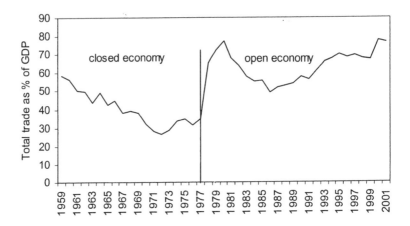

Figure 8.1   Openness of the Sri Lankan economy

BENEFITS OF GLOBALISATION

As many Sri Lankan observers have demonstrated, there are obvious achievements of globalisation of the Sri Lankan economy in terms of some macroeconomic indicators. As shown in Figure 8.2, the economic growth immediately after 1977 and before the escalation of civil war and the Southern insurrection during the late 1980s was impressive, if not spectacular. Even with civil war the economy managed to maintain a satisfactory growth rate in the 1990s.

During the closed economy, one of the main economic problems in Sri Lanka was the higher unemployment rate. It was around 20 per cent just before the introduction of the reform package in 1977. As shown in Figure 8.3, the aggregate unemployment rate in the economy continuously declined from around 20 per cent in the mid-1970s to 8 per cent in 2001. This is a very impressive achievement. There are some combined factors of globalisation contributing to this impressive achievement of employment. There is no doubt that the export-oriented economic policies have created employment opportunities, particularly in the garment industry. In addition, an increase in the number of people permanently leaving the country, temporary migration for overseas jobs, an increasing number of people joining the army and the LTTE and the disappearance of more than 50 000 youth in the 1980s can be regarded as factors contributing to the lower unemployment rate in Sri Lanka.

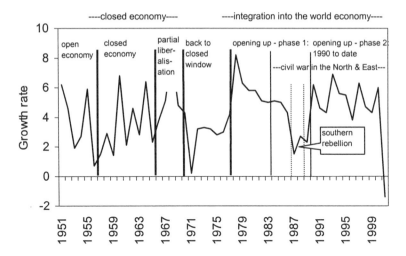

Figure 8.2   Real GDP growth in Sri Lanka, 1951–2001

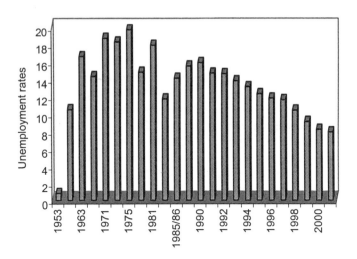

Figure 8.3   Unemployment in Sri Lanka

The other impressive achievement of the economy is the flow of FDI. Before 1977 the net flow of FDI to Sri Lanka was virtually zero. However, the flow has increased since 1977 with some fluctuations due to civil war (see Figure 8.4). FDI generated employment opportunities and assisted industrialisation in Sri Lanka.

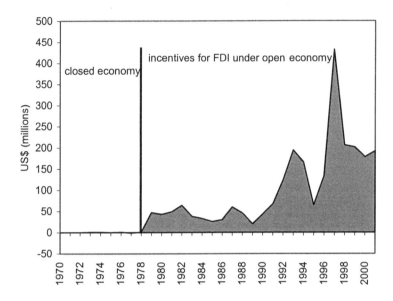

Figure 8.4   Net foreign direct investment in Sri Lanka

The overall domestic investment in the economy has increased. As shown in Figure 8.5, while the aggregate investment ratio to GDP was around 15 per cent during the closed trade policy regime, it increased to more than 25 per cent after 1977. However, the domestic savings ratio did not increase much, creating a domestic resource gap.

Figure 8.6 demonstrates the behaviour of other macroeconomic aggregates such as inflation, the current account deficit and budget deficit. Many observers believe that the huge budget deficit has been the result of defence expenditure. The government has not been able to control inflation.

Athukorala and Rajapathirana (2000) have examined the link between liberalisation and industrialisation in Sri Lanka. According to them Sri Lanka's performance in manufacturing is very impressive during the post-liberalisation period. Exports of industrial products have increased considerably (see Figure 8.7). They have highlighted the following favourable outcomes during the liberalised regime:

- there is greater capacity utilisation of the manufacturing sector;
- manufacturing output has increased;
- the ratio of exports to gross manufacturing output has increased;
- manufacturing exports from Sri Lanka are heavily concentrated in clothing;

- FDI has played an important role in the expansion of manufacturing exports;
- the manufacturing sector has created a large number of jobs.

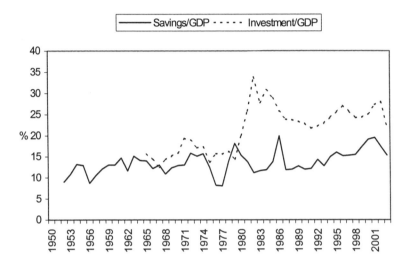

Figure 8.5   Domestic savings and investment as a percentage of GDP in Sri Lanka

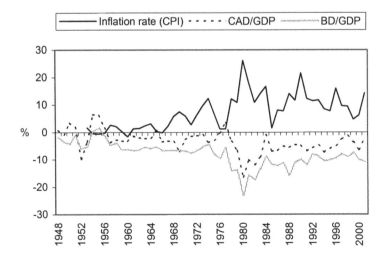

Figure 8.6   Inflation, current account deficit and budget deficit in Sri Lanka

Their study has praised the achievements of the post-liberalisation period in terms of industrial growth, export-oriented industrialisation, employment generation and the role of FDI in industrialisation. They further conclude that

> the economic outcome of reform would have been much more impressive had it not been for policy inconsistencies, delays in the implementation of some key elements of the initial reform package, and perhaps more importantly, the continuing ethnic conflict since 1983 and the radical youth uprising during the period of 1986–89. (Athukorala and Rajapathirana 2000, p. 189)

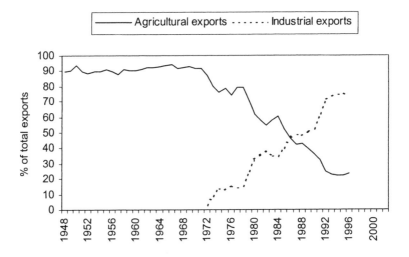

Figure 8.7   The changing composition of exports in Sri Lanka

The above mentioned benefits of the liberalised regime can be considered as achievements of aggregates. Consideration of achievements alone, however, is not sufficient. It is important to evaluate the impacts of Sri Lanka's integration into the world economy on poverty, income distribution and regional disparities. In the next section we examine the impact of globalisation on inequality and poverty.

IMPACT OF GLOBALISATION ON INEQUALITY AND POVERTY

As in many developed and developing countries, household expenditure and income surveys provide data on poverty and inequality in Sri Lanka. These surveys were carried out by the Department of Census and Statistics (DCS) and the Central Bank of Sri Lanka (CBSL) at regular intervals over the last few decades. Despite some problems and inconsistencies involved in income and expenditure surveys in Sri Lanka (see Dunham and Jayasuriya 2000), we use Gini coefficients data estimated using different income and expenditure survey data by the CBSL and the DCS to understand what has been happening in terms of equality in the post-liberalisation period. During the welfare-oriented protectionist policy regime up to the late 1970s Sri Lanka experienced a trend towards relative equality in income distribution as indicated by Gini coefficients, which demonstrate the overall position of income distribution, shown in Table 8.2.

For example, the Gini coefficient declined from 0.46 in 1953 to 0.35 in 1973, indicating a significant move towards lower income inequality during the period of closed economy. However, it increased in the 1980s, fell moderately in the middle of the 1990s and rose with the dawn of the new millennium, during the process of globalisation of the Sri Lankan economy, as shown in Table 8.2. Overall, on the basis of evidence, there is no doubt that inequality has increased in Sri Lanka during the post-liberalisation period with a weak trickle-down effect of economic growth. Using Gini coefficient data for the last two decades, the latest CBSL annual report notes the trend in inequality and growth effect as follows: 'The estimated Gini coefficient, which measures the inequality in income distribution, increased from 0.43 in 1980/81 to 0.46 in 1995/96 and further to 0.48 in 2002, demonstrating an increase in the inequality in income distribution, indicating low trickle-down effect of the benefits of economic growth' (CBSL 2004, p. 20).

One of the most salient features of income distribution in Sri Lanka is the significant difference in Gini coefficients in three major sectors of the economy (urban, rural and estate). This can also be observed from Table 8.2. The inequality in the urban sector is higher than that of the rural and estate sectors.

As has been pointed out further in the latest annual report of the CBSL, 'the income distribution is skewed more towards the high income categories' (CBSL 2004, p. 14). This can be observed clearly when examining the income shares of different income deciles. For example, the share of highest income decile in the total income was 38.6 per cent in 2002. This was 23 times higher than the share of lowest income decile in the total income, that is, 1.7 per cent (DCS 2003). Disparities in terms of income between sectors have also been visible. For example, the average household income of the urban sector was about twice as high as that of the rural sector and three times as high a than that of the estate sector in 2002 according to DCS's latest survey (CBSL 2004, p. 20).

Table 8.2 *Gini coefficients of incomes*

Gini coefficient	1953	1963	1973	1978/79	1980/81	1985/86	1990/91	1995/96	2002
GC of household income									
All island	0.46	0.45	0.35	0.43	0.43	0.46	0.47	0.46	0.48
Urban	n.a.	0.49*	0.40*	0.51*	0.44	0.47	0.62	0.47	0.51
Rural	n.a.	0.44*	0.37*	0.49*	0.38	0.43	0.42	0.46	0.46
Estate	n.a.	0.47*	0.37*	0.32*	0.27	0.31	0.25	0.34	0.32
GC of income receiver's income									
All island	0.50	0.49	0.41	0.49	0.43	n.a.	0.52	0.52	0.55

Note: * For income receiver's income

Sources: SLBS (various reports) and DCS (2003)

While income received by the poorest 40 per cent of spending units had also increased from 14.5 per cent in 1953 to 19.3 per cent in 1973, income received by the richest 20 per cent of the economy had declined from 53.8 per cent in 1953 to 42.95 per cent in 1973, during the welfare-oriented protectionist policy regime (see Table 8.3). This was due to the equity emphasis of government policy during the 1960s and 1970s.

With the beginning of the new globalisation process, however, the income share of the poorest 40 per cent started to decline (despite a moderate improvement in the mid-1990s). Recently this share has declined from 15.2 per cent in 1995/96 to 13.8 per cent in 2002, the lowest in post-independence Sri Lanka. On the other hand, the income share of the richest 20 per cent increased from 49.9 per cent in 1995/96 to 53.7 per cent in 2002, the highest in the last four decades. This trend is alarming in terms of inequality in Sri Lanka. This new evidence suggests that Sri Lanka is facing a considerable degree of income inequality.

Previous studies carried out in Sri Lanka revealed that poverty is primarily a rural phenomenon.[2] The estimates of poverty measures computed for Sri Lanka in various years are given in Table 8.4. However, these measures are not comparable as different studies have adopted different definitions of the poverty line, such as, income/expenditure cut-off point or dietary energy cut-off point. Furthermore, there is a wide variability in poverty measurements as a result of sampling problems and other inconsistencies in defining different sub-groups.[3] When we consider the proportion of the population in poverty estimated using the poverty line based on Rs 791.67/person/month at 1995/96 prices, it can be observed that total poverty dropped from 30.9 per cent in 1985/86 to 19.9 per cent in 1990/91. Yet it is evident that poverty grew again up to 25.2 per cent in 1995/96.

According to the latest DCS data, the poverty head count index is 28.1 (based on the national poverty line) in 2002. There are disparities of income poverty between sectors (urban, rural and estate). For example, poverty in the rural sector is nearly four times as high as in the urban sector. Urban poverty seems to have declined over time. Nevertheless, poverty among rural and estate sector households has fluctuated. As 90 per cent of the poor live in rural areas (CBSL 2004, p. 20), the current trend in poverty incidence attracts grave concern.

Furthermore, as evaluated by a recent World Bank study, one-quarter of the total population in Sri Lanka is living below the poverty line and 'a large part of the population remains vulnerable to income fluctuations' (World Bank 2000, p. 27). Using the results of ongoing poverty-related research jointly undertaken by the Sri Lankan government and the World Bank, this study (p. 28) summarises the main features of poverty in Sri Lanka as follows:

Table 8.3 Income shares of the poorest 40 per cent and the richest 20 per cent of spending units

Income groups	1953	1963	1973	1978/79	1981/82	1986/87	1995/96	2002
Poorest 40%	14.5	14.7	19.3	16.1	15.2	14.1	15.2	13.8
Richest 20%	53.8	52.3	43.0	49.9	52.0	52.3	49.9	53.7

Sources: CBSL (1998) and DCS (2003)

Table 8.4 *Estimates of the proportion of the population in poverty (in percentages)*

Base/year		Households			
		Urban	Rural	Estate	Total
Income/expenditure based poverty line					
1969/70	(1)	5.0	12.8	11.1	11.2
1973	(3)	22.7	31.6	8.1	27.6
	(4)	4.0	26.1	1.7	19.1
1978/79	(3)	24.4	23.8	8.9	22.7
	(5)	16.0	22.7	5.9	19.5
1980/81	(1)	16.9	25.9	25.0	24.1
1981/82	(3)	19.6	23.2	13.8	21.9
	(4)	17.7	26.1	12.3	23.6
Dietary energy based poverty line					
1969/70	(2)	58.3	52.3	38.5	52.0
1980/81	(6)	49.0	42.9	32.6	–
1985/86	(5)	12.3	32.4	5.9	27.4
1986/87	(8)	10.5	28.7	11.1	24.1
1990/91	(7)	18.2	34.7	20.5	30.4
Rs 791.67/person/month at 1995/96 prices taken as poverty line					
1985/86	(9)	18.4	35.6	20.5	30.9
1990/91	(9)	15.0	22.0	12.4	19.9
1995/96	(9)	14.7	27.0	24.9	25.2
Poverty head count index based on national poverty line					
2002	(10)	8.6	31.3	28.0	28.1

Sources: This table draws heavily from Tudawe (2000) and Gunetilleke (2000). (1) Bhalla and Glewwe (1986); (2) Visaria (1981); (3) Anand and Harris (1990); (4) Marga (1981); (5) Gunaratne (1985); (6) Sahn (1984); (7) DCS (1993); (8) Edirisinghe (1990); (9) Gunetilleke (2000); (10) DCS (2003)

- Income poverty remains high in Sri Lanka.
- The long-term trend in overall poverty levels shows a decline over the period 1985–96.
- Urban and rural poverty is declining, with significant fluctuations in rural poverty over the period 1985–96.
- Income poverty in Sri Lanka is primarily a rural phenomenon.
- Acute regional disparities in poverty persist and widened between 1990 and 1996.

A number of poverty alleviation programmes have been implemented by successive governments since the late 1980s to protect vulnerable groups in the country. However, these programmes have suffered from design problems and implementation weaknesses leading to inefficiency. The World Bank study of 2000 has found three specific flaws in the poverty alleviation programmes implemented during the period 1989–95 (*Janasaviya* programme) and from 1995 to the present (*Samurdhi* programme). They are (i) the political bias in implementing state-sponsored programmes, (ii) the non-materialisation of the expected improved quality of decentralised public services and the state's increased accountability to the poor and (iii) the failure of these large costly programmes to give sufficient opportunities for creating employment opportunities for the poor (see World Bank 2000 for details).

Recent studies indicate that poverty has declined when averaged across sectors over the post-liberalisation period, though it is still high and volatile. However, the aggregate analysis based on income poverty is misleading. In the next section we review the trends in geographical disparities in income poverty and disparities in human poverty during the post-liberalisation period on the basis of recent studies.

EXCLUSION AND REGIONAL DISPARITIES

After the introduction of liberalisation and economic integration into the world economy in 1977 and implementation of structural adjustments in the 1980s, the rate of economic growth in Sri Lanka initially rose, compared with the pre-liberalisation growth rate, as expected. However, this should not be read as being purely the result of liberalisation. The higher growth was partly attributable to the investment boom in the late 1970s and the early 1980s. New evidence has also emerged that this growth strategy created significant regional disparities. The majority of the population in the south was excluded from reaping the benefits of liberalisation. In the initial period of reforms, the government implemented three leading projects: the massive Mahaweli irrigation project, the establishment of a free trade zone and the construction of 100 000 urban houses. The economic benefits of these projects were limited to certain areas like the Colombo District and some administrative districts of other parts of the country. However, not only were the mostly Tamil-dominated Northern province and some parts of the eastern districts excluded, but also the hardcore Sinhalese-dominated Southern province and some parts of rural North Western province were excluded. Similarly, some regions did not reap the benefits of trade liberalisation. Lakshman (1997, p. 191) finds the 'economic growth that took place during this period appears to have been strongly biased toward the Colombo metropolis'. He further points out that the Tamil-dominated area was relatively neglected by the economic reform package and there was no alternative package to compensate the adverse impact of policy reforms. This helped the Tamil separatist movement to gather momentum in the Tamil-dominated areas. According to Lakshman (ibid., p. 213), 'certain social groups appear to have been favoured and certain others systematically excluded from the limited income earning opportunities created'. Some of the groups are middle-aged married women, the youth educated in *Swebhasha,* a large section of small farmers living in traditional villages, and people living in Sri Lanka's Northern, Eastern, Southern and North Western provinces.

The World Bank (2000) study finds that some poor communities have been either marginalised or excluded during the last two decades. There are about 15 000 villages in Sri Lanka and 50 per cent of these villages are categorised as '*purana*' or traditional villages. As Gunetilleke (2000, p. 8) notes, about 10 per cent of these *purana* villages are isolated and they are vulnerable to acute deprivation. As a result of globalisation, industrial and services sectors have grown rapidly in urban areas rather than these villages. These villages have poor access to human and physical infrastructure such as education, health and transport. The best way to analyse multi-dimensional aspects of rural poverty is to look at the provincial and district level income poverty and human development data. Before examining multi-dimensional aspects of poverty, it is interesting to look at regional shares of GDP in Sri Lanka.

In Sri Lanka, there are nine provinces (or regions). The Western province is the most urbanised province and Colombo (capital city) in the Western province is the political, commercial and banking centre. The Northern and Eastern provinces, which are basically rural provinces, are dominated by the minority Tamils and they are the centres of the ethnic conflict. The main agricultural activity of the Central province is tea and the estate sector (based on Indian Tamils – mainly labourers) dominates this province. All other provinces can be considered as rural provinces. Until recently, Sri Lankan statistical authorities and the CBSL did not estimate regional

GDP annually. Following a systematic study by Mutaliph et al. (2001, 2002) the CBSL started to publish regional GDP in its annual report from 2003. Table 8.5 summarises recently published regional GDP data by the CBSL and it demonstrates the economic strength of each province in terms of the shares of GDP. As pointed out by Mutaliph et al. (2001, 2002, p. 4), the data shown in Table 8.5 and Figure 8.8 clearly demonstrate an uneven distribution of GDP among provinces. The Western province contributes nearly 50 per cent of the total GDP in Sri Lanka and it has become the most prosperous province in the island. On the other hand, rural provinces such as Uva, North Central, Northern and Sabaragamuwa contribute only a small proportion of the total GDP (see Table 8.5). While the GDP of the Western province has increased recently, the GDP shares of rural provinces have declined or stagnated. Mutaliph et al. (2001, 2002) find that there is a considerable regional disparity in Sri Lanka in terms of regional distribution of GDP, regional per capita income and regional productivity.

Some of these rural provinces and their districts are poor for a number of reasons. Firstly, these provinces are missing out on globalisation because of their geographical distance from the hub of economic activities in the Colombo-based Western province. Secondly, their economic growth and development have been constrained by the lack of access to physical and human infrastructure. Thirdly, some of these provinces have not been economically stimulated by other supplementary locally led projects such as the massive Mahaweli irrigation project initiated in the 1970s. Finally, the low productivity of agriculture compared with manufacturing and services has contributed to the low income levels of rural provinces.

Table 8.6 shows annual average growth rates and poverty incidence related to different provinces in Sri Lanka. While only the Western province achieved higher growth and reduction in poverty during the first half of the 1990s, rural provinces such as North Western and Uva provinces recorded low regional growth and an increase in poverty incidence (except the North Central province). Around 80 per cent of the Sri Lankan population still live in rural provinces and rural poverty is an important issue in Sri Lanka. Despite the decline in the importance of agriculture in terms of share of GDP, a large proportion of rural households still depend on agriculture. A recent World Bank study (2003, p. xi) found that 'income from agriculture was critical in some provinces, particularly in the North and Eastern (67 per cent), Sabaragamuwa (60 per cent), Uva (59 per cent), Southern (48 per cent) and Central (47 per cent) provinces'. Figure 8.9 also demonstrates the dominance of agriculture in rural provinces.

Table 8.5 Shares of GDP by province (at factor cost prices), 1996–2002

Province	1996	1997	1998	1999	2000	2001	2002	Annual average GDP share	Average % change of share
Western	43.7	44.3	45.3	48.7	49.6	48.3	48.1	46.9	1.7
Southern	9.0	8.8	9.3	9.6	9.4	9.7	9.7	9.4	1.3
Sabaragamuwa	9.0	7.6	6.7	6.4	6.7	6.4	6.9	7.1	-4.0
Central	10.0	10.5	9.8	9.2	9.4	9.4	9.4	9.7	-0.9
Uva	5.1	5.0	4.9	4.1	3.9	4.6	4.3	4.6	-2.3
Eastern	4.8	5.0	5.5	5.0	4.5	5.0	4.9	5.0	0.7
North Western	11.3	12.1	12.0	10.4	10.4	10.7	10.1	11.0	-1.6
North Central	4.6	4.0	3.6	4.1	3.9	3.7	3.9	4.0	-2.3
Northern	2.4	2.8	2.9	2.5	2.2	2.4	2.6	2.5	2.0
Total	100.0	100.0	100.0	100.0	100.0	100.0	100.0	100.0	

Source: CBSL (2004)

189

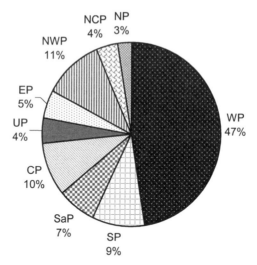

*Figure 8.8 Average provincial contribution to the national GDP, 1996–
          2002*

Table 8.6 GDP growth and poverty incidence by region

	Annual average growth 1990–95 (%)	Growth ranking	Poverty incidence (%)	
			1990/91	1995/96
North Central	9.9	1	18.2	31.2
Western	6.4	2	15.2	13.6
Southern	6.1	3	23.7	26.5
Sabaragamuwa	5.3	4	23.1	31.6
Central	5.0	5	23.5	27.9
Eastern	5.0	6	n.a.	n.a.
North Western	4.3	7	18.0	33.9
Uva	3.5	8	23.7	37.0
Northern	−6.2	9	n.a.	n.a.

Source: World Bank (2000)

These are the provinces with higher poverty rates in Sri Lanka. As noted
in a recent World Bank study, the surprising finding is that poverty
levels have not declined even in high performing provinces such as
North Central and Southern provinces, 'indicating that the poor are unable
to take full and sustained advantage of gains from economic growth'
(World Bank 2000, p. 35).

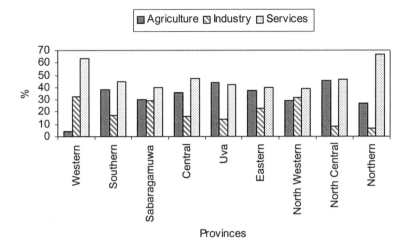

Figure 8.9   Sectoral GDP shares by province, 2002

The World Bank study (2000, p. 38) concludes that 'acute regional disparities in poverty persist and widened between 1990 and 1996'. Most economic activities stimulated by globalisation are still based in the Western province and it is known as the 'economic hub' of Sri Lanka. The main commercial and administrative centre of Colombo is in the Western province. Northern and Eastern provinces have rarely benefited from the globalisation process and these areas are the main conflict zones of the ethnic conflict in Sri Lanka. Until recently they have been severely affected by the eruption of civil war since 1983. Other rural provinces such as North Western, North Central, Sabaragamuwa and Uva are dominated by domestic agricultural activities such as paddy farming, subsidiary crops, minor export crops and rubber production. Income poverty in these provinces is relatively high. As shown in Table 8.6, there exist significant disparities in income poverty among these provinces.

As noted before, the rural provinces are dominated by agricultural activities (see Figure 8.9). Poverty rates are highest in provinces such as Uva and Sabaragamuwa provinces with the highest percentages of agricultural households. Developments in the manufacturing and services sectors and international migration with globalisation have led to a massive labour migration away from agriculture. While the percentage share of labour employed in agriculture has declined from 47 per cent of total employment in 1990 to 36 per cent in 1999, agricultural productivity per worker stagnated around Rs 53 000 (in constant 1996 rupees) over the 1990s decade. Further, Sri Lankan productivities for a large number of agricultural commodities are lower than in many other South and East Asian countries (see World Bank 2003, pp. ix and 12, for details).

Access to human and physical infrastructure can be measured approximately by the human poverty index (HPI). This index has been constructed at provincial and district levels in Sri Lanka in a recent study (UNDP 1998). Conceptually, as considered by this study, 'human poverty is considered to exist if people are deprived of the opportunity to lead a long and healthy life, access information and knowledge through the world of reading and communication and obtain economic and social resources needed to attain a decent standard of living' (UNDP 1998, p. 28). To construct the HPI at provincial and district levels in Sri Lanka, the UNDP study team has covered deprivation in survival, knowledge and access to drinking water, safe sanitation, adequate basic health care and electricity. We use the results of this study to demonstrate disparities between regions and districts in terms of human poverty.

The overall level of human poverty is around 18 per cent in Sri Lanka and this can be considered moderate. However, data given in Table 8.7 on the HPI at provincial and district levels demonstrate that large-scale regional disparities in human poverty exist as emphasised in UNDP (1998). While the HPI is low (13.98) in the Western province (the most urbanised and rich province in Sri Lanka), it is very high in rural and estate provinces such as Uva (27.46), North Central (24.10) and Sabaragamuwa (23.34). Many gainers of globalisation live in the Western province and they have greater access to human and physical infrastructure than people in rural provinces. The results of HPI related to different districts show the existence of significant disparities in human poverty at district level. The HPI ranges from 12 in Gampaha district (in Western province) to 31 in Nuwara Eliya district (in Central province). Rural districts such as Monragala (29), Polonnaruwa (28), Badulla (27), Ratnapura (27) and Kegalle (24) are ranked as poor in terms of human poverty. Thus the degree of variation in human poverty is significant. These province and district level disparities suggest that Sri Lanka has not managed to reduce human poverty evenly using gains from globalisation.

Before concluding this section, it is critical to note one more aspect of globalisation, which cannot be captured properly in the above indices. The material benefits brought about by the opening up of the Sri Lankan economy are well known and these benefits have raised the aspirations of rural youth in particular. Globalisation has led to aggressive consumerism in society after 1977. The modern urban lifestyle has been highly visible in contrast to the traditional rural lifestyle with very basic standards of living.

Table 8.7   The regional pattern of per capita GDP, human development and human poverty in Sri Lanka, 1994

Provinces and their districts	Per capita GDP (Rs)	Human development index	Human poverty index
Western	n.a.	0.864	13.980
Colombo	154 545	0.847	13.016
Gampaha	14 880	0.851	12.040
Kalutara	13 480	0.893	16.208
Central	n.a.	0.727	23.081
Kandy	6 664	0.649	17.391
Matale	1 592	0.727	21.581
Nuwara Eliya	13 987	0.806	30.545
Southern	n.a.	0.728	20.375
Galle	7 125	0.736	18.611
Matara	6 780	0.705	19.324
Hambantota	7 119	0.742	23.333
North Western	n.a.	0.804	21.446
Kurunegala	8 905	0.883	22.215
Puttalam	7 314	0.726	19.048
North Central	n.a.	0.859	24.098
Anuradhapura	10 832	0.854	21.313
Polonnaruwa	9 047	0.865	27.685
Uva	n.a.	0.705	27.463
Badulla	7 742	0.717	27.052
Moneragala	6 659	0.692	28.728
Sabaragamuwa	n.a.	0.746	23.338
Ratnapura	7 315	0.751	25.300
Kegalle	7 062	0.741	24.076
Sri Lanka		0.730	17.756

Note: Northern and Eastern provinces are not included owing to war.

Source: UNDP (1998)

The poor in the rural areas, who have not benefited from globalisation, tend to perceive that the new material gains of globalisation are limited to the urban rich and 'opportunistic and self-serving politicians' (see Dunham and Jayasuriya 2000 for details). As Dunham and Jayasuriya (ibid., p. 107) correctly point out, 'the lower incidence of absolute poverty that has recently been recorded in large-scale surveys seriously understates the frustrations and pressures building up in Sri Lankan society'. As they have further noted, society releases these frustrations and pressures in various forms, such as armed insurrections, communal riots, election related violence, increased levels of crime, increased rates of suicide and desertions from the army.

After the opening up of the economy to the rest of the world in 1977, a new class, what Hettige (1998) labels the New Urban Middle Class (NUMC), emerged. This class includes private sector middle and higher rank executives (most of them educated in English), the upper layer of foreign funded NGOs, high ranking state officials, expatriate skilled and professional workers and other new segments of society who have benefited from economic reforms. This class is different from the traditional middle class that was established for decades. The emergence of private schools (commonly known as international schools) and private educational institutions linked with universities in America, England and Australia has catered to the requirements of the NUMC's children and allowed them to study in English, while the children of the poor have only been educated in *Swebhasha*. While the majority of English-educated, rich children manage to go to Western countries for university education, the children of the poor struggle to get into local universities, owing to the highly competitive environment. Further, it takes a longer time for *Swebhasha*-educated poor children to complete their degrees, owing to student unrest, strikes, closures and disputes between different student groups in local universities. Recent violent activities in local universities are a reflection of local students' frustration and anger. A new phenomenon has emerged to make the situation worse, namely, 'overseas qualifications syndrome'. Both the private and public sectors tend to give priority to overseas-qualified graduates ahead of local graduates, considering their English knowledge, training in Information Technology and, more importantly, political and family connections. This process systematically excludes the bright young children of poor families in both Sinhalese and Tamil communities. This exclusion has given rise to further conflicts and destruction of social capital. In particular, the exclusion of less tolerant young groups has led to conflicts. This situation has emerged partly as a result of globalisation.

CONCLUDING REMARKS

Our descriptive analysis in this chapter suggests that:

- poverty is still a main problem in Sri Lanka and globalisation did not help much to reduce poverty;
- despite the implementation of various poverty alleviation programmes by successive governments from the late 1980s onwards, about 45 per cent of

the Sri Lankan population are poor according to the higher poverty line, that is, US$2 per day (see CBSL 2004, p. 20);

- since Sri Lanka gained independence in 1948 poverty has been a rural phenomenon;
- differences in poverty, income, living conditions and access to physical and human infrastructure that had existed between three sectors (rural, urban and estate) and between regions (provinces and districts) are continuing;
- living conditions and income in some sections of sectors, regions and districts that have had access to new economic opportunities because of globalisation are improving compared with other sections that have been plagued by the lack of new economic opportunities;
- inadequate access to physical and social infrastructure has not been eliminated significantly in Sri Lanka;
- so-called 'trickle-down' effects of the benefits of growth have not been working properly in Sri Lanka towards reducing rural poverty;
- disparities in human poverty at province and district levels suggest that Sri Lanka has not managed to reduce human poverty evenly using gains from globalisation;
- it is important for Sri Lanka to stimulate the rural sector to reduce rural poverty through higher economic growth;
- an increase in agricultural productivity is important to reduce rural poverty.

Even though Sri Lanka was the first country in South Asia to open up its economy to the world economy, it cannot be proud of its record of achievements in reduction of inequality and elimination of poverty over the last two and a half decades. While the Sri Lankan experience under the closed economy indicates that there was a trend of declining inequality within a stable social and political environment, its experience of globalisation suggests that achieving higher economic growth, lowering the unemployment rate and promoting industrialisation are only aggregate benefits of globalisation. A trend of increasing inequality and geographic disparities, together with other social costs, has put pressure on the social and political stability in Sri Lanka in the process of globalisation.

NOTES

1. At the time of the writing of this chapter, the Sri Lankan government and the Liberation Tigers of Tamil Eelam (LTTE) are engaged in a peace process to find a permanent solution to the conflict.
2. For instance, see Gunewardena (2000) and Kelegama (2001).
3. See Gunetilleke (2000) for a discussion on problems related to different poverty estimates.

REFERENCES

Anand S. and C. Harris (1990), 'Food and standard of living: an analysis based on Sri Lanka Data', in J. Dreze and A. Sen (eds), *The Political Economy of Hunger*, Oxford: Oxford University Press, 297–350.

Anand, S. and S.M.R. Kambur (1991), 'Public policy and basic needs provision: intervention and achievement in Sri Lanka', in J. Dreze and A.K. Sen (eds), *The Political Economy of Hunger*, vol. 3, Oxford: Clarendon Press.

Athukorala, P. and S. Jayasuriya (1994), *Macroeconomic Policies, Crises and Growth in Sri Lanka, 1969–90*, Washington, DC: World Bank.

Athukorala, P. and S. Rajapathirana (2000), *Liberalisation and Industrial Transformation: Sri Lanka in International Perspective*, Delhi: Oxford University.

Bhalla, A.S. (ed.) (1998), *Globalisation, Growth and Marginalization*, New York: St. Martin's Press, Inc.

Bhalla S.S. and P. Glewwe (1986), 'Growth and equity in developing countries: a reinterpretation of the Sri Lankan experience', *World Bank Economic Review*, 1 (1), 35–63.

CBSL (Central Bank of Sri Lanka) (1998), *Economic Progress of Independent Sri Lanka*, Colombo: Central Bank of Sri Lanka.

CBSL (Central Bank of Sri Lanka) (2004), *Annual Report 2003*, Colombo: Central Bank of Sri Lanka.

Chen, S and M. Ravallion (2004), 'Welfare impacts of China's accession to the World Trade Organization', *The World Bank Economic Review*, 18 (1), 29–57.

Cuthbertson, A. and P. Athukorala (1991), 'Sri Lanka', in D. Papagergious, A. Choksi and M. Michaely (eds), *Liberalizing Foreign Trade: The Experience of Indonesia, Pakistan and Sri Lanka*, Oxford: Basil Blackwell.

DCS (Department of Census and Statistics) (1993), *Household Income and Expenditure Survey 1990/91*, Final Report, Sri Lanka: Department of Census and Statistics, Ministry of Policy Planning and Implementation

DCS (Department of Census and Statistics) (2003), *Household Income and Expenditure Survey 2002*, Preliminary Report, Colombo: Department of Census and Statistics.

Dollar, D. and A. Kraay (2001a), 'Trade, growth and poverty', paper presented at the World Institute for Development and Economic Research (WIDER) Conference on Economic Growth and Poverty Reduction, Helsinki, 25–26 May.

Dollar, D. and A. Kraay (2001b), 'Trade, growth and poverty', *Finance & Development*, 38 (3), 16–19.

Dunham, D. and S. Jayasuriya (2000), 'Equity, growth and insurrection: liberalization and the welfare debate in contemporary Sri Lanka', *Oxford Development Studies*, 28 (1), 97–110.

Easterly, W. and L. Pritchett (1993), 'The determinants of economic success: luck and policy', *Finance & Development*, **30** (4), 38–41.

Edirisinghe, H. (1990), 'Poverty in Sri Lanka: its extent, distribution and characteristics of the poor', paper submitted to the World Bank for the Sri Lanka Poverty Alleviation and Employment Project, Colombo.

Gunaratne, I. (1985), 'Present status of knowledge on poverty, income distribution and welfare in Sri Lanka: a statistical review', mimeo, Colombo.

Gunetilleke, R. (2000), *Basic MIMAP Poverty Profile: Sri Lanka*, Colombo: Institute of Policy Studies.

Gunewardena, D. (2000), 'Consumption poverty in Sri Lanka, 1985–1996: a profile of poverty based on household survey data', mimeo, April.

Hettige, S. (1998), 'Introduction: youth, nation-state and globalisation', in S.T. Hettige (ed.), *Globalization, Social Change and Youth*, Colombo: Karunaratne and Sons, pp. 1–11.

Isenman, P. (1980), 'Basic needs: the case of Sri Lanka', *World Development*, **8** (3), 237–58.

Kelegama, S. (2000), 'Development in independent Sri Lanka: what went wrong?', *Economic and Political Weekly*, **35** (17), 1477–90.

Kelegama, S. (2001), 'Poverty situation and policy in Sri Lanka', paper presented at the Asian and Pacific Forum on Poverty: reforming policies and institutions for poverty reduction, Manila: Asian Development Bank.

Lakshman, W.D. (1997), 'Income distribution and poverty', in W.D. Lakshman (ed.), *Dilemma of Development: Fifty Years of Economic Change in Sri Lanka*, Colombo: Sri Lanka Association of Economists, pp. 121–222.

Lubker, M., G. Smith and J. Weeks (2002), 'Growth and the poor: a comment on Dollar and Kraay', *Journal of International Development*, **14**, 555–71.

Marga Institute (1981), *An Analytical Description of Poverty in Sri Lanka*, Colombo: Marga Institute.

Masson, P. (2001), 'Globalisation: facts and figures', IMF Policy Discussion Paper, PDP/01/4, Washington, DC: IMF.

Mutaliph, T.M.Z., D. Wasantha and A.D. Bandaranayake (2001, 2002), 'A provisional estimation and analysis of regional economic activity in Sri Lanka (1996–2000)', *Staff Studies*, **31** and **32**, 1–14.

Ravallion, M. (2001), 'Growth, inequality and poverty: looking beyond averages', *World Development*, **29** (11), 1803–15.

Sahn, D.E. (1984), *Food Consumption Pattern and Parameters in Sri Lanka: the causes and control of malnutrition*, Washington, DC: Food Policy Research Institute.

Sen, A.K. (1981), 'Public action and the quality of life in developing countries', *Oxford Bulletin of Economics and Statistics*, **43** (4), 287–319.

Snodgrass, D. (1999), 'The economic development of Sri Lanka: a tale of missed opportunities', in R. Rotberg (ed.), *Creating Peace in Sri Lanka: Civil War and Reconciliation*, Washington, DC: Brookings Institution Press, pp. 89–107.

Stiglitz, J.E. (2002), *Globalisation and Its Discontents*, New York: W.W. Norton and Company.

Streeten, P. (1979), 'From growth to basic needs', *Finance & Development*, **16** (3), 28–31.

Tudawe, I. (2000), 'Review of poverty related data and data sources in Sri Lanka', MIMAP Sri Lanka Series No. 4, Colombo: Institute of Policy Studies.

UNDP (1998), *National Human Development Report 1998: Regional Dimensions of Human Development*, Colombo: UNDP.

Visaria, P. (1981), 'Some aspects of relative poverty in Sri Lanka 1960–1970', World Bank Staff Paper No. 461, Washington, DC: World Bank.

Wade, R.H. (2002), 'Globalisation, poverty and income distribution: does the Liberal argument hold?', paper presented to the Reserve Bank of Australia Conference on Globalisation, Living Standards and Inequality: Recent Progress and Continuing Challenge, Canberra, 27–28 May.

Wei, S.-J. (2002), 'Is globalisation good for the poor in China?', *Finance & Development*, **39** (3), 26–9.

World Bank (2000), 'Sri Lanka – recapturing missed opportunities', Report No. 20430-CE, Washington, DC: World Bank.

World Bank (2003), 'Sri Lanka: promoting agricultural and rural non-farm sector growth', Report No. 25387-CE, Washington, DC: World Bank.

9. It's the government, stupid! Globalisation, government and equality in Australia

Tom Conley

INTRODUCTION

From the perspective of many policy-makers, business people and commentators, Australia's embrace of globalisation and economic liberalism has been an unequivocal success.[1] Australian Prime Minister John Howard (2003b) declared that:

> We are now in the 12th unbroken year of economic growth. Australia is now experiencing what I can without any fear of contradiction describe as the longest, unbroken period of economic growth since the late 1960s. In many ways Australia is now enjoying the best economic period that our country has seen since the end of World War II. The growth of the last 12 years is more soundly based and in many ways more meritorious than the long economic growth of the 1950s and 1960s ... We now have an economy which is operating in a competitive global environment.

In terms of growth, the story is an accurate one: the Australian economy grew by 51 per cent between June 1991 and June 2003.[2] There is, however, another, darker side to the story. Despite the long period of growth, inequality is increasing in Australia. This rising inequality presents a problem for those propounding the success story of globalisation and liberalisation because it makes clear that changes in economic and social policy since the 1980s have produced losers as well as winners.

For some, the less benign assessment is either premature or irrelevant. They argue that either the benefits of increased growth resulting from liberal policy changes will eventually improve the lot of most citizens or inequality is simply an unfortunate by-product of otherwise necessary policy changes. As senior Howard Government Minister Tony Abbot reveals, 'The other thing we have to face up to is that in the end we have to be a productive and competitive society and greater inequality might be inevitable'.[3] Rather than increasing inequality being a problem, it is viewed as an unavoidable component of efficient and globalised capitalism. The costs of doing something to seriously address inequality would be too high in a globalising world economy.[4]

Globalisation can provide a simple explanation for the rise in inequality in developed countries. Both proponents and opponents of globalisation make such arguments. Proponents argue that globalisation is a marker of a changed and constantly changing world, where the past goal of government to redistribute equitably the fruits of growth is no longer possible or even desirable. Instead, garnering growth in a globalised economy means governments must intervene less in market processes.[5] Opponents argue that globalisation increases inequality and that better outcomes are only possible if countries take a step back from globalisation and liberal capitalism.[6] Many others, less certain about costs and benefits, still believe that governments are increasingly constrained by global developments and forces.[7]

The idea of globalisation has become a framework for understanding a whole range of trends in the domestic and international spheres. It can be seen as a set of material developments whose causes lie in inextricably intertwined political, economic, cultural and technological processes. Globalisation, however, is much more than this. It is also an ideological construction that is used to explain and justify domestic and international developments and the way they interact. Globalisation is both a process and a contestable concept.[8] To understand the effect of globalisation on social outcomes, therefore, requires a consideration of both its ideological dimensions and its material underpinnings.

The relationship of globalisation to social outcomes in developed countries has sparked a large literature across sociology,[9] political economy,[10] political science[11] and economics.[12] Much of this literature is empirically based and often attempts to isolate the impact of finance, investment and trade on social outcomes. The aim of this chapter is to augment this empirical story by considering the wider discursive impact of globalisation and its relationship to domestic politics and policy inaction. The chapter makes a case for the significance of the *discourse* of globalisation, particularly the rhetoric of constraint, for outcomes.[13] Despite much evidence that globalisation does not lead to government powerlessness, the assessment that it does carries much weight in business, government and media circles (Watson and Hay 2003). The pessimistic appraisal of governmental capacities fits well with an economic liberal agenda of limited government.

The chapter makes a series of connected claims. Firstly, the policy response to the related issues of globalisation and the structural inadequacies of the Australian economy may have led to a more dynamic economy and economic growth, but it has also been accompanied by an increase in inequality in Australia. Secondly, although globalisation in the form of finance and trade has placed significant pressures on policy-making, it has also provided an important explanation of, and justification for, the rise in inequality. In Australia and elsewhere, globalisation has been the essential component in the explanation of why governments must limit their role. Thirdly, globalisation and liberalisation have not led to a reduction in the size of government, in terms of taxation and spending, thus indicating the general possibilities of increasing social spending and other programmes and policies that could improve social outcomes.

The chapter proceeds by briefly outlining the context of the restructuring of the Australian political economy before assessing poverty and inequality in Australia. This is followed by an analysis of the diverse ways globalisation affects outcomes in developed countries. The chapter then shifts to an examination of the continuing role of government and the domestic sources of inequality.

THE RESTRUCTURING OF THE AUSTRALIAN POLITICAL ECONOMY

Australia's fate has always been comprehensively shaped by developments in the world political economy. Throughout the twentieth century, Australia developed a protective policy structure that aimed to deal with problems associated with Australia's position in the world economy. While motivations of policy-makers and voters varied, the aim was to redistribute Australia's resource wealth to the population through the protection of manufacturing industries. It was these industries that provided employment and higher wages, giving rise to what Castles (1985) has called the 'wage earners' welfare state'. The protectionist policy structure enjoyed bipartisan support until the 1960s, when the white Australia policy began to be seen as unequivocally racist, Britain abandoned Australia for the European Economic Community, tariff protectionism was increasingly attacked by economists as an inefficient and inappropriate tool for industrial development, and the industrial relations and welfare systems were criticised by both the Right and the Left as either too restrictive and costly or not comprehensive enough.

The Whitlam Government challenged industry protectionism by cutting tariffs by 25 per cent in 1973. In response to the economic crisis of the mid-1970s, however, first his government and then its conservative successor reinforced the idea that protectionism was the fallback solution to Australia's economic woes. The Liberal Prime Minister, Malcolm Fraser, may have been seen as Australia's equivalent to Margaret Thatcher at the time, but he still supported a heavily regulated and protected Australian capitalism, as had his conservative forebears. Fraser and many others believed that primary resources would continue to provide for Australian abundance.

Confronting the structural and cyclical economic crises of the early 1980s, the Hawke Labor Government turned to economic liberalism. It increasingly gave greater scope to market forces and imposed adjustment on business, workers and the wider Australian community through the liberalisation of trade, financial and industrial relations regulations, privatisation, and competition reforms. The uncompromising embrace of economic liberalism by the Liberal–National Coalition Opposition during the 1980s and early 1990s helped the Labor Government to appear moderate in comparison, even whilst radically restructuring the Australian political economy. Bipartisanship gave the Labor leadership leeway to embrace policies that were anathema to many of its traditional supporters, who were concerned, among other things, about rising inequality (Conley 1999, Ch. 5).

Labor claimed that increasing income inequality was a global development and that it had done much to ameliorate the worst effects of this structural change. The outcomes, it argued, were much better than would have been the case if the Coalition had been in office. In relation to the gap between the rich and poor, Keating explicitly made the point:

> Yes, the gap has widened, but nothing like it would have widened . . . This is now an international country and the wage spectrum reflects that which exists in a lot of other countries . . . but what we have done, unlike the United States, unlike . . . the Thatcher's Britain which John Howard would seek to emulate, or Ronald Reagan's America, we have brought the bottom two income deciles . . . up immeasurably. (cited in Taylor 1995)[14]

In other words, Labor had succeeded where governments in other countries had failed: it had managed the transition to increased economic and social polarisation more fairly.

Since coming to office in 1996, the Howard Liberal–National Coalition Government has not enjoyed the same level of policy bipartisanship that Labor did in government. Alongside the lessons learned from losing the supposedly unlosable election in 1993 under John Hewson, the lack of support from Labor and minor parties in the Senate has forced the Howard Government to modify many of its policy preferences, especially in the areas of industrial relations, health and welfare policy. Changes in these areas have also forced the Government to take account of widespread opposition to continuing reform. Despite these difficulties, the overall thrust of Coalition policy has undoubtedly been a consolidation and extension of Labor's liberalising and globalising agenda. The Howard Government has further liberalised the industrial relations system, extended privatisation, shifted the focus of the tax system from direct to indirect taxation, and rationalised the welfare system and made it more punitive. In social and health policy, the Coalition appears to be waiting for the opportunity to extend its programme of reform.

Despite differences in emphasis, there is a new bipartisanship in Australian economic policy – economic liberal rather than protectionist. The election of a Labor Government could involve the development of a more elaborate and protective social policy framework to accompany the current policy direction. A change in government, however, would not result in the de-globalisation of the Australian economy. Neither political party in Australia advocates a shift in direction away from economic liberal globalisation. The new policy consensus does not yet have the universality of the protectionist consensus that existed for most of the twentieth century. Although there has been much popular concern about the course of policy in the last 20 years, there is no political force that is currently capable of challenging the new orthodoxy. What does exist is a rearguard action, a conservatism of the Left and Right, to maintain traditions of Australian egalitarianism in the face of far-reaching economic and social policy changes.

One reason for the failure to generate a new society-wide consensus is the perceived negative effects of the economic liberal changes associated with globalisation. To assess the validity of these perceptions it is pertinent to examine social outcomes in Australia and determine whether inequality has indeed increased.

ASSESSMENT OF INEQUALITY AND POVERTY IN AUSTRALIA

There is much controversy about the measurement of inequality and poverty in Australia.[15] In a period of fundamental structural change, it would be surprising if there were not substantial changes to social outcomes. Governments throughout the developed world have aimed to increase the outward orientation of their economies and to maintain low inflation. There has been a general shift in attitude of even supposed left-wing governments to unequivocal support for business and, in particular, profitability.

On a broad level, there has been a significant shift in the wage to profit ratio (see Figure 9.1). The share of wages in total factor income was 54.4 per cent in 2002–03 compared with 61.5 per cent in 1974–75. The share of profits was 25.0 per cent in 2002–03, the highest level since 1959–60 (ABS 2003c). These shifts were engineered by the Labor Government with the active participation of the union leadership in Australia (Dabscheck 1995).[16] The explicit aim of Labor through its Accord with the Australian Council of Trade Unions was to lower real wages in Australia in exchange for social and taxation advantages for workers.[17] This effectively meant that social outcomes were, to a greater extent, directly reliant on government. This change occurred at the same time as policy-makers were arguing that government was being forced to do less. There is significant doubt that Labor sufficiently compensated for declining real wages.

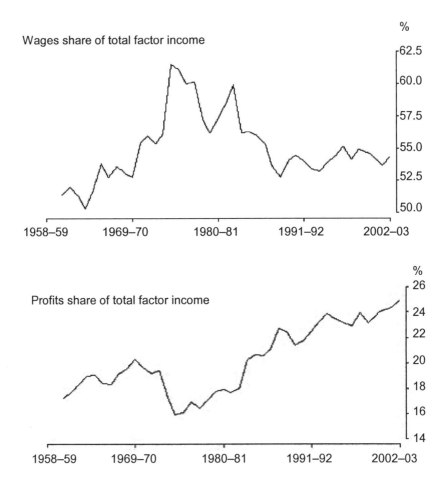

Source: ABS (2003), *Australian System of National Accounts 2002–03* (5204.0)

Figure 9.1   Wages and profits shares of total factor income

An analysis of the academic literature reveals wide-ranging and often contradictory assessments of what has happened to the detail of social outcomes in recent years. Such polarisation of assessments is evidenced by two accounts of poverty in Australia in the 1990s. A Smith Family/NATSEM[18] study led by Harding found that poverty had increased from 11.3 per cent to 13.0 per cent during the 1990s (Harding et al. 2001). Researchers for the Centre for Independent Studies (CIS) criticised this report for assessing poverty on the basis of a figure of half of average income (Tsumori et al. 2002). The half average measure is more indicative of inequality and leads to a higher poverty figure because higher incomes have been rising much faster than lower incomes. However, as Harding (2002) points out, using the CIS's preferred figure of half of median income still produced an increase from 8.2 per cent to 8.7 per cent. Saunders and Tsumori (2002) from the CIS freely admit that inequality has risen but argue that 'the poor don't get poorer simply because a few people get richer'.

There are undoubtedly a wide variety of ways to measure poverty and inequality. Harding et al. (2001, pp. 18–19) canvass a range of measures and find that, on 12 different measures, poverty rose in 11 of them. Particularly significant is the measure of poverty including the cost of housing, which increased the poverty rate to 17.5 per cent. The official assessment of income inequality by the Australian Bureau of Statistics (ABS) since 1994–95 has gone from 'no significant change' to 'some possible rise in income inequality' (ABS 2001, 2003e).[19] Interrogating the most recent ABS figures, Saunders (2003, p. 7) argues that there has been a significant rise in inequality. Depending on the methodology used, it is evident that despite real disposable incomes increasing across the board, income inequality fell between 1994–95 and 1995–96 and then increased. From 1994–95, mean income in the top quintile increased by $111 a week – more than eight times the increase of $13 a week in the lowest quintile. Since 1995–96 'almost half (47.3 per cent) of all the income produced by a growing economy was received by those in the top quintile'.[20] As Saunders (ibid., p. 9) points out, considerable scope existed for the Howard Government 'to improve the living standards of those at the bottom of the income distribution by putting a break on the large increases that have gone to those at the top'. It is clear that 'some dimensions of inequality have grown faster since the mid-1990s than during the 1980s' (Saunders 2003, p. 16). The major difference between the 1980s and the mid- to late-1990s is that the middle (the third and fourth) quintiles have seen their declining income shares halted.

The CIS researchers point out that income statistics do not match consumption figures, providing evidence, they suggest, of the under-reporting of incomes. As Krugman (2002) points out, however, under-reporting of incomes does not just apply to the 'poor'. Barrett et al. (2000, pp. 116–38) argue that to get a better understanding of inequality it is necessary to focus on consumption rather than income because 'utility is typically defined over consumption rather than income and ... resources consumed in a period are not necessarily the same as those received in a period'.[21] Their study period covers 1975 to 1993 and they find that, although under this measure inequality was less than for income, it had still risen. There are also, of course, problems with consumption/expenditure measures. Saunders (2004, p. 12) proposes that a more satisfactory approach may be to combine income and expenditure measures into what he calls a 'restrictive core poverty approach'. Under this approach, the level of poverty is halved, but differences between family types 'are more pronounced'. Another possibility is to 'incorporate direct observations on deprivation' (Saunders 2004, p. 17).

Saunders (2003, p. 16) argues that there seems to be a lack of concern in Australia about rising inequality. He posits three possible explanations: firstly, statistical issues have blurred the picture of inequality; secondly, there has been a 'generalised growth in real incomes since 1994–95'; and thirdly, the 'free market, pro-choice ideology of the Howard Government ... has detracted attention away from what has been happening to outcomes'. He asserts, perhaps hopefully, that the most likely explanation is the lack of clear data.

Many Australians have done well in the restructured Australian economy and it is to be expected that such 'winners' will be supporters of the economic liberal direction of policy. There is evidence to suggest, however, that Australians are worried about the rise in inequality. Pusey (2003) contends that many middle-class Australians have significant concerns about the direction of policy and outcomes.[22] In 2000 Newspoll reported that 83 per cent of people surveyed believed that 'the rich are getting richer, and the poor are getting poorer' and 70 per cent said that 'they would prefer the gap between rich and poor to get smaller, compared with 28 per cent who would rather see the overall wealth of Australia grow as quickly as possible'. A majority believed that the distribution of wealth was less fair than it was in 1990, compared with 10 per cent who believed it was fairer (Steketee 2000b).[23] Such figures give some indication, at least in principle, of the desire for greater equality in the Australian community.

Others argue that rising inequality is not necessarily a problem. Edwards (2000, p. 55) maintains, 'increasing inequality is not of itself a bad thing, if even the poorest are markedly better off as a result of the forces that have made the rich richer'. Secretary to the Treasury, Ken Henry (2002, pp. 31–2), argues that rising inequality should not be seen as a problem for policy-makers:

even supposing income inequality had increased slightly over the second half of the 1990s, should this be of concern to economic policy makers? The answer to this question is not clear-cut. Importantly, there is no clear consensus on what an acceptable level of inequality is ... Moreover, the policy lesson to be drawn from a reform-induced widening of income inequality is not obvious. Policy makers are very likely to believe that the market liberalising reforms of the past couple of decades in Australia have contributed to rising average incomes, and that the income gains have been widely shared. Is anybody seriously suggesting that those reforms should be reversed, in the certain expectation of significantly reduced average incomes and the highly speculative hope of a more egalitarian distribution of a smaller cake?

The Howard Government also aims to downgrade concerns about poverty by arguing that, because poverty is not increasing significantly, no government action is required. In dismissing the findings of a Senate Inquiry into Poverty that concluded that 3.5 million Australians live in poverty, Howard (2004b) explained that:

There is little doubt that the low levels of unemployment Australia is now enjoying mean that more and more people have work. That doesn't mean that there aren't people who are living in poverty. It doesn't mean that there aren't people who are missing out, if I can use that expression. Of course there are. But it's very important to get this income distribution thing in perspective. To the extent that any gaps have widened, it has been that people at the top – there are more of them, and they're doing better. It's not that there has been an inadequacy of support at the bottom. It's fair to say that the rich have got richer, but the poor have not got poorer.[24]

This assumes that existing levels of poverty were, and are, not a problem; that those slightly above poverty lines are living adequately by community standards; that prices of essential services have not increased faster than wages; that housing affordability has not shifted many out of areas they would like to live; and so on.

The contention of many others is that, while poverty may be of some concern, inequality is not. But perceptions of poverty are closely related to inequality: what is available to the majority of citizens shapes perceptions of deprivation. Poverty, even in an 'absolute' sense, is 'relative' over time and space. For example, absolute poverty today in Australia is different from what it was 50 years ago, and there are differences between rural and urban Australia and between Australia and sub-Saharan Africa. Most importantly, rising inequality is a problem because it divides societies and opens up the possibilities of eventual reactionary responses to economic and social problems.

Despite Henry's concern about reversing the direction of policy and the mooted 70 per cent who would prefer slower growth if it produced better social outcomes, advocating greater equality does not imply being in favour of slowing the growth process. Rather, *the major concern is that the growth should lead to lower levels of poverty and inequality*. Opponents of economic liberal reforms argue that policy changes made in response to structural economic weaknesses and globalisation have led to an increase in inequality and to increased insecurity for those less able to take advantage of the opportunities provided by liberalisation. They argue that attempts to compensate the losers, so integral to Labor's reform agenda, have been inadequate.

Saunders (2003, p. 9) alleges that supporters of liberal policy changes, such as Henry, imply that attempts to improve social outcomes have a negative effect on growth and that therefore a bit of inequality can help to increase the growth rate. He counters that 'The view that growth in inequality has been the *only* (or even primary) cause of Australia's economic growth thus seems highly implausible, lending weight to the argument that Australia could have chosen less inequality if it had wanted'. It is this view, however, that economic liberals dispute, pointing to the 'new realities' of globalisation. Just what these impacts are continues to be contentious.

IMPACTS OF GLOBALISATION ON INEQUALITY

Just as there is some agreement that inequality (although not poverty) has risen in Australia, '[t]here is a broad consensus that income inequality has risen in OECD countries since 1980' (Weller and Hersh 2002, p. 6). There is, however, no consensus over the culpability of globalisation in this rising inequality and about the possibilities of government ameliorating negative social outcomes. What is the relationship between globalisation and growth? Does increased trade bolster growth and therefore lower poverty? What about investment? What is the role of technological change and should it be regarded as intricately related to the process of globalisation? Should the focus be on trade, finance and investment or on the impact of liberalisation? In sum, the major issue is how to assess whether globalisation is the causal variable. There are a number of ways to measure the impact of globalisation and how we define globalisation is obviously going to have significance for our perception of its impact.

Dollar and Kraay (2002) argue that in the developing world increased trade has spurred growth, which has in turn reduced poverty and inequality.[25] Weller and Hersh (2002, pp. 1, 16) argue to the contrary that 'trade in a more deregulated environment lowers the income share of the poor' and that capital and current account liberalisation has 'hurt the poor'. Lundberg and Squire find that greater openness to trade is correlated negatively with income growth among the poorest 40 per cent of the population, but strongly and positively with income growth for all other groups, in a sample of 38 countries between 1965 and 1992. The costs of adjustment are borne exclusively by the poor, regardless of how long the adjustment takes.[26]

Reuveny and Li (2003, pp. 577–83, 593–4) argue that globalisation and democracy should be studied together to understand income inequality. Based on reviews of the literature, their initial hypotheses are that more democracy should lower inequality, that trade and investment should increase inequality in developed countries and lower it in developing countries, and that foreign financial capital should increase inequality because countries engage in liberal reforms to attract capital. They find that 'democracy reduces the level of income inequality . . . trade openness is associated with more equitable income redistribution within countries, FDI is associated with greater income inequality, and foreign financial capital inflows have no statistically significant effect on income inequality'. Their overall contention is that 'economic openness may improve or worsen income inequality, depending on its type'. The most important factor in doing something about inequality remains government action.

Alderson and Nielsen (2002, pp. 1246, 1284, 1286–8) investigate the relationship of globalisation to the 'great U-turn' in 16 OECD countries. They argue that the 'recent experience of some industrial societies suggests radical reversal of the Kuznetsian scenario of the declining inequality with development'. They find that between 1967 and 1992 'direct investment and North–South trade have played a role in the determination of income inequality. Our results suggest likewise for immigration.' They argue that their findings give credence to arguments that globalisation increases inequality by exacerbating deindustrialisation, weakening labour bargaining power, expanding the percentage of income going to capital and intensifying the divide between skilled and unskilled labour. They also argue that for the OECD countries as a whole, the 'strongest effect on inequality corresponds to [the percentage of the] labour force in agriculture . . . The next two most important factors are institutional: union density and decommodification . . . Next come two globalization factors: southern import penetration and [FDI] outflow.' However, they contend that globalisation is a more important factor in explaining inequality over time within countries that experienced a rise in inequality: 'Thus for countries that experienced an inequality upturn during the period, the upward inequality trend may be attributable in substantial part to aspects of globalization we have distinguished, primarily North–South trade and FDI outflow, and to a lesser extent immigration.'

Moller et al. (2003, p. 39) disagree that globalisation is a significant factor, contending that developing country exports, capital mobility and immigration do not 'explain variations in poverty rates across [advanced capitalist] countries during the latter third of the twentieth century'. Their study considers pre- and post-tax/transfer poverty. They avow the importance of de-industrialisation and unemployment in pre-tax/transfer poverty and the significance of welfare state generosity and constitutional structure in post-tax/transfer poverty. In conclusion, they stress

> the importance of polity in reducing levels of poverty, which is largely created by economic structures ... the more generous the welfare state, the greater is the extent of poverty reduction. In addition, long-term incumbency of left parties affects poverty reduction positively by giving the tax and transfer system a particularly redistributive profile. (ibid., p. 44)

What these perhaps obvious conclusions highlight is something that is often submerged in the globalisation debate – explicit efforts to reduce poverty continue to make a difference. Popular support for parties with the goal of redistribution continues to matter.

Galbraith (2002), however, holds that it is global factors rather than national economic policies that have exacerbated inequality. He contends that neither growth of trade nor accelerating technological change are responsible: 'the evidence of timing points toward the effect of rising real interest rates and the debt crisis. For this the stage was set by the dissolution of the Bretton Woods framework of fixed but adjustable exchange rates and international supervision of capital flow'. Such trends, he contends, were made worse by the 'triumph of neoliberalism' (ibid. 2002). But how should the triumph of neoliberalism be seen? Though its rise has been a global phenomenon, the extent of its adoption has differed remarkably between countries, as has the extent to which policies have been accompanied by efforts to compensate the losers of policy changes. In this sense neoliberalism should be seen as a domestic rather than a global factor.

As many writers point out, the problem occurs in determining the direct impact of globalisation: correlations are no proof of causation. Lundberg and Milanovic (2000) argue, 'whether inequality goes up or down while globalisation proceeds is no proof of causality'. Smeeding (2002) also maintains that 'globalisation is one force among many which accounts for widening income inequalities in the rich countries of the OECD'. He highlights the fact that

> social policies, wage distributions, time worked, social and labour market institutions, and demographic differences all have some influence on why there are large differences in inequality among rich nations at any point in time. In contrast, trade policy has not been shown to have any major impact on economic inequality.

According to Dollar and Kraay (2004), there is 'no evidence whatsoever of a systematic relationship between changes in trade and changes in inequality'. Henry (2002, p. 15) also argues the case for uncertainty about the relationship: 'Even the direction of the impact of globalisation on income distribution before taxes and transfers is not clear cut, depending on the country's starting point, its comparative advantages, and the nature of its international economic links.' Many of the same authors, however, appear keen to claim at other times a role for globalisation in reducing poverty and inequality.[27]

Adding further to the difficulties of assessing the relationship between globalisation and social outcomes is the fact that the impacts of globalisation may not always be directly measurable. For example, while it is possible to measure the impact of capital account liberalisation on inequality within nations (Weller and Hersh 2002), it is more difficult to measure the wider impact of financial globalisation on the policy-making process. How do we measure the impact of financial market preferences on government policies and in turn on social policy? Global financial markets have a huge impact on a wide range of policies and attitudes about the viability of redistribution (Conley 1996; Argy 1995; CEDA 1998).

Governments have been increasingly pressured to avoid policies that cause negative financial market reactions and exacerbate volatility, because instability in capital and foreign exchange markets can create difficulties for governments and firms alike. Rising interest rates deter investment and excessive exchange volatility may discourage exporters, especially smaller companies and those without financial expertise. Adverse reactions in financial markets can severely impair the benefits of expansionary policies, especially in relation to the costs of borrowing. In general, financial market pressures have helped to bolster domestic claims about the need for lower taxation on capital gains and higher incomes and for cutting government spending, especially on policies of redistribution and social services.

Milner and Keohane (1996) argue that financial market concerns about Left-wing programmes act to limit the ability of Leftist governments to extend borrowing to a greater extent than governments of the Right. This explains why social democratic governments have often been so keen to court and give advantage to financial market actors. Many economic policy-makers and commentators see the discipline of a globalised financial system as an unequivocally positive development, forcing governments to abandon 'unsustainable' policies. This argument has been well used in Australia.[28] Supporters of financial discipline can even see irrational financial reactions as beneficial if they force governments to abandon 'inappropriate' policy choices. The persuasive substance of financial market discipline is well illustrated by Kelly's (1994, p. 220) description of the government's reaction to the 1986 currency crisis:

> The currency crisis hit Australia on Monday 28 July when the ERC ministers[29] were finalising the budget. Keating had his little Reuters screen on the cabinet table and kept pointing to the falling $A rate ... The cabinet was infiltrated by a distinct mood of panic. Keating's banana republic warning had never seemed so real ... The response took two forms – immediate and budgetary ... [I]t was decided that Keating would announce his more liberal foreign investment policy, ease the withholding tax provision, and that the Reserve would throw a lot of money to hold the dollar rate. It was Keating who synthesised these responses. The upshot was a stabilisation of the currency and a gradual rise ... At the same time the crisis led Hawke and Keating to reopen the budget deliberations to tighten fiscal policy even further.

Financial pressures have been seen as particularly important in the short-term disciplining of government and economic actors in relation to fiscal and monetary policies and also in relation to industrial relations and competition policy more generally.

Unequivocal assertions about the increasing disciplinary effects of international finance on states are complicated, however, by the fact that the ratio of rich-country government debt to GDP has expanded enormously during the supposed era of financial discipline (*Economist* 2004).[30] Increased financial market discipline on the expansion of public debt in OECD countries has just not happened. Australia's debt to GDP ratio has fallen markedly during the years of the Howard Government to 3 per cent, after reaching a high of 19.1 per cent of GDP in 1995–96 (Treasury 2004, p. 2.10) (see Figures 9.2 and 9.3). While there are many benefits of a low level of debt, the current low level of debt provides possibilities for significant new spending on improving social outcomes, if that were to be a goal of government.

The increase in debt levels in many countries indicates that increased levels of spending have been possible. Even if expansionary policies were constrained, it would still be possible to redistribute wealth within a tighter fiscal framework. Conceptions of policy autonomy have shifted in response to the changing financial environment, but, rather than being outrightly constrained by financial globalisation, governments continue to make trade-offs between financial stability and domestic priorities.

Constructions of trade and investment competition have also been used to argue that governments should be more liberal and more disciplined in all areas of policy, which generally means they should spend less on redistribution. Trade pressures have been used to make the case that protections for workers need to be downgraded and minimum wages abandoned. Undoubtedly there is much evidence to suggest that trade liberalisation in Australia has led to a more dynamic, trade-focused economy: productivity growth has been significant and exports have expanded from around 15 per cent of GDP, for the 20 years between 1960 and 1980, to over 20 per cent in recent years (ABS 2003a). Freer trade brings many benefits to an economy, but it has many short-term and conspicuous costs. Increased competitive pressures lead to continual pressures for governments, industries and workers to adjust, but do not compel a reduction in the role of the state.

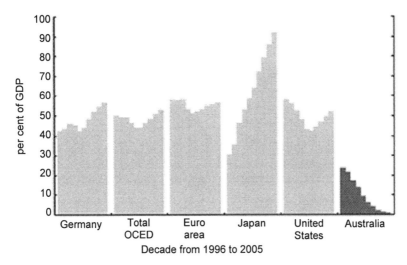

Source: Treasury (2004) *Budget Paper No. 1*, Canberra, Commonwealth of Australia, p. 1.6, available at www.budget.gov.au/2004-05/bp1/download/bst1.pdf

Figure 9.2 General government net debt levels in selected countries

States continue to mediate the effects of the world political economy and to shape the competitiveness of the domestic economic environment and firms. As Evans (1997) attests, 'Existing cross-national statistics suggest that greater reliance on trade is associated with an increased role for the state rather than a diminished one.' Indeed, he argues, the evidence appears to run the other way: significant state involvement 'may even be a competitive advantage in a globalized economy'.[31] By providing infrastructure, education, training and health care, research and development support, effective legal structures and various types of industry assistance, states can bolster the competitiveness of firms. Further, as UNCTAD (1994) acknowledges, it is 'through national institutions that the potential gains (or losses) from increased international economic integration are distributed'. Trade competition does not force governments to cut social spending. In fact, spending may help to compensate the losers from reforms and buttress support for trade openness. Government actions can ameliorate the negative impacts of the reforms that deliver improved trade performance. Efforts are not likely to be made, however, if it is believed that globalisation makes increased spending counterproductive, unviable or a restriction on growth.

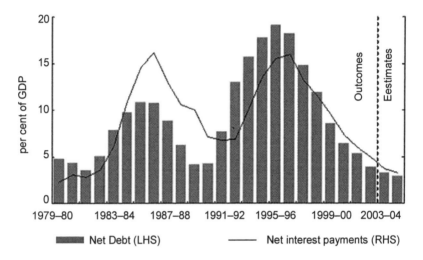

Source: Treasury (2004) *Budget Paper No. 1*, Canberra, Commonwealth of Australia, p. 2.10, available at www.budget.gov.au/2004-05/bp1/download/bst2.pdf

Figure 9.3   Australian general government sector net debt and net interest payments

What is clear from the above review is the uncertain nature of the effects of globalisation on social outcomes. Differing aspects of globalisation have varying effects, but all are mediated through the framework of the domestic political economy. It is government that shapes the impact of globalisation, but this fact has often been overlooked in Australian debates about the impact of the international political economy.

GLOBALISATION, GOVERNMENT AND INEQUALITY IN AUSTRALIA

There is no doubt that rich countries like Australia can afford to abolish poverty. The financial cost of doing so represents only a small fraction of our national income or gross domestic product . . . Even an exaggerated estimate of the poverty gap thus represents less than 2.4 per cent of GDP, with the true figure probably below 2 per cent. We can thus pay to remove all Australians from poverty if we want to: the fact that we don't do so is a matter of choice, not affordability. (Saunders 2004, p. 2)

The idea of globalisation has dominated debates about Australian political economy in recent years.[32] Reflecting trends in the international literature, many accounts have treated globalisation as a clear imperative forcing economic liberal policy change and an acceptance that governments should or must do less to structure egalitarian social outcomes. The impact of globalisation is seen as divorced from what happens in the domestic polity – that it is a new structural reality to which domestic politics reacts. This position is a form of (global) economic determinism, which downgrades the importance of domestic policy choices at the expense of an accurate analysis of the interaction between the state and international and domestic level variables.

Kelly (1994, p. 2) argues that certainty for Australians, represented by the protectionist policy structure, is gone forever because of developments in the world economy. Although there were policy choices to be made, there was no 'real' choice: the progressive embrace of economic liberalism was unavoidable (ibid., p. 209). The forces of the world political economy made economic liberal policy change inevitable and, once enacted, irreversible. Studies by Catley (1996) and Bryan and Rafferty (1999) see policy change in Australia in a similar manner – as a response to the imperatives of global accumulation. Catley's argument is that the Labor Government finally pushed Australia to accept the inevitable outcome of global processes. Bryan and Rafferty (1999, p. xiv) have a different, but equally determinist, view of globalisation. They see the intensification of globalisation and the shift to economic liberalism as involving 'a limitation on the state's capacity to effect desired national outcomes', meaning that policy-makers are incapable of delivering 'systematic outcomes'. For them, domestic politics has become insignificant. Although the global-determinist view has been widespread in academic and journalistic analyses, perhaps the biggest proponents of the argument have been the policy-makers themselves.

Globalisation, constructed as an overwhelming constraint on all areas of policy, is useful for governments and interest groups that want to reduce the role of government in improving social outcomes. The 'domestic politics of globalisation' in Australia has involved efforts by policy-makers to open Australia to world political economic pressures and force domestic economic and political adjustment (Conley 2001). With assistance from a loose coalition of supporters of globalisation and economic liberalism, policy-makers have increasingly sold the message that there is a distinct limit to what government and the wider political process can achieve.

Political rhetoric has aimed to lower popular expectations about what is politically possible in a globalising world economy. The Howard Government has been adamant that in a globalising world economy, government must play a limited role in the determination of social outcomes. Howard argues that Australia 'needs a new style of government, one which acts strongly within the realms of the possible, one with a disposition towards individuals finding their own solutions . . . Only in this way will we have the strength to face the future, to face the challenges of globalisation.'[33]

Globalisation emerges as a framework within which all arguments about activist government can be confronted. The discourse of global constraint and state powerlessness is significant and needs to be considered together with the material process of globalisation itself. Authoritative pronouncements and comprehensive efforts to persuade have important impacts in and of themselves, but dominant interpretations can also act in a self-fulfilling way as policy decisions based on such interpretations transform policy structures and coerce adaptation (Conley 2004). As governments act as though globalisation makes it more difficult to improve social outcomes, the result, unsurprisingly, is poorer outcomes. Such attitudes also contribute to greater acceptance of rising inequality as a natural phenomenon in a globalising world economy.

What governments say – the rhetoric they use, the overall discourses they contribute to – has a profound impact on the way debates are framed. The attitudes of policy-makers to the sources of poverty and inequality are pivotal to whether efforts are made to improve social outcomes for the poor. Alongside contentions about global constraints are efforts to blame the poor for their plight. Criticism of the unemployed as 'job snobs', indolent or responsible for their own fate helps to reinforce prejudices against the less fortunate. Such rhetoric aims to place the causes of poverty and inequality in the realm of the individual and to increase the acceptability of deteriorating outcomes. It is also an attempt to distinguish a deserving from an undeserving poor. As Howard (2004a) makes clear, 'Our belief in self-reliance and individual responsibility means we favour private initiative, competition and choice over government direction of resources and of society.'

How accurate is the contention that globalisation leads to a weakened state? Despite the contentions of many analysts that globalisation would force a reduction in the role of the state, it is clear that this has not occurred. Table 9.1 makes this point very clearly in terms of total government outlays, current taxation and social outlays. Government's ability to tax has not been reduced. The pertinence and power of fiscal policy remains in today's globalised Australian economy.

Table 9.1 Government outlays, total current taxes and social assistance benefits in cash (percentage of GDP – 5-year averages*)

	1961–65	1966–70	1971–75	1976–80	1981–85	1986–90	1991–95	1996–2000	2001–03
Government outlays	23.1	24.9	27.4	31.0	32.8	34.8	33.0	35.5	34.8
Total current taxes	10.4	12.1	14.2	15.8	15.9	17.4	16.0	17.7	17.3
Cash benefits	4.3	3.9	4.4	6.9	7.3	6.9	8.4	8.5	8.9

Notes:
* Except for 2001–03
Based on 5204.0 'Australian System of National Accounts Table 8 Gross Domestic Product Account, Current prices ($M)' and 5204.0 'Australian System of National Accounts Table 39 General Government Income Account, Current Prices ($m)'. Ratios compiled by James Dentrinos, Australian Bureau of Statistics; 5-year averages compiled by the author.

Arguments, therefore, that the state is weakened by globalisation are really arguments that the state should do less. Globalisation and liberalisation have placed pressures on government to at least maintain social spending because of increasing market inequality. According to the ABS (2003b): 'In 1998–99, the gap in gross incomes received by the top 20 per cent of households (by gross income) compared with the bottom 20 per cent was reduced by one-third through the taxation and indirect benefits attributed to households'. Between 1984 and 1998–99, government benefits had the effect of negating much of the potential increase in income inequality. This was especially the case for the second and third income quintiles (ibid.). Despite constraints and attempts to lower expectations about the possibilities of policy, government action continues to be pivotal to improving social outcomes. At the same time, it is evident that these efforts have not been comprehensive enough to stop poverty and inequality from increasing. Indeed, there has been an increase in the percentage of non-cash benefits (government services, spending on health and education, and so on) going to higher-income households. The value of benefits going to the bottom quintile increased by 37 per cent, while the value going to the top quintile increased by 47 per cent (Harding 2002, p. 8).

Policy-makers have aimed to remove their level of culpability. As Howard (2000) maintains, 'Few Australians still believe that the answer to pressing social problems lies solely in the hands of government. Even fewer believe that simply spending more taxpayers' money is the answer. That is why the Government has fostered the notion of a social coalition.' Howard's social coalition aims to downgrade the responsibility of government and to give precedence to non-government organisations:

> There is a role for the Government. There are things that governments can do that nobody else can do. There are things that governments do that you all wish they didn't do. I recognise that. But there are also some things that governments aren't very good at, and my experience has been that the coalface delivery of human compassion and looking after those in society who need particular help, that kind of assistance is always best delivered by those who have the motivation and some kind of personal moral commitment to doing that kind of thing. (Howard 2003a)

The attempt to shift responsibility is illustrated by the fact that in October 2000 the Catholic charity St Vincent de Paul sent a letter to all MPs expressing concern about the 80 000 people in social distress who had been sent to them by the government's welfare agency, Centrelink, which could not cope with demand for financial assistance. In the previous year, St Vincent de Paul had distributed $77.4 million in assistance but had only received $2.6 million in emergency relief funding from the government (Haslem 2000a).[34] Previously people who were waiting for benefits to come through were given a payment to see them through, now they are referred to a welfare agency (Steketee 2000a).

CONCLUSION

The argument of many policy-makers, business people and analysts in recent years has been that, in an economically liberal, globalised society where citizens increasingly succeed and fail on market terms, there is less room for concern about equality. The best that governments can do is to foster increasing self-reliance and self-provision. This chapter has argued to the contrary that globalisation does not necessarily or directly lead to rising inequality. There can be no doubt that governments face a multitude of domestic and global pressures and constraints. States and societies wanting to increase living standards have little choice but to engage with the global economy. However, the debate about globalisation and inequality obscures the most important variables in the determination of outcomes – government and societal choices. To understand the impact of globalisation on social outcomes, it is still necessary to focus on the impact of policy changes, rather than on globalisation as a stand-alone variable. The determination of the level of inequality in a society has more to do with domestic political struggles than with globalisation.

While governments may make certain policy decisions that have negative impacts on social outcomes, there is no reason why they cannot make other policies to compensate for these impacts. Social outcomes are determined through a range of policy areas. Globalisation does not force particular policy responses or reductions of spending on governments. Rather than being forced in an absolute way, what seems to be evident is that governments in developed countries have abandoned the goal of greater equality in rhetoric and action. Governments could still ameliorate the negative impacts of market outcomes but, in recent years, they seem increasingly less willing to do so, often arguing that such efforts will impede the growth process.

The fact that government in Australia has abandoned the attempt to increase equality is more important than any impact of globalisation. Globalisation as an ideological and political construction is important as a constraint, but also as a framework to make the case that egalitarian policies are no longer possible. Such aspects of globalisation are, of course, much more difficult to 'measure', but are no less important because of this. Attempts to improve social outcomes have given way to attempts to explain inequality. Scepticism should prevail about the contention that globalisation compels governments and societies to idly accept inequitable outcomes. It is even more doubtful that the best response is to increase inequality by downgrading existing government efforts to improve social outcomes in the name of incentive and efficiency.

Alternative globalisation strategies are available for Australia: economic liberalism is not always the best strategy. For globalisation to continue in Australia and throughout the world, efforts must be made to ensure that it creates benefits that are more widely distributed. Just as the concept of globalisation is contested and multifaceted so are the choices available to citizens and governments.

NOTES

1. See Edwards (2000).
2. Author's calculations based on Australian Bureau of Statistics (2003d).
3. Abbott, cited in Steketee (2003).
4. See for example Henry (2002) and Wood (1997).
5. See for example Friedman (1999), Ohmae (1995), O'Brien (1992) and Drucker (1989).
6. See for example Klein (2001), Germain (2000), Gray (1998) and Lang and Hines (1993).
7. See Greider (1997), Cerny (1997), Strange (1996), Keohane and Milner (1996) and Ruggie (1993).
8. See Conley (1999, 2002).
9. See for example Moller et al. (2003) and Alderson and Nielsen (2002).
10. See for example Scharpf (2000), Bryan and Rafferty (1999) and Garrett (1998).
11. See for example Reuveny and Li (2003), Pierson (2001) and Crepaz (2001).
12. See for example Rodrik (1997), Cline (1997) and Wood (1994).
13. For a detailed explication, see Conley (2004).
14. For a sympathetic view of Labor's social policies, see Castles (1996); for one less so, see Bryson (1996).
15. For discussion see Trigger (2003).
16. See also Keating (1985). This was a theme Keating constantly reiterated when speaking to business audiences. See also Keating (1988). Keating (1993) argued that 'Corporate profits before tax and interest over the last decade were much higher than in the 1970s . . . Wage restraint was a major factor in lifting the corporate profit share to high levels around 17 per cent, after it had fallen to a low of 12.4 per cent in the September quarter 1982.'
17. For an account of the various versions of the Accord see Conley (1999, Ch. 6).
18. The Smith Family is a social welfare organisation, NATSEM is the National Centre for Social and Economic Modelling and the CIS is an economic liberal think tank.
19. Cited in Saunders (2003, p. 7).
20. It needs to be noted that there are two Peter Saunders writing on these issues in Australia with very different interpretations of the data.
21. The authors do not measure 'households' consumption of public goods (such as recreational and cultural facilities) or non-cash benefits (such as education and health care)'.
22. See also Gregory (1993).
23. See also Kelly (2000).
24. Howard was commenting on the Senate Community Affairs Reference Committee (2004).
25. See also World Bank (2002).
26. Reported in Lundberg and Milanovic (2000).
27. For a critique, see Milanovic (2003).
28. See for example Keating (1986a, 1986b), Hawke (1994, p. 236), Kelly (1994, Ch. 4), Grattan (1994), *Economist* (1994) and Roger Hogan (1995).
29. The ERC was the Expenditure Review Committee of Cabinet.

30. See also Woodall (1995).
31. See also Porter (1990) and Michie and Smith (1998).
32. See for example EPAC (1995), Catley (1996), Capling et al. (1998), Wiseman (1998), Latham (1998), Tanner (1999), Bryan and Rafferty (1999) and Frankel (2001).
33. John Howard cited in Shanahan (1997).
34. See also Haslem (2000b, p. 4).

REFERENCES

ABS (Australian Bureau of Statistics) (2001), 'Income Distribution 1999–2000 (Cat. No. 6523.0)', February.
ABS (Australian Bureau of Statistics) (2003a), *5206.0 Australian System of National Accounts – Analysis and Comments*, September, available at www.abs.gov.au/Ausstats/abs@.nsf/Lookup/51C21550F77FDEA8CA2568A9001393E9.
ABS (Australian Bureau of Statistics) (2003b), 'Australian Social Trends: Economic Resources – Income Distribution: Taxes and Government Benefits: the Effect on Household Income', *Australia Now*, available at www.abs.gov.au/Ausstats/abs@.nsf/Lookup/8C901B170F9B0A34CA25688800285CA6.
ABS (Australian Bureau of Statistics (2003c), *Australian System of National Accounts 2002–03*, (5204.0).
ABS (Australian Bureau of Statistics) (2003d), 'Australian System of National Accounts Table 1, Gross Domestic Product and Associated Statistics (5204.0)', available at www.abs.gov.au/ausstats/abs%40.nsf/lookupresponses/24fd4d48443cff63ca256dd4007bc534?opendocument.
ABS (Australian Bureau of Statistics) (2003e), 'Household Income and Income Distribution (6523.0)', July.
Alderson, Arthur S. and François Nielsen (2002), 'Globalization and the great U-turn: income inequality trends in 16 OECD countries', *American Journal of Sociology*, **107** (5).
Argy, Fred (1995), *Financial Deregulation: Past Promise – Future Realities*, Sydney: CEDA.
Barrett, Garry F., Thomas F. Crossley and Christopher Worswick (2000), 'Consumption and income inequality in Australia', *Economic Record*, **76** (233), 116–38.
Bryan, Dick and Michael Rafferty (1999), *The Global Economy in Australia: Global Integration and National Economic Policy*, Sydney: Allen & Unwin.
Bryson, Lois (1996), 'Transforming Australia's welfare state', *Just Policy*, 6.
Capling, Anne, Mark Considine and Michael Crozier (1998), *Australian Politics in the Global Era*, Melbourne: Addison Wesley Longman.
Castles, Francis (1985), *The Working Class and Welfare: Reflections on the Political Development of the Welfare State in Australia and New Zealand, 1890–1980*, Sydney: Allen & Unwin.
Castles, Francis (1996), 'Australian social policy: where are we now?', *Just Policy*, 6.
Catley, Bob (1996), *Globalising Australian Capitalism*, Melbourne: Cambridge University Press.
CEDA (1998), *Australia at the Crossroads: Radical Free Market or a Progressive Liberalism?*, Sydney: Allen & Unwin.
Cerny, Philip G. (1997), 'Paradoxes of the competition state: the dynamics of political globalization', *Government and Opposition*, **32** (2).

Cline, William R. (1997), *Trade and Income Distribution*, Washington: Institute for International Economics.

Conley, Tom (1996), 'The politics of international finance', *Flinders Journal of History and Politics*, 18.

Conley, Tom (1999), *'Economic discipline and global punishment: globalisation and Australian economic policy during the Hawke and Keating years'*, unpublished PhD dissertation, Department of Politics, University of Adelaide, June.

Conley, Tom (2001), 'The domestic politics of globalisation', *Australian Journal of Political Science*, 36 (2).

Conley, Tom (2002), 'Globalisation as constraint and opportunity: the restructuring of the Australian political economy', *Global Society*, 16 (4).

Conley, Tom (2004), 'Globalisation and the politics of persuasion and coercion', *Australian Journal of Social Issues*, 39 (2).

Crepaz, Markus M.L. (2001), 'Veto players, globalization and the redistributive capacity of the state: a panel study of 15 OECD countries', *Journal of Public Policy*, 21 (1).

Dabscheck, Braham (1995), *The Struggle for Australian Industrial Relations*, Melbourne: Oxford University Press.

Dollar, David and Aart Kraay (2002), 'Spreading the wealth', *Foreign Affairs*, January/February.

Dollar, David and Aart Kraay (2004), 'Trade, growth and poverty', *Economic Journal*, 114, 27.

Drucker, Peter (1989), *The New Realities*, Oxford: Heinemann.

Economist (1994), 'Leaders should be used to economic understeer', 22 June, 11.

Economist (2004), 'The rising tide of red ink', 23 August, 56.

Edwards, John (2000), *Australia's Economic Revolution*, Sydney: University of New South Wales Press.

EPAC (1995), *Globalisation: Issues for Australia*, Canberra: AGPS.

Evans, Peter (1997), 'The eclipse of the state? Reflections on stateness in an era of globalization', *World Politics*, 50, 67–8.

Frankel, Boris (2001), *When the Boat Comes In: Transforming Australia in the Age of Globalisation*, Sydney: Pluto Press.

Friedman, Thomas (1999), *The Lexus and the Olive Tree: Understanding Globalisation*, New York: Farrar, Strauss, Giroux.

Galbraith, James K. (2002), 'A perfect crime: inequality in the age of globalization', *Daedalus*, Winter, 23.

Garrett, Geoffrey (1998), *Partisan Politics in the Global Economy*, New York: Cambridge University Press.

Germain, Randal (ed.) (2000), *Globalization and Its Critics: Perspectives from Political Economy*, London: Macmillan.

Grattan, Michelle (1994), 'The float: an economic and political discipline', *Economic Papers*, March, 13 (1), 42–3.

Gray, John (1998), *False Dawn: The Delusions of Global Capitalism*, London: Granta.

Gregory, R.G. (1993), 'Aspects of Australian and US living standards: the disappointing decades 1970–1990', *Economic Record*, 69 (204).

Greider, William (1997), *One World, Ready or Not: The Manic Logic of Global Capitalism*, New York: Simon and Schuster.

Harding, Ann (2002), 'Research highlights a nation growing apart', *Australian*, 25 February.

Harding, Ann, Rachel Lloyd and Harry Greenwell (2001), *Financial Disadvantage in Australia 1990–2000: The Persistence of Poverty in a Decade of Growth*, Smith Family/NATSEM.

Haslem, Benjamin (2000a), 'Charities fear return to 1930s-style welfare', *Australian*, 24 October, 4.

Haslem, Benjamin (2000b), 'Go to Vinnies, Centrelink told mother', *Australian*, 24 October, 4.

Hawke, Bob (1994), *The Hawke Memoirs*, Melbourne: William Heinemann.

Henry, Ken (2002), 'Globalisation, poverty and inequality: friends, foes or strangers', Towards Opportunity and Prosperity Conference, University of Melbourne, April.

Hogan, Roger (1995), 'RBA: deregulation the answer to lobby bias', *Australian Financial Review*, 28 April, 12.

Howard, John (2000), 'Quest for a decent society', *Australian*, 12 January, 11.

Howard, John (2003a), 'Address at the launch of the Queensland Deaf Foundation', Brisbane, 7 April, available at www.pm.gov.au/news/speeches/speech83.html.

Howard, John (2003b), 'Address to Ryde Business Forum', Sydney, 21 November, available at www.pm.gov.au/news/speeches/speech588.html.

Howard, John (2004a), 'Address to the Committee for Economic Development of Australia', Melbourne, 25 February.

Howard, John (2004b), 'Joint press conference with Brendan Nelson', Canberra, 11 March, available at www.pm.gov.au/news/interviews/Interview744.html.

Keating, Paul J. (1985), 'Speech to Institute of Directors', *Commonwealth Record*, 2–8 September, 1533.

Keating, Paul J. (1986a), 'Speech to Australian Bankers' Association', *Commonwealth Record*, 16–22 June.

Keating, Paul J. (1986b), 'Speech to Banking Summer School', *Commonwealth Record*, 10–16 February, 173.

Keating, Paul J. (1988), 'Address to the Asia Society and American/Australian Society, New York', 4 October, pp. 4–5.

Keating, Paul J. (1993), *Investing in the Nation*, Canberra: AGPS, 27.

Kelly, Paul (1994), *The End of Certainty: Power, Politics and Business in Australia*, 2nd edition, Sydney: Allen & Unwin.

Kelly, Paul (2000), 'Rhetoric is no remedy for inequity', *Australian*, 21 June, 13.

Keohane, Robert O. and Helen V. Milner (eds) (1996), *Internationalization and Domestic Politics*, New York: Cambridge University Press.

Klein, Naomi (2001), *No Logo*, London: Flamingo.

Krugman, Paul (2002), 'For richer', *New York Times Magazine*, 21 October, available at www.nytimes.com/2002/10/20/magazine/20INEQUALITY.html.

Lang, Tim and Colin Hines (1993), *The New Protectionism: Protecting the Future Against Free Trade*, London: Earthscan Publications.

Latham, Mark (1998), *Civilising Global Capitalism: New Thinking for Australian Labor*, Sydney: Allen & Unwin.

Lundberg, Mattias and Branko Milanovic (2000), 'Globalization and inequality: are they linked and how?', World Bank, p. 1, available at www.worldbank.org/poverty/inequal/abstracts/milanov.htm.

Michie, Jonathon and John Grieve Smith (eds) (1998), *Globalization, Growth and Governance: Creating an Innovative Economy*, Oxford: Oxford University Press.

Milanovic, Branko (2003), 'The two faces of globalization: against globalisation as we know it', *World Development*, **31** (4), 676.

Milner, Helen V. and Robert O. Keohane (1996), 'Internationalization and domestic politics: an introduction', in Robert O. Keohane and Helen V. Milner (eds), *Internationalization and Domestic Politics*, New York: Cambridge University Press, 18.
Moller, Stephanie et al. (2003), 'Determinants of relative poverty in advanced capitalist democracies', *American Sociological Review*, 68.
O'Brien, Richard (1992), *Global Financial Integration: The End of Geography*, London: Pinter.
Ohmae, Kenichi (1995), *The End of the Nation State: The Rise of Regional Economies*, London: Harper Collins.
Pierson, Chris (2001), 'Globalisation and the end of social democracy', *Australian Journal of Politics and History*, **47** (4).
Porter, Michael E. (1990), *The Competitive Advantage of Nations*, London: Macmillan.
Pusey, Michael (2003), *The Experience of Middle Australia: The Dark Side of Economic Reform*, Melbourne: Cambridge University Press.
Reuveny, Rafael and Quan Li (2003), 'Economic openness, democracy and income inequality: an empirical analysis', *Comparative Political Studies*, **36** (5), 577–83, 593–4.
Rodrik, Dani (1997), *Has Globalisation Gone Too Far?*, Washington: Institute for International Economics.
Ruggie, John Gerard (1993), 'Territoriality and beyond: problematizing modernity in international relations', *International Organization*, **47** (1).
Saunders, Peter (2003), 'Examining recent changes in income distribution in Australia', Social Policy Research Centre Discussion Paper No. 130.
Saunders, Peter (2004), 'Towards a credible poverty framework: from income poverty to deprivation', SPRC Discussion Paper, No. 131, January.
Saunders, Peter and Kayoko Tsumori (2002), 'For richer or poorer, we're still a lucky country', *Australian*, 16 January, 11.
Scharpf, Fritz W. (2000), 'The viability of advanced welfare states in the international economy: vulnerabilities and options', *Journal of European Public Policy*, **7** (2).
Senate Community Affairs Reference Committee (2004), *A Hand Up Not a Handout: Renewing the Fight Against Poverty (Report on Poverty and Financial Hardship)*, Canberra: Commonwealth of Australia.
Shanahan, Dennis (1997), 'Strength, not size, Howard's way', *Australian*, 6 May, 7.
Smeeding, Timothy M. (2002), 'Globalisation, inequality and the rich countries of the G-20: evidence from the Luxembourg Income Study', in David Gruen, Terry O'Brien and Jeremy Lawson (eds), *Globalisation, Living Standards and Inequality: Recent Progress and Continuing Challenges*, Proceedings of a conference held in Sydney 27–28 May, Reserve Bank of Australia and Australian Treasury, 201.
Steketee, Mike (2000a), 'The poor deserve a fairer go', *Australian*, 27 October, 11.
Steketee, Mike (2000b), 'Unhappy days are here again', *Australian*, 17–18 June, 22.
Steketee, Mike (2003), 'Still work in progress', *Australian*, 7–8 June, 22.
Strange, Susan (1996), *The Retreat of the State: The Diffusion of Power in the World Economy*, Cambridge: Cambridge University Press.
Tanner, Lindsay (1999), *Open Australia*, Sydney: Pluto Press.
Taylor, Lenore (1995), 'PM admits gap between rich and poor has widened', *Australian*, 6 October, 2.

Treasury (2004), *2004 Budget Overview*, Canberra, Commonwealth of Australia, available at www.budget.gov.au/2004-05/bp1/download/bst2.pdf.

Trigger, David (2003), 'Does the way we measure poverty matter?', Discussion Paper No. 59, November, National Centre for Social and Economic Modelling.

Tsumori, Kayoko, Peter Saunders and Helen Hughes (2002), 'Poor arguments: a response to the Smith Family Report on poverty in Australia', *Issue Analysis*, (21), 16 January.

UNCTAD (1994), *World Investment Report 1994*, New York: United Nations, 119.

Watson, Matthew and Colin Hay (2003), 'The discourse of globalisation and the logic of no alternative: rendering the contingent necessary in the political economy of new labour', *Policy and Politics*, **31** (3).

Weller, Christian E. and Adam Hersh (2002), 'The long and short of it: global liberalization, poverty and inequality', Economic Policy Institute Technical Papers.

Wiseman, John (1998), *Global Nation: Australia and the Politics of Globalisation*, Melbourne: Cambridge University Press.

Wood, Adrian (1994), *North–South Trade, Employment, and Inequality*, Oxford: Oxford University Press.

Wood, Alan (1997), 'Why we can't help everyone', *Australian*, 14 March, 13.

Woodall, Pam (1995), 'Who's in the driving seat? A survey of the world economy', *Economist*, 7 October.

World Bank (2002), *Globalization, Growth and Poverty: Building an Inclusive World Economy*, World Bank and Oxford University Press.

Index